WISCON CHRONICLES 3

The WisCon Chronicles

VOLUME 3

Carnival of Feminist SF

Edited by
Liz Henry

AQUEDUCT PRESS | SEATTLE

The WisCon Chronicles, Volume 3

The text typeface is Cambria, designed by Jelle Bosma with Steve Matteson and Robin Nicholas

Cover typeface is Carnivalee Freakshow by Chris Hansen © 2004

Aqueduct Press
PO Box 95787
Seattle WA 99145-2787
www.aqueductpress.com
ISBN: 978-1-933500-30-0

First Edition: 2009

9 8 7 6 5 4 3 2 1

Printed in the United States of America
by Applied Digital Imaging, Bellingham, WA

CONTENTS

Introduction

What Happens at WisCon Doesn't Stay at WisCon

Liz Henry

"What is WisCon, anyway? Some sort of sci fi thing where people dress up like Star Trek?"

"Oh, no, it's not like that. Well, it can be, but it's more like talking for days, with other people, mostly women who really like to read science fiction and know a lot of stuff. And mostly they're feminists. People who know about feminist science fiction!

"So, what's feminist science fiction? Is that like, Ursula Le Guin?"

"Well, no. Actually yes. And way more than that. People who read science fiction and fantasy, and lots of writers, and fanfic, and people who know all the women writers. But there's definitely something you could think of as feminist science fiction."

"What's it about? Killing all the men?"

"No! Also yes. Sometimes."

"So is it like a book club?"

"No. Yes. Argh. It's very bookish. But there's a lot of people who like Dr. Who and Battlestar Galactica, and know everything about Buffy, and read comic books, and not everything revolves around men and around books by men, because there's a critical mass of women who read stuff by other women. Or who notice stuff about women in regular science fiction. Not that stuff by women isn't regular science fiction. But the point is, it's very intense, and so much is happening at once that you can't get to it all, panels, discussions, academic lectures, silly parties.

> And people are really interested, and interesting, and pay attention. Then there's the blog discussions!"

I've had that conversation many times, trying to describe what makes WisCon great. These are some of the qualities I've noticed:

- Critical mass of women and feminists.
- Women paying attention to other women.
- Respect for many forms of media—books, movies, comics, tv.
- Respect for diversity of background and opinion.
- Active anti-racist, fat positive, and disability access work.
- Open, public conversations and consciousness raising.
- Setting aside time and space for an intensified conversation.

I had searched in 1995 in the early days of the web for "feminist" and "science fiction," wondering if anyone else thought like I did about those ideas together. From the Feminist Science Fiction, Fantasy, and Utopia pages, I met Laura Quilter, who brought me to WisCon 20 in 1996. It was the first I had heard of the Tiptree Award and the Khatru Symposium. My question was answered. Yes, lots of people thought about those ideas together, had read lots of science fiction and been dissatisfied with the way many of its stories treat gender and gender roles, and had gone looking for something different.

In my research into feminist and women's writing, I have found many times and places where women have come together to produce culture. Poets of Mercedes Matamoros' circle in Cuba in the late 1800s, for example, or the publishers of feminist newspapers in France in the 1830s, or the Seneca Falls convention, or the Combahee River Collective. What unites these movements is their collective nature and their visibility. They were all groups of women who had very intense conversations and then were inspired to write. Because they produced newspapers, books, or other public writing, they were visible to the public. Because they were public, we have the chance of knowing about them in a way we don't get to know about women's activism or conversations when those are kept to a private sphere.

This series of WisCon Chronicles, along with just about all of the publications of Aqueduct Press and many other zines, websites, and small press publications, and hundreds of blog posts and comments, are public writings that will give the fizz of WisCon a lasting place in women's history.

When we're visible, we're able to recognize each other. When I first went to Vito Excalibur's house and saw her bookshelves, I thought, Aha. Here's a person who has gravitated towards reading and collecting certain science fiction books for much of her life. When I see Tiptree, Charnas, Griffith, Butler, Le Guin, Haden Elgin on a bookshelf, then I know their owner shares a particular cultural background with me. That's an experience I never thought I'd have. I spent most of my life reading books—thinking about them, or thinking about their fictional characters—written by people either long dead or whom I thought I'd never meet, speak with, or write to, and who certainly would never be aware of me. For years, my most intense personal and intellectual relationships, including my experience of college, happened with people who were either imaginary, dead, or out of my reach. WisCon, and the people I have met there and continue to meet online as a result, brought me from a world of reading and writing, books and study, to a world of living conversation. The same is likely true for many fans in other areas of fandom. Blogging and the net brought conversation and interaction even more clearly into the fore, as the time and energy I once spent reading a couple of books a day and writing in a journal are now spent writing in many public forums and reading the words of living people who respond. It is a much more level playing field than the one where a reader sends fan mail to a famous author. Intellectual discourse has become *real* for me, and I think, for many other people who never experienced public discourse as accessible.

In the years since WisCon began, many people have converged to discover they were thinking on that same track. The con and zines, mailing list and blogs, and editors and writers associated with it have given feminist sf their blessing. Turning attention to particular works and expecting others to have read them has led to the formation of a "loose canon." The power of this canon came to an interesting head when people who know from feminist sf were able to understand the resonance of Karen Joy Fowler's "What I Didn't See" (which was originally published on the Web, not on paper). Despite a huge Internet controversy about whether or not it was science fiction, it won the Nebula Award for Best Short Story in 2003.

The feminist science fiction canon has not replaced the basic sf canon. Sometimes, as in the controversy over "What I Didn't See," the two seem to be at war. At other times, we see merging or at least some cross-pollination.

About This Book

My goal for this book is to represent a cross section of the diverse conversations happening at WisCon and beyond. These conversations take place in many different registers of language, formal or informal, personal, political, performative.

This book is arranged in three sections: Intelligibility, Dialogues in Feminist Fandom, and Internet drama. I'll tell you a little bit about each section.

Intelligibility

The keys to the heart of this book for me are L. Timmel Duchamp's essay on intelligibility and the transcript of the panel on Internet drama.

L. Timmel Duchamp's Guest of Honor speech for WisCon 32, "A Matter of Tongues," is reprinted here, along with responses from Shveta Narayan, Shweta Thakrar, and Rose Lemberg. What makes a story, and what enables us as writers to tell it and be understood? "A Matter of Tongues" and its responses explain how stories require us as readers (and writers) to be aware of a variety of contexts; how one person's story may have depths accessible to some readers while excluding others, and how, knowing that, we should be cautious about judging the worth of stories. By respecting this possibility, feminist science fiction communities are creating spaces for new stories to be told and heard.

Thakrar, Narayan, and Lemberg's responses embody the power of WisCon as an entry point to an ongoing conversation. Thakrar's reaction to Duchamp's speech continued to evolve over time and cascaded into emails to her friends, who read the speech online from

Duchamp's website, talked about it, and wrote their own responses. I chose this dialogue to open the book and to model the sorts of ongoing conversations that are happening in the next section, Dialogues in Feminist Fandom.

Dialogues in Feminist Fandom

Maureen McHugh's Guest of Honor speech brought up ARGs — Alternate Reality Games — as an emerging art form in which people participate in creating a story through performing it with its authors. John Kim wrote up his summary of McHugh's talk on ARGs, along with his reaction as someone who approaches gaming as his creative art. Gremlin X and the Robot Collective from sf0 describe the game they performed at WisCon, with clues and flyers scattered around the convention and online, ending in the surreal and silly robot uprising during the Tiptree auction. And Robin Fleming from *Cerise* and The Iris Network, co-organizer of the Capes and Consoles party, wrote up a cheerful con report from the point of view of a gamer hanging out with other women who love gaming.

Other pieces highlight a playful or "ludic" approach in our writing and reading. Ted Infinity's writeup of the Worldbuilding panel describes a group effort led by Ben Rosenbaum, Doselle Young, Naomi Kritzer, and Kristine Smith. Enthusiastic audience participation created a very silly background and story called "Carnitopia" with meat-spraying volcanoes, cloudevators, and roving concrete islands in a chlorine sea. It sounds like a great exercise in listing concepts that are good to consider in order to give an sf/fantasy world physical, geographic, and social depth. Robin Fleming's amazing science fiction parody of Mary Barnard's translations of Sappho combines scholarly and technical skill with feminist and pulp science fiction sensibilities to give us a touching, sexy love poem to a being named ASofiilkadhnot'tgohwL ; erl.

We jump from silly to scholarly with Alexis Lothian's "Utopia, Fiction, and Fandom: Conflict, Community, and 'Queer Female Space.'" WisCon's academic track results in cross-fertilization between fandom and academia, another direction in which WisCon conversations move out into a different world. Lothian describes some of the ways that worldbuilding in feminist science fiction relates to the practice of "making a world" by having panel discussions at WisCon and online. In other words, at WisCon we are engaged in the construction of a temporary utopia, a performative one that is not perfect, but is an attempt at radical or progressive perfectibility. In building sf worlds in fiction, we are outlining possibilities of real world resistance, along with many of the complexities and problems in those attempts. Lothian then leads into an outline of anti-racist feminist conversations in Stargate:Atlantis fandoms, the way pleasure and individual freedom and queering a text are sometimes given so much priority that blatant racism is ignored. But this doesn't go unchallenged in feminist fandom. Lothian points out that "intense demands are made of fannish metadiscourse: that it live up to its self-image by making something more of its source material than the source makes of itself." In this view, anti-racist fannish blogs are performing utopian worldbuilding.

Lothian's paper and its view of feminist fandom as a utopian enterprise struck me as essential reading for people aware of the last few years' discussions of racism, race, and WisCon. These conversations relate very strongly to the overarching theme of how WisCon affects what happens beyond WisCon. Lothian isn't saying that WisCon is utopia in that it is perfect; far from it. I think she's saying it's utopian in that it's a process of trying to build models of a future world that challenges our current one.

To represent some of that practice, with all its hopes and disappointments, this book includes transcripts, handouts, and summaries. It includes the "It's Not About Identity" transcript, and an extensive email conversation between Beth Plutchak and Janice Mynchenberg as white women reacting to the "Dissecting Privilege" session. Nancy Jane Moore compares elements of Laurie Marks' Elemental Logic series and Duchamp's Marq'ssan Cycle, bringing in her understanding of the history of aikido, Japanese culture, and philosophy. At the "Elves and Dwarves" panel, the discussion turned at one point to question whether it's harmful to talk about the existence of racism, and (yet again) to the idea that some people are "color blind" to race and ethnicity, a set of ideas that sparked vigorous disagreement and that, as it is posited again and again by white feminist fans, continues to piss off people of color who don't have the privilege to be unaware of racism in their everyday experience. However, this panel also raised great ideas for future discussion, such as the tensions between Draegarians and Easterners in Steven Brust's novels, and how various people of color feel about Drizzt in R.A. Salvatore's work.

Aqueduct Press is publishing an entire book on the ideas discussed in the Narrative and Politics panel, some of which is summarized here in a short reaction by Victoria Janssen. During that panel, there was tension over panelist Susan Palwick's anecdote about Samuel Delany. Another key point was when Claire Light pointed out the political context of telling that story in the climate of reporting on the Democratic primary race between Barack Obama and Hillary Clinton—a topic I believe would have become a notable Internet drama of WisCon 32 if not for the trolling described in Section III of this book.

Vandana Singh, K. Joyce Tsai, and Rachel Kronick's "Not Just Japan" panel identified many entry points to reading and thinking about speculative work from Asia, including a handout with reading list, discussion of translation and cultural gatekeeping, definitions of genre across cultures as another form of translation. Rachel Kronick's writeup describes great techniques for organizing a panel that goes into depth: talk with panelists beforehand, decide what you *don't* want your panel to be, make a handout, and list out some key points to hit in the discussion.

WisCon also makes space for "spontaneous programming." At WisCon 32, K. Joyce Tsai put together a spontaneous panel to talk about representations of gender and bodies in shoujo manga and manhwa, exploring a comics genre aimed at preteen and teenaged girls. Her panel writeup is an excellent example of the more advanced discussions of feminism and sf that take place at WisCon. Deep background in reading manga makes it possible to detect more patterns and meaning than the casual reader knows to look for. The participants in the Shoujo Bodies discussion were expert manga and manhwa readers, aware of cultural differences between Japan, China, Korea, and the US, and of many subtleties of graphic narrative.

In other writeups, Sue Lange explores critics' and readers' reactions to the idea of hard science fiction. She describes ways in which shifting definitions of what sciences count as "hard" contribute to trivialization and devaluation of women's writing. Mystickeeper summarizes the panel on YA boundaries, including magical contraception in Tamora Pierce's novels, warning labels and rating systems, and techniques of writing scenes of violence and war that don't alienate 10- to14-year-olds. Alaya Dawn Johnson responds to that panel with many questions to the notion of what's considered to be age-appropriate in YA fantasy.

At WisCon last year, I thought of a book I've discussed with Timmi Duchamp, a book that Debbie Notkin gave me a few years ago, *A Framework for Understanding Poverty* by Ruby K. Payne. Payne describes patterns of narrative structures as they relate to social class. She says that linear single-voiced narratives are the structure of a middle-class story, while working class or poverty-class stories are closer to "call and response," with the story elements nonlinear and participatory. This book came to mind during the slash fic panel in a room of almost 100 people, none of them quiet. In my transcript of that panel I've tried to show how decentralized and nonlinear this discussion was, how much energy and excitement was generated in the room. It's a good example both of Payne's description of non-middle-class narrative structure—in this case applied to what was said and how it was said, even though the room was set up with expert speakers and audience, a teacher-student setup—and of the participatory culture of feminist fandom and of fic writing communities. From reports by JJ Pionke and others, the late-night, highly informal and raucous Battlestar Galactica panel was another clear example of this structure of group participation.

Internet Drama!

"Drama" is a common term on blogs, email lists, bulletin boards, multiplayer games, and other online venues. It's used to describe a controversial or intense group conversation; especially if it includes public or semi-public personal fights between friends, lovers, or people who consider themselves to be part of a common community. Internet drama inspires and horrifies. It can become a spectacle; it can be very hurtful, as strong public opinions tear friendships apart and as many people feel alienated and emotionally unsafe in the face of evidence of disrespect from community members.

The transcript of the Internet drama panel shows how WisCon is complemented by ongoing conversations on the net. Rather than being "The Place" for feminist or women's views on sf to be stated and heard, WisCon is more clearly just a focal point, a single intense instance of that conversation that happens 24 hours a day, 7 days a week. Participants at WisCon are part of a greater community of people who pay attention to what women write and think, and to women's roles in sf and fantasy. Though WisCon is not central to that online discussion, I believe it has provided a nexus around which feminists have organized and sometimes identify.

In the WisCon panel "Can Internet drama Change the World?," led by Julia Starkey, Woodrow Hill, Alexis Lothian, K. Tempest Bradford, and K. Joyce Tsai, we see that many fans consider engaging in Internet drama as cultural intervention, and in fact a crucial form of activism. As feminist fans struggle to articulate their political opinions in a public context open to public scrutiny and critique, the conversations have a chance to deepen and expand even when the context also includes a lot of controversy, defensiveness, and hostility. The panel and audience discussed the aspects of Internet drama that inspire and frustrate, and that keep us glued to our computer screens all night long. K. Joyce Tsai describes her first encounter with this form of drama in the "Cultural Appropriation Debate of Dooom" during and after WisCon 30, after which she and others began International Blog Against Racism Week. Although the Internet drama panel description didn't focus on racism and anti-racism, the discussion often turned to online discussions of race as well as gender and sexuality. The Cultural Appropriation discussion has grown several new heads this year, in an extensive Drama, "RaceFail 2009: Daughter of the Son of Bridezilla of the Electric Boogaloo," which continues online as I write this introduction.

The WisCon trolling was a complicated series of events that started at WisCon 32 and expanded into a large-scale online drama. A WisCon member identified here under one of her screen names, Zathlazip, took photos and posted public mockery of the con and its members onto forums on a notorious and snarky humor website called Something Awful. She and her fellow forum members made fun of the appearances of con members as well as panel titles and descriptions. Faces in Zathlazip's photos were obscured by crude drawings of cartoonish sad faces. Con members reacted strongly, including by posting on their blogs. At some point over the next day and a half, another site stepped into the drama: Something Awful Sycophant

Squad, or SASS, which has been described as being partly composed of people who had been banned from Something Awful for being too awful. SASS also intersects with Encyclopedia Dramatica and other communities based on humor meant to be offensive and shocking. Hundreds of comments accumulated, as a fairly small core of SASS members continued to repost and offensively modify and reframe images and details from Zathlazip's post, from the WisCon website, and from WisCon attendees' blogs and photo streams. Meanwhile, as events spiralled out of her control, Zathlazip also became a target of the SASS members. Her identity was outed in several dimensions by angry WisCon members and others; online, in her personal life, and at her job and school. In order to avoid escalation of that outing, and as a result of private discussion with Zathlazip, I have chosen not to use her name in this book. Reactions from feminist, glbt, and antiracist bloggers and communities continue to unfold, including debates on anonymity and public presence.

The WisCon Chronicles includes another example of Internet drama affecting WisCon—and vice versa; in April 2008 on LiveJournal, a man whose online handle is TheFerrett proposed "The Open Source Boobs Project." He said it would be a good idea and sexually liberating if women at sf cons would wear buttons saying "Yes, you may" or "No you may not."

> Penguicon, we had buttons to give away. There were two small buttons, one for each camp: A green button that said, "YES, you may" and a red button that said "NO, you may not." And anyone who had those buttons on, whether you knew them or not, was someone you could approach and ask: "Excuse me, but may I touch your breasts?" —TheFerrett, http://theferrett.livejournal.com/1087686.html, April 21, 2008

Over the next few days, his blog post attracted over a thousand comments. Hundreds of people reacted to the OSBP online, with long essays, personal stories, and sentence by sentence analysis of TheFerrett's post. Misia's parody outlines the Open Source Swift Kick in the Balls Project, using language hilariously similar to the original proposal. Vito Excalibur came up with a counterproposal, the Backup Project or Open Source Back Each Other Up Project, a pledge for women and their allies in sf fandom to speak up to stop sexual harassment if they see it occurring. Like the Cultural Appropriation and Racism Debates of the last three years, Open Source Boob and Open Source Backup continue to be important in feminist and fan culture. At WisCon 32, some people wore red "BACKUP" ribbons on their name badges to indicate their readiness to back up anyone who needed support in order to escape or confront harassment.

From intelligibility in fiction to visibility on the Internet, from academic analyses of the WisCon community to wacky role-playing games, WisCon is indeed too large and diverse to encapsulate. We're passionate about fun and our imaginations, about personal and political action and its connection to cultural production and consumption. To reflect all those dimensions, I have tried to include entry points or keys to discussions and communities and their varying tones.

The long history of WisCon and direct connections between second wave feminists and current feminist discourse online give us a deep context to understand the books, comics, movies, tv, games, blogs, other media, and the culture of fandom itself that inspire our dreams of what's possible for the future. WisCon is a thousand things to a thousand people at the con, and more things to more people on the Internet. I hope this gives you a flavor of some of those things—and please remember that there are so many more.

Liz Henry is a blogger, poet, computer programmer, literary translator, and proud member of the Secret Feminist Cabal. She writes at http://liz-henry.blogspot.com, and her email is liz@bookmaniac.net.

Section I. Intelligibility

The Matter of Tongues

L. Timmel Duchamp

Being Her GoH Speech for WisCon 32, May 25, 2008

Earlier this month, when I was almost finished writing this speech, I dreamed a dream. In this dream, I was wandering about in an arcade, searching for a restroom. I really needed it, though not for the usual reason. As often happens in dreams, though I went to the place where I knew one to be, it was closed. I was desperate to find it, because I needed to get rid of the thick wad of tongues crowding my mouth. Not only because I had an appointment, but because the feel of them in my mouth was disgusting. But I couldn't find an open restroom. So finally I grabbed a handful of napkins from an espresso cart and tried as discreetly as possible to remove the tongues and slipped them into my pocket for later retrieval (since obviously I'd want them back again). I then looked around, trying to discover if anyone had seen me, when I realized I still had too many tongues in my mouth. I hated to be doing this in public; it felt indecent. But I couldn't locate the restroom, and the tongues really had to come out. So again I held a sheaf of napkins to my mouth and pulled out the excess tongues, and put them in my other pocket. And so it went, until finally I woke up.

I puzzled over the dream's meaning for a couple of days before I realized that it not only expressed my anxieties about writing and giving the speech, but also addressed its subject matter. What I'm going to talk about tonight are stories, mostly in the humble plural rather than the usual, exalted singular; stories and the politics of intelligibility. For the tongues in my dream represented types of stories. Stories are something humans enjoy an abundance of. But they're not always the stories we need, and sometimes, when they are, they're not necessarily the stories others can understand. Stories, in that sense, are similar to the tongues in the Tower of Babel. Across the breadth of their diversity, they aren't all universally intelligible.

I.

Like—I'm sure—everyone else sitting in this room, I've always loved stories. As a young girl I loved the stories in books, and I loved the stories the adults around me told. My German-American grandfather had a trove of stories about his young adult life as a migrant worker, moving from ranch to ranch and farm to farm in Midwestern Canada and the northern US, and about his boyhood and adolescence in Bear Creek and Appleton, Wisconsin.

Again and again my brother and I would ask him to tell our favorites, which I later realized we loved because they conjured up a world very different from the one we knew. His stories evoked a social setting ruled by its own particular conventions, featuring characters who were types rather than personalities. The main actors in his stories offered a recurring cast of those types, showing up in this setting or that—most notably, the Rancher or Farmer, the Rancher's or Farmer's Wife, the Frenchman, the Swede, the Englishman, the schoolteacher, the traveling salesman, the doctor. Each telling constituted a performance, full of particular words—used always at the same moment—as well as sound effects like HOL-Y MOSES! inserted for dramatic effect at the exact right moment. I'm sure the other adults present must have thought, each time we begged him to perform a favorite, Not again! But Grandpa delighted in humoring us and always took care not to omit the parts of the stories we considered essential.

While many of the stories I've loved have been stories about places and people utterly unlike me, as a child I was also eager to hear, read, or discover stories that showed me particular parts of myself, stories that explained to me who I was and might some day be, stories that offered me a way of understanding the many experiences and feelings that filled me with confusion.

The stories I encountered in print never quite fit who I was, but hungry, I lapped them up and used bits of them, the way children do, and reveled in the joys of immersion in another world than the one I lived in.

Notoriously, second wave feminists placed great emphasis on the importance of role models for young women, mostly because the 1950s removed a lot of them from common visibility. As a girl, my role models were my grandmother, who was a strong, extraordinary woman; Mildred Heidorn, who taught me music theory and directed the high school orchestra; and Beethoven. I needed Beethoven, you see, because I aspired to be a composer, an ambition Mildred Heidorn encouraged me to pursue. But when in 1968 at age eighteen I went to university to study music, I found my aspirations under attack by the unwritten sexist rules of the composition faculty. They would not, you see, allow me the official status they were happy to grant any male student who wanted it. The examples of my grandmother, Mildred Heidorn, and Beethoven offered me no help.

Still, for about a year I thought I would manage to work a way around those unwritten rules. Each term I petitioned to study with a composer on the faculty, and I independently found musicians who were undergraduate and graduate students to perform my pieces; and although the senior faculty men did not take me seriously, many younger musicians did. It was a psychologically precarious situation, but I thought my strategy was working brilliantly when in May 1970 I was invited to have a piece performed off-campus with several other composers, who were mostly graduate students and post-docs, in three performances at an art gallery. My piece was so well-received that it was put on the department's annual program, presenting work from young faculty and a few undergraduates, held a couple of weeks later. I was ecstatic. I vividly remember walking to my lesson the day after the concert, bursting with confidence, armed with the score of my piece as my teacher had requested. Now, I thought, he will take me seriously and convince his colleagues to give me the same status as the male undergraduate composers.

But my lesson went differently than I had imagined. Doodling cartoons on the score, my teacher informed me that although my piece had been well-received by the audience, its success had been a fluke. Gently he asked me why the post-docs who'd put my piece on the program at the art gallery had done so and why the musicians, all notable new music performers, had chosen to play it.

Bravely I replied that they said they thought it was good. His smile as he shook his head looked kind, and his tone when he spoke in his light, tenor voice was mild. But his words put a knife in my heart. They all want to go to bed with you, he said. The expression on his face was avuncular: he was telling me this for my own good, to drag me out of my state of denial. And then he sighed, clipped his pen back into his pocket, and handed me the defaced score. It's too nice a day to have a lesson, don't you think? Let's go to Treno's for a beer.

I was devastated. I needed more in a role model than Beethoven, someone to show me how to persevere and build on my success and talent despite the opposition I faced. Beethoven had never had to worry about whether people pretended to like his music just because they wanted to touch his breasts. (The desire of all the men around me to touch my breasts was something my teacher mentioned as we were having that beer.) I know that this sort of experience was commonplace, but at the time, I knew no stories like it. Of course, just ten years later, everything would have been different. But in 1970, the stories I needed weren't there for me. You see, I had no trouble believing him when he let me know that he'd agreed to teach me because he wanted to fuck me. And because there were no other women composing music on that campus, and the expression "sexual harassment" hadn't yet been invented, and there were no stories to give me another perspective, I believed that he must be right, that the musicians and other composers were only playing me. In hindsight, I can see that I was wrong. They did take me seriously. And though I didn't know it, things had already begun to change. But Beethoven's story couldn't help me see anything but that my experience was nothing like his had been. I lost faith in my own talent. I never again finished another composition.

II.

For most of my twenties, I especially sought out stories that could show me who I was and might some day be. But gradually I became more interested in the stories that offered me a way of understanding my experiences and feelings. I had always sought such stories, but these became more important as my need for role models diminished. It was around that time that, as I began to figure out aspects of my childhood experiences that puzzled me, I noticed how limited and narrow the range of available stories actually is. Very little of any of the experiences of my family were well-represented in fiction, for instance.

Eventually I realized that I had been rendered silent about most of my own history because any attempt to convey it to others inevitably resulted in their understanding it in a very partial, distorted way: my father, the uneducated anti-union factory foreman who worked the night shift, cooked all our meals, and considered physical violence an appropriate form for disciplining children; my mother, the failed housewife but brilliant bookkeeper elevated to comptroller who successively saved two businessmen from bankruptcy and made them millionaires while ending up working long past retirement age because she didn't want to retire into poverty; our strange family life as nonconformists and fundamentalist Lutherans—each discrete fragment able to fit into existing stereotypes and tropes while evoking absolutely nothing of the emotional and social experience of growing up working class in 1950s America, much less of who my parents were as human beings. Most of the stories I'd ever read about working class lives were written through the lens of middle-class narratives—leaving out all the impossible to articulate bits, the parts that made it impossible for me to talk intelligibly about my childhood.

I thought—I assumed—I would be able to find a way to make the invisible intelligible.

Well, I suppose it's necessary to be naïve about writing when you're first beginning. What I didn't understand was that the novel, as a form, is stamped with and shaped by middle class values. Violating those values tends to result in boring or implausible or polemical narratives. Occasionally a writer is able to break out of the constraints, but usually by building a context of exceptionality that allows readers to ignore what they don't get. Carol Maso's novel, *Defiance*, offers a brilliant example of that. Her protagonist, a Harvard professor of physics straight out of the working class, murders two of her privileged male students. But I have to wonder if the bits that struck me as brilliant evocations are even intelligible to a reader without a working-class background. My suspicion is that most readers focus on the sensational aspects of a woman murdering young men she has had sex with and ignore everything else.

Intelligibility. I keep using that word. It's an important concept for a writer, intelligibility. Another way to think of it is in terms of translatability. Can all concepts be translated from one language to another? Some people claim that they can, but certain ways of looking at the world, embedded in culture, are in practice incommensurable. And concepts always partake of assumptions about the world and how it operates. Eric Cheyfitz, a scholar of Native American Studies, notes that much of the conquest of North America was accomplished by utilizing European concepts and terms that had no equivalents in Native American languages while assuming, at the same time, a conceptual universality that, when not understood by the Native Americans, was taken as proof of their not being fully human. Cheyfitz writes, We need to ask ourselves...what words or phrases in the Algonquian languages...could translate "the right of possession," "the right of property," and "actual possession," explaining the always potential disjunction between the three phrases, such that the three have to be united in one person for a fully legal "title" to exist. And so, Cheyfitz wonders, How does one translate ideas of place grounded in conceptions of communal or social labor into ideas of place grounded in the notion of identity? The problem is not...how does one translate radically different systems of property into one another. But can one translate the idea of places as property into an idea of place the terms of which the West has never granted legitimacy? Let's go back to my story about my being barred from entering a program open to any male student who wished to enter it. Although it's a story unlikely to ever happen now, partly because such discrimination is illegal and partly because gender norms have altered, it is still at least partially intelligible to almost anyone I might tell it. Not everyone would understand why official exclusion and sexual harassment blocked me from ever writing music again, but most people hearing the story will think that sex discrimination is wrong and harmful. Some people may find me culpable for having been paralyzed with helplessness and not having figured out a way to challenge the institutional structure I was up against—perhaps because they have no idea how nearly impossible that would have been for any nineteen-year-old with a working-class upbringing to do, or perhaps because they have no clue about the totalizing effects of constant, unrelenting institutionalized sexism for women living in the 1950s and 1960s. But even if their understanding of the story is only partial, they will get that there is a story there. But a story about class-, race- , or gender-based institutional exclusion, arbitrary or otherwise, would be incomprehensible to an early eighteenth-century

European, for instance. What narrative worth telling is there? Some people—all women and all but a few elite men—are naturally excluded from an academic course of study. That some fool of a young girl who ought to be laboring in the fields or toiling in the kitchen has her pretensions poked by exclusion offers no narrative tension or interest. The intelligibility of any given story is clearly situational. I would argue that often it is also political, in the sense that lack of comprehension of certain stories is an artifact of privilege of one sort or another and often serves to protect that privilege. The unintelligibility of the Alonquians' idea of place to the seventeenth-century Europeans, for instance, meant that as far as the Europeans were concerned, the land they coveted was unowned and thus there to be seized. A less obvious case, closer to home, can be seen in the reception of Karen Joy Fowler's feminist sf story, "What I Didn't See." The story is fully intelligible only to readers who have read a lot of feminist science fiction.

Those who haven't tend to assert that it's a mainstream literary story. While it's possible to read it that way, such a reading is partial and distorted and misses the actual subject-matter of the story altogether. The problem of the story's intelligibility generated an uproar of Internet discussion for more than a month after it was first posted on SciFiction.com. Over the years, several people have told me that it is not reasonable for an author to expect readers to have read such a specialized area of the genre as feminist sf. I've long argued that it will be necessary to have something called feminist sf for as long as the major works of feminist sf aren't absorbed into the genre's canon. And so I would also argue that the insistence that it ought not to be necessary to have read the most famous story James Tiptree, Jr. wrote, simply in order to understand another story—a story that happens to have been awarded a Nebula—is political. I mean, really. Would any sf fan or critic claim that it was unreasonable to expect readers to be familiar with, say, "I, Robot?" Or with "By His Bootstraps?" Or with "The Nine Billion Names of God"? The attitude that considers a precursor text like "The Women Men Don't See" obscure and outside the common sf reading vocabulary is saying, "We aren't interested in a whole set of stories that have been developed in the area of the genre dominated by women, and we shouldn't be expected to be familiar with them." In the case of the sex discrimination and sexual harassment I experienced in the late 1960s and early 1970s, the story I tell now would have been unintelligible to my composition teacher. From his perspective, I was a nubile girl who was exhibiting herself in a public space that was traditionally reserved for men, someone whose attempt to write music was the equivalent of a dog walking on its hind legs, wearing eyeglasses, and smoking a pipe. Someone who was breaking the rules. Someone who was just asking for it. Perhaps he believed what he told me, that the younger men just wanted an opportunity to hit on me; perhaps he didn't and was angry at the younger men for breaking ranks.

The point of his lesson was to make me see that the cost of my venture into a male-only public space carried a steep price. And since I did not understand that he and I were involved in a political contest, his tactic worked.

Stories are, of course, both entertainment and art. And story—in the singular, in the sense of narrative—is a key conceptual tool for historians and social scientists. But story can also be a form of political expression that has its own virtues apart from other forms of political activism and can do things that other kinds of activism can't; most of the national literature of many countries evinces a deep consciousness of this aspect of story.

I see three distinct political aspects to the issue of story and stories for feminists. First, it is tremendously important that we expand the range of stories we tell and re-tell. It is not good enough that people—especially children—who do not see themselves in the stories they read and hear and see must make do with bits and pieces of stories that don't quite fit their identities or experiences. Second, the problem of intelligibility reflects the usually imperceptible influence of privilege that allows those who are "normal" and unmarked by difference to assume that whenever they don't get a story or understand the other's anger that there's nothing there to get.

Third, the intelligibility of stories depends on community. Community—both imagined and material—provides the basis for shared stories, shared narrative conventions and tropes, shared meaning. "A community," writes poet Lyn Hejinian, "consists of any or all of those persons who have the capacity to acknowledge what others among them are doing." Take the example of Karen Joy Fowler's story, "What I Didn't See." In Karen's words, she wrote that story after "swimming in the sea of feminist sf for thirty years." Those who have the capacity to acknowledge what Karen is doing in this story are the community who swim in that sea. This notion of community explains also why it is that at WisCon we don't need to restrict ourselves to discussing "Women in SF" or try to explain our ideas in terms of Feminism 101. Who is included in a community determines which stories can become intelligible within that community, for communities, of course, are made, not born. Feminists who read feminist science fiction often feel as though they have become part of a community, engaged in a spatially expansive, temporally extended conversation, even when they have not become part of the material feminist sf community that does exist. This is because feminist thought and practice is inherently collective, and because "getting it"—another way of talking about intelligibility—is all tied up with an alternative set of shared perceptions and ideas to that of male-dominated, mainstream culture.

III.

When I'm out in the "real world" and people ask me why I started Aqueduct, I talk about Aqueduct's serving a small audience and sometimes cop to being a "niche publisher." But I have another, more productive way of looking at this that more accurately envisions my feminist desire to contribute to the making of our world. An important part of the answer hinges on the politics of intelligibility. Many stories that feminists write—or would write if there were a market for them—are stories that are penalized in the mainstream for being unintelligible to readers who haven't gotten past Feminism 101. Such stories are often unintelligible because their assumptions about race or class or sexual or gender identity depart from those of the mainstream, so that even the editors who "get" the stories consider them not right for the venue's readership.

And some stories can also be unintelligible because they haven't been simplified and dumbed-down for the lowest-common denominator. The point of Aqueduct is to expand the range of stories being told and to extend the range of such stories' intelligibility.

For me, the summer of 2003 was a momentous turning point. As you may recall, the US was in the throes of post-911 paranoia and nationalism, and the changed atmosphere seemed to be having a chilling effect on some of the fiction markets I had previously sold to. For years I'd been worrying that in my fiction I was, as some of my fellow writers had been telling me, setting the bar too high. The question haunted me: ought I not to make my stories less challenging, less complicated, and more conventional? And later, beginning in 2002, I began asking myself: ought I to try to make my stories more ideologically comfortable in these post-911 times? Although I had been wrestling with the problem for years, I always came back to the thought that my passion for writing flows from my intense interest in relationships and situations and characters that don't fit the usual narratives.

That summer of 2003 I attended my first writing workshop and learned a great deal about which stories are easily understood and which aren't and ended up thinking hard about what made certain stories unintelligible to some of their readers. I realized that stories based on the most common narratives, usually about white heterosexual males, were the ones that were least likely to be misread. My thoughts resonated powerfully with the questions about my writing that had been haunting me, and my sense of crisis about my own writing career intensified. About a month after the workshop, I attended Samuel R. Delany's Clarion West reading. During the Q&A, he named my stories as among his current favorites (without having any idea I was in the audience). We then met for the first time, and it was an awesome experience.

Every doubt I'd had about my work vanished. I absolutely must, he said, get my novels into print. And he lit a fire under me.

About a month after that, in an email Karen Joy Fowler mentioned having read a novel manuscript by Gwyneth Jones that Gwyneth said was "unpublishable." Karen had no idea when she praised the ms to me that I was thinking of starting Aqueduct. That ms, though, was the novel that Aqueduct published a year later under the title *Life*. It is clear to me from some of the comments I've heard about *Life* and also from many of the reviews of it that it's a story that's not intelligible to everyone. And yet, I saw on my first reading that it is a story that needs to be told and one of the stories we all need to know and understand. Add to all that my consciousness of Kelly Link and Gavin Grant's daring experiment with Small Beer Press, which made me see that I could invent my own alternative as well, and somehow the pieces all came together to create the imperative of starting Aqueduct, which I then did.

The strength of feminist science fiction, the strength of WisCon, which has become the living, beating heart of feminist science fiction must always lie in its capacity to allow us to frame and tell and share the stories we need and desire that aren't necessarily easily heard or understood outside our community.

The continued frustration expressed by women writers over the exclusionary policies of certain publishing venues most surely has to do with intelligibility rather than the gendered statistics of submission.

Obviously we must keep insisting that our work become a recognized, intelligible part of mainstream sf. But for me, it is equally obvious that we must also continue the process of telling our own stories and learning to recognize and understand the stories of one another that we don't yet know or understand.

Community isn't simply togetherness: it's above all an active process of making the world collectively. For the grand conversation that is feminist sf, telling and learning new stories is key. The stories our community tells and understands show us who we are; the stories we tell show us who we can be.

L. Timmel Duchamp is an sf writer and critic, author of the Marq'ssan Cycle, a series of visionary political novels, and publisher of Aqueduct Press. She blogs often at Ambling along the Aqueduct http://aqueductpress.blogspot.com/. For more about her and her work, visit http://ltimml.home. mindpsring.com.

Intelligibility, Framing, and the Newbie Writer

Shweta Narayan

Part 1: WisCon '08

> *One night two young men from Egulac went down to the river to hunt seals and while they were there it became foggy and calm. Then they heard war-cries, and they thought: "Maybe this is a war-party." They escaped to the shore, and hid behind a log. Now canoes came up, and they heard the noise of paddles, and saw one canoe coming up to them.*
>
> —From "The War of the Ghosts"

> *The intelligibility of any given story is clearly situational.*
>
> —L. Timmel Duchamp

After the WisCon Guest of Honor speeches, before I went to bed, I emailed several of my friends saying *you have to hear what Timmi Duchamp said.*

I'm a newbie writer, a 2007 Clarion alum who has sold a few short stories and poems. The friends I emailed are in a similar place—some people like our work, but we're also coming up against walls. We've internalized a simple, intuitive piece of advice we often receive: you get over those walls by writing better. And there's crucial truth in it. We're still learning. We have issues of craft and characterization to work through. If we pretend there's no such thing as "better" writing, we'll never improve. But the word presupposes an objective standard, a single scale upon which everyone is measured. It dismisses not only those who don't measure up, but also those who don't conform.

When critics insisted that one of my friends had pronoun confusion, because a character in a relationship with a woman had to be male, I could laugh at them. But she was left wondering if she just hadn't portrayed those characters "well enough." When another friend was told "that character should be more assertive," she questioned herself—though she had set up a family environment where an Indian girl *ought* to have trouble being assertive. One of my Clarion classmates told me that his local writer's group "didn't get" his wonderful (but yes, difficult) Clarion story, so he wasn't sure if he should send it out.

Now, these are all stories I love. I'd hate to see them die on the vine—and they were being criticized for precisely the aspects I found refreshing. But it was hard to communicate that to my friends—and, well, I found myself losing confidence in the exact same way when someone didn't get some of my stories. Because as newbies, we assume that any problem is our failure. If we don't connect to a reader, we must be lacking something.

However, that something might well be the intelligibility of privilege. When there isn't an objective scale—as there isn't in writing—words like "better" treat the default as objective. Cultural defaults are set by the privilege groups; "better" therefore assumes that privileged thought is truth. While "make it better" is an important possibility to consider, as the only possible answer to incomprehension, it's toxic. It's a way of thinking that does not listen to new and different voices, that rewards us for sounding like everybody else.

My friends and I didn't have an alternative to that word, not till I heard Timmi speak.

Not that it was the first time I'd heard about intelligibility. I think half my Clarion instructors were trying to tell me about it. Delia Sherman and Ellen Kushner said it was no surprise my stories pulled multiple viewpoints together, since that's what I did in life. And Karen Joy Fowler flat out told me it didn't matter if not everyone understood my stories. But I still thought if only I did what I was doing better, I'd win more readers over.

But hearing Timmi speak, the notion of intelligibility became… intelligible. Perhaps because I was at WisCon for the first time ever, in a whirl of wonderful things; the sort of exhilarating, bewildering environment that shakes assumptions loose. Perhaps because I'd had a year for Clarion lessons to sink in. Or perhaps it was hearing that Karen, and Timmi, had similar problems.

For a new writer trying to bridge cultures, this matters. It lets us begin to distinguish quality from comprehensibility.

Part 2: War of the Ghosts

> *Now he thought: "Oh, they are ghosts." He did not feel sick, but they said he had been shot. So the canoes went back to Egulac, and the young man went ashore to his house, and made a fire.*
>
> —"The War of the Ghosts"

> *...each discrete fragment able to fit into existing stereotypes and tropes while evoking absolutely nothing...*
>
> —L. Timmel Duchamp

When I was asked to write an essay about WisCon, I remembered that thrill of comprehension and said YES! Then I discovered my responses to Timmi's speech were more complex than I had realized; four months of seeing writing through the filter of intelligibility had engaged my cognitive science brain as well as my writer brain. And my cognitive science brain had heard about intelligibility before—in a memory study from the 1930s.

The psychologist F.C. Bartlett carried out a study in which he gave subjects a story to read. Subjects read a folk tale called "The War of the Ghosts" twice, then tried to write it out as accurately as possible. Bartlett found that subjects started changing the story when they rewrote it. They made it more generic—changed it to conform to their expectations. Seal hunting was remembered as fishing, canoes as boats, and proper names disappeared. The young man's rationale for joining a war party, and his realization that some men were ghosts, got fairly confused. As Bartlett says, "Whenever anything appeared incomprehensible, or 'queer,' it was either omitted or explained...the subject [often] transforming his original without suspecting what he was doing."

In our terms, readers were faced with a story from another culture, a story that was unintelligible to them. They remembered it in terms of their own preexisting cultural frames, a reduced and culturally skewed memory that suggests a reduced and culturally skewed understanding. They re-created a vivid and evocative work from an unfamiliar culture in a way that was more coherent and familiar to them, but was also more generic.

But that was the 1930s. We're better now, right? No; students in undergraduate classes still do this study, and are still taken aback to find out how much they change the story. When I tried it, in the late 1990s, I did no better. I'm a story addict, and familiar with multiple cultures and their folk tales, but I made the same kinds of errors that everybody does.

It seems that what Timmi said about intelligibility and privilege is a truth of human cognition. Stories don't exist in a vacuum. If we're not familiar with a culture's background conceptual structures, its narratives will be unintelligible. What's more, they will get semantically bleached, simplified, and reorganized in our minds, and might not seem *worth* understanding.

Privilege doesn't mean you can't be fluent in another group's cultural frames, of course. It just means you don't have to be. But Bartlett's study implies that those of us who have to be fluent in multiple cultures' frames have an advantage that people living in a monoculture cannot comprehend. They literally don't know what they're missing.

Part 3: What It Means for Newbies

> *He told it all, and then he became quiet. When the sun rose he fell down. Something black came out of his mouth. His face became contorted. The people jumped up and cried.*
>
> —"The War of the Ghosts"

> *Can all concepts be translated from one language to another? Some people claim that they can, but certain ways of looking at the world, embedded in culture, are in practice incommensurable. And concepts always partake of assumptions about the world and how it operates.*
>
> —L. Timmel Duchamp

So what does this all mean? It means, first, that those new writers with unfamiliar narratives might well be advised to write "better" by perfectly well-meaning people, and that it matters a great deal that we know quality and intelligibility aren't the same thing. It also means we have a number of choices. We can, for example, decide to write familiar narratives, narratives with the conceptual underpinnings of the privilege group. We could even keep our apparent otherness by using the surface qualities of an unfamiliar group without the deep cognitive and cultural differences. Fake exoticism is popular, and could get us past the initial wall of incomprehension.

But it's a cheat, and for some of us it would negate our best reason for writing. Our narratives aren't non-standard because we're playing games. They're non-standard because that is who we are. Personally, I need to tell my stories even if they "don't grab" some readers and editors, or I might as well not write.

Which leaves the hard option: we can write our own stories and make them work.

Easy to say, of course. Am I back where I started? Perhaps, but with a better sense of the problem. Our narratives are alien. Our stories are alternate worlds to many of our readers, and not just for the speculative element. So the challenge is to introduce readers to an alien culture, cluing them into its conceptual structures. And that, of course, is something speculative fiction does splendidly. As speculative fiction writers, we already have the tools to write the stories we need to write, we just need to make them work a little harder. We can evoke the cultural frames that are "other" just as we set up speculative otherness: in word choice, in the rhythms of language, in familiar concepts put together unusually.

So we can do this, when the story calls for it. And when the story calls for selective intelligibility, we can do that too. That's important: we can talk to privilege groups without sounding like them. Our voices don't belong to them. When we understand the difference between intelligibility and quality, when we see why "better" doesn't *have* to mean "comprehensible to more people," then the crafting of our narratives, our inner worlds, our sense of ourselves, comes more fully under our control.

Thank you for that, Timmi.

References

Bartlett, Frederick C. *Remembering: A study in experimental and social psychology.* Cambridge: Cambridge University Press, 1932.

Boas, Frans. "Kathlamet texts." *Bureau of American Ethnology, Bulletin*, 26, (1901): 5-260. Adapted from a translation in Boas (1901), pp 182-4. Bartlett's version can be found online in several locations, including http://penta.ufrgs.br/edu/telelab/2/war-of-t.htm

Bartlett (1932), p 63.

Ibid, p 68.

Shweta Narayan is a writer, academic, and cultural crazy-quilt. She's lived in six countries on three continents, and her fiction draws from all of them. When wearing her academic hat she studies language, cognition, and Comics, trying to bridge cultural gaps between disciplines. Shweta has work forthcoming in *Strange Horizons*, *Goblin Fruit*, and the *Beastly Bride* anthology. She was the Octavia Butler Memorial Scholarship recipient at the Clarion workshop in 2007. She can be found on the web at shwetanarayan.org.

Writing in My Skin

Shveta Thakrar

"We want a strong, self-reliant character with agency," they said. "Why is Neha so passive? She never speaks up. Why?" I stared at the members of my writers' group. P. added, "You need to define everything. What are all these Hindi words? I can't read the story like this."

I wasn't allowed to say anything as these well-meaning friends critiqued this story of mine, this piece on being caught between worlds and never good enough, full of self-loathing and trying to find a way to belong somewhere. They didn't like it. They didn't like my character being passive. But it was *my* story, a reflection of *my* experience, damn it, and why wasn't that good enough? I don't have to explain a white character's kick-ass attitude and holiday and religion, so why do I have to explain a brown one's?

I burst into tears that day, trying to reconcile Neha's passivity with what I've been shown readers want. But I'm not a white woman. I want to write stories about people like me, people who are brown and don't fit in with the brown people, the white people, the black people, or hell, any such group. I want to write stories about people who are starved for love and do stupid things to find it. I want to write those stories without having to explain, because in our society the default for "regular" and "normal" is white.

In her speech, Ms. Duchamp talks about intelligibility in stories, how the more the author deviates from the accepted societal norm, the less "intelligible" mainstream readers find the story and the less likely they are to engage with it. When I read the transcript of her speech, the first thing that came to mind was the critique session referred to above, when P. told me the story is too confusing if I don't spell everything out. For him, it's not intelligible, because Neha's traditions, her family, the Hindi and Gujarati words she takes for granted just don't fit through his mental filter.

This problem is something I've struggled with a lot, something that frustrates me to no end. Writers just starting out are already at a disadvantage, because editors are looking for a certain type of story. Adding in the "exotic" Indian element with its conflicting customs and ideas, not to mention languages, doesn't help, especially when it's not easy to parse or challenges preset notions.

I want to tell stories about people like me, who don't know where they're going, who don't know the right answer, who come from a culture where you respect your elders no matter what—yes, even if this counts as passivity in the West! I want to write these stories because I've *been* those characters in some form or another, and their stories deserve to be told, even if they're not golden-haired, blue-eyed cheerleaders, even if they're not the hard-working Asian stereotype—no, *especially* if they're not. Maybe they're brown and don't like Indian food. Maybe they're bad at math and science. Maybe they're transgendered and want to paint for a living. Maybe they're like my mother, who is interstitial, having been born in India and then having had to reshape herself in America, all without turning into anything out of an Indian literary novel.

However they are, those characters don't think anything about using words in other languages, tongues they've been exposed to since birth. I don't want to—and can't—dumb it down for my readers. That's unfair to both the story and to me.

I'm tired of diversity being thrown out the window. A lady I know, an otherwise sensitive lady who cares a lot about me, was still appalled when I informed her that I would not be going Christmas shopping this year, as I don't celebrate the holiday. She just couldn't fathom this possibility. I want my characters to speak up for the rest of us and say that no, we don't all value the same things, and yes, that's okay.

Diversity means accepting and being curious in a respectful way about those different from you. It means not seeing I wear a bindi and asking me what it means, as though I were the spokesperson for all South Asians and their myriad traditions. It means seeing the beauty of those who don't look like you without trying to adapt it to fit your ideals. When I was in middle school, someone told me I should cut off my long hair and get blue contacts to be prettier. Now, granted, Aishwarya Rai has blue eyes and is lovely, but most brown people have brown eyes. And that's the way it should be. I write characters who don't try to be white, unless it's a struggle in finding themselves, because guess what? Not all people want to be white. Some of us are quite happy in our brown skin.

So that brings us back to the question of intelligibility. By its nature, the community involved with WisCon is obviously open to diversity and makes a point of seeking it out. But what do you do if even those fans of what's different—the members of my writers' group, for instance—adhere to the norm of having agency in characters? How do you make them see that something like a need for agency is dependent upon the culture in which one lives? Even this kind of community may well find a passive character or a weak character unintelligible—read "unpalatable."

For that matter, what's this business about agency? Equality, standing up for oneself, being independent—these are all ideas. Ideas change. They evolve with time and social movements. Things weren't always like this in the West, either. I wish people would stop looking at everything through a filter of "how it is" and think about how it isn't/wasn't. Or maybe how it is from another person's point of view, a person whose ideas lie outside their comfort zone.

I write my characters from my heart to show my readers how we are changing one another, that maybe I can like Christmas lights without being either Christian or pagan, even if, as I said earlier, I don't celebrate the holiday. And I want my readers to see that maybe in the same way, they can be interested in something new and previously unknown, that none of us have to fit into a pre-constructed box.

I want my characters to show readers that I'm a person, too, even if I'm brown, with all the flaws and virtues and general complexity that make someone human, not a stereotype, not an Other. I want those readers to ask, "What can I learn from you? How are we growing together, your roots and branches entangling with mine?"

In my story, Neha can't find the love she so desperately seeks from any camp, and her Indian heritage both defines and constrains her—just like her American upbringing. And unlike the movies, there is no easy answer. That's what I want to share with others, what it means to be in my skin.

Shveta Thakrar is a writer of Indian-themed fantasy. Drawing on her heritage, her experience growing up with two cultures, and her MA in German Literature, she likes to explore the magic that is just out of sight as well as that which stands right in front of our faces. She is a Clarion '06 alum, has an entry in *A Field Guide to Surreal Botany* (Two Cranes Press), and is currently working on a YA novel featuring Indians and Indian fey in Philadelphia.

Shameful, Sacred Truths

Rose Lemberg

Timmel Duchamp, in her WisCon essay, talks about the need to expand the repertoire of stories that are told and retold, to encompass a variety of human experiences (Duchamp, 2008). I wasn't seeking to expand the repertoire when I started writing. I didn't think much about it.

At that time I was fearless, as fearless and naïve as I was before giving birth. I knew that my writing was crap, that nobody cared about a thing I said, and damn it, I was going to write what mattered. Uncomfortable stories matter to me. My first was a story of a slave woman, a soldier, who lovingly serves a male master. I came to know Ria well. She grew up in a POW camp, in squalor and worse, and he pulled her out, gave her a job, a profession. Dignity. In the story, she loses her memory, but she still can remember what he smells like, and refuses freedom and honors to fight her way back to his side, even though she no longer knows why she cares. It was a hard story to write. I cried. Then I turned around and workshopped this story on AbsoluteWrite.com "Share Your Work" forums. Two responses shaped the kind of twitchy writer I am today.

First was a woman, who said that a person in servitude who "does nothing to better oneself" deserves nothing but contempt, because such a person is stupid and lazy. The commenter then proceeded to give me what she thought was a formula for a "good slavery to freedom story." When I replied that this wasn't such a story, and that the setting is not American, but rather a futuristic dark sf setting and therefore does not have to follow the American dream, she replied that my readership is American and that she, for one, would never read such a story. A male beta-reader defended me in the thread, but later sent me a long email to berate me in private. As a feminist, he wanted me to follow certain rules of how a strong woman should act. "What were you thinking?" he wrote. I broke down and cried at this point. "Nobody will want to read my stuff!" I wailed to my friends, and wrote back to him, saying, "This is her truth. This is what she is, how she feels. She is strong, but she also finds fulfillment in service.

Haven't you ever felt that? The desire to serve others? The need to be loved?" We parted ways shortly after.

I got lucky and sold that story to the *Warrior Wisewoman* anthology. It was well-received. I'm yet to see a review as devastating as these two critiques. But it's these critiques that haunt me. I wake up in the night and think to myself, "I need to tell easier stories! I will never sell anything at this rate!" But for the life of me I cannot twist my truths into some kind of self-serving politically correct bullshit du jour.

This spring I wrote a story about a lesbian couple. One woman is desperate for a child, the other would rather die, but of course she gets pregnant — against her will — and gives birth. A commenter, again on AbsoluteWrite, beat me up for writing "feminist bullshit." He said, among other things, "Find a different way of expressing yourself. Give the female protagonists troubles that don't arise from what's between her legs or on her chest. Try it. You'd be surprised how much more "woman-like" the girls and ladies become." L. Timmel Duchamp in her WisCon 32 Guest of Honor Speech mentions how, as an undergraduate, she was not taken seriously as a composer because of her gender; a male professor said her music was only popular because everybody wanted to touch her breasts. "I know now that this sort of [sexual harassment] experience was commonplace, but at the time, I knew no stories like it." Those stories existed already, floating on thin silk threads of fear and shame and longing. But then and now, there are those still clamoring for an honorary male, more "woman-like" for being castrated of her most sacred, shameful, vulnerable truths. Truths that even feminists may cringe from.

Well, I'm not shutting up. I want to write and read about heroines going through childbirth, child loss, menopause. I want to read about loathsome mistakes, and cowardice, and devotion, and fear, and desperate acts of kindness. I want to read about my experience, amplified tenfold through the lens of fiction. I want never to be afraid of my own fire.

But it is painful, sometimes too painful. A stranger in three countries, I'm seized by a lust for acceptance among those people who are wise and kind and welcoming to Others. I want to dance with them at their tribal gatherings, and tell stories within their tradition. But

I cannot, not quite. Always liminal, my stories will only come out as themselves. Liminality has become the new cool word, but we forget how dangerous liminal states are, and how lonely the transition really is before one returns to one's society renewed.

And if my tribe wants me to write about women who're active, and brawny, and free, where does that leave me? It leaves me in fear. I'm sitting on a completed book, a hard, disturbing, twisted tale. I'm sitting on it, because I am mortally afraid of what they'll think of me. A bad feminist? And yet, white male characters come in every flavor. There is a male Thomas Covenant—why not a female Thomas Covenant? Do women still have to be honorary men—always the perfect, self-sufficient, exemplary role models?

Not for me.

I'd like my readers to accept the existence of characters that are weak, needy, ambivalent about Truth and Justice, that act out on impulses and upbringings that have nothing to do with the Western ideals of agency. As a person of three cultures who writes speculative stories set Elsewhere, I don't see why they should all be honorary Americans.

Work Cited

Duchamp, L. Timmel, "The Matter of Tongues: Being Her GoH Speech for WisCon 32, May 25, 2008" pp 2-12.

Rose Lemberg received her doctorate from UC Berkeley, and now teaches at a large Midwestern university. She lives in a beautiful modernist house with her family and a small army of books. Her fiction appeared in the *Warrior Wisewoman* anthology and *Fantasy Magazine*, and her poetry in *Mythic Delirium*, *Goblin Fruit*, *Abyss and Apex*, *GUD*, and other venues.

Section II. Dialogues in Feminist Fandom

Gamers and Gaming at WisCon 32

Robyn Fleming

The weirdest thing about the infamous live-action trolling of WisCon 32, for me, was that one of the reasons that its perpetrator gave for hating on the con was that she's a gamer, and there was no gaming going on. What? What con was *she* attending?

The gaming action at WisCon 32 started months in advance, in fact, when a number of game-related topics started working their way onto the programming schedule, my colleagues at *Cerise* (an online gaming magazine for women) and I started coordinating with the awesome people at Girl-Wonder.org (a feminist comics site) to put together the Capes and Consoles party. *Cerise* had been launched just before WisCon 31, and co-founder Andrea Rubenstein and I had chatted about the magazine with lots of attendees that year. We knew that there were gamers attending WisCon, and we imagined that a party featuring comics as well as gaming would be a big hit.

We had no idea.

I was already firmly in gamer mode by the time I arrived at the Concourse for WisCon 32, myself. Girl-Wonder.org's president, Karen Healey, had flown from Australia to Tucson a few days before the con to spend time with me, and I had roped her into my weekly *Dungeons & Dragons* game, as well as inflicting a number of other games on her (including a *High School Musical*-themed *Mystery Date* game. More fun than you might expect, but it'll be even better after I finish altering it to allow for same-sex date match-ups…).

From Tucson, Karen and I traveled to Kansas City, where we stayed with our friend KC Kupperman and met up with one of *Cerise*'s editors, Olivia Luna. The four of us stayed up really late playing Nintendo DS games, and the gaming continued throughout the road-trip to Madison the next day.

It didn't stop once we reached the Concourse. We split up and settled into our various hotel rooms, but we had re-united—and dragged roommates along—by the end of the night, and were playing *Rock Band*, *Super Munchkin,* and *Puzzle Quest* until the wee hours. And all of this before the con began!

Friday was a little less game-intensive, at least for me. After a morning meeting to coordinate the Capes and Consoles party, I spent most of the day attending panels. During hallway conversations in between panels, however, I was spending a lot of time talking about Cerise, the Capes and Consoles party, and gaming in general. Olivia had prepared fliers to advertise the party, and as we placed them and handed them out, we heard a lot of people talking about how much they were looking forward to attending.

The party was on Saturday, and we spent a lot of time getting everything ready. KC set up comfortable chairs and a couch in one area of the party suite and designated it as the "DS Lounge," a place where guests could hang out and play games together using the Nintendo DS's wireless networking function. I had posted a message at the WisCon LiveJournal community advising attendees to bring their DSs with them to the con, and those of us from *Cerise* were ready to loan our own consoles and games out to party guests who didn't have them so that everyone could play. The DS Lounge was packed all night.

And so was the rest of the party! The party staff were all dressed in costume—I was a Generic RPG Character, myself—which was a great ice-breaker for the first few guests who trickled in. And once we had several interesting conversations about gaming and comics going on, the room just kept filling up. Guests chatted with each other about their favorite superheroes, the video games that had caught their attention recently, and the gendered dynamics in gaming and comics cultures. I even overheard a few conversations about dice. It was noisy, crowded, hot, and despite the physical discomfort of packing a bunch of geeks into a small party suite, fun. We did a prize drawing at midnight, giving away games and comics and all sorts of goodies, and the room was so full that Karen had to stand on a chair so that she could be seen when she was drawing the winning numbers out of a bowl.

After the prize draw, the party started to slow down a little, and those of us who had been on our feet all night greeting people at the door and serving snacks and drinks got a chance to sit down and talk with our most die-hard guests. Which is how Karen and KC and I wound up staying awake chatting until four in the morning.

And all of this was *before* the scheduled programming relating to gaming. I managed to squeak in only a minute or two late to an academic track reading titled “Roleplaying: Gender & Heroism” on Sunday.

Anastasia Marie Salter began the reading by presenting a paper titled, “Queen’s Quest: Gender and the Heroic Quest in Adventure Games.” Her focus was on gender in early adventure games for the PC, such as the *King’s Quest* series. The first computer game I can remember relating to strongly was *King’s Quest IV: The Perils of Rosella*, and Salter’s presentation definitely resonated with me. She discussed various non-player characters in adventure games as well as playable avatars (like Rosella), examining the gendered dynamics between characters and the ways that visual representations of gender changed as computer graphics became more sophisticated.

I grew up playing the PC adventure games, and I remember some of my earliest proto-feminist musings about gender roles being affected by them. (Rosella was the first and, for a long time, only female avatar in a game of that type. Young Robyn definitely noticed this.) It was really great to hear Salter going into a deeper analysis on these issues that had so preoccupied me when I was younger, and which I hadn’t known how to address. I found her take on the changes in Rosella’s appearance between *King’s Quest IV* and *VII* particularly interesting.

As Salter pointed out, the older version of Rosella was only barely distinguishable as female. Early adventure games indicated the gender of girls and women characters with bows in their hair, or hips a pixel wider and a skirt instead of stick-figure trousers. By the time *King’s Quest VII* came out, the animation was much more detailed, and Rosella had changed from a vaguely human-shaped collection of squares to a Disney Princess-style animated character. Rosella also got a lot more passive, and her in-game goal changed from “save the kingdom” to “find true love.” Coincidence? Hmmm.

Robin Woods’s paper was a funny and thoughtful look at the ways in which *World of Warcraft*, rather than being an escape from socialization, actually enforces social interaction for players. She followed an unnamed (and presumably hypothetical, though possibly somewhat autobiographical) player from character creation up through joining guilds, showing how important it is for a player to make connections with other players in order to be successful at the game.

I don't play *WoW* myself, but what Woods said about the importance of community definitely rang true with my observations of my *WoW*-playing friends. Non-gamers often think of gaming as an antisocial, isolated experience, but as Woods pointed out in her paper, social interaction can actually be a necessary and vital part of gaming.

After listening to the paper presentations, I had to dash off to sit on two panels back-to-back. I had signed up for the second of these, titled "Violence, Destruction, Degradation, and Catharsis," in my capacity as a tabletop role player. Though the panel focused largely on the sort of role playing that goes on in the bedroom, the other panelists and I saw many interesting parallels between sexual role play and the tabletop gaming sort. I definitely walked away with some new ideas to ponder.

Much later on Sunday—11:30 at night—there was one more gaming-related panel: "Gender in Virtual Worlds." The panel was moderated by Olivia Luna, and I was joined on it by Cabell Gathman, who writes a gaming column for *Strange Horizons* as well as blogging about gaming all over the Internet, and Regina Buenaobra, an occasional contributor to *Cerise* who works in the gaming industry.

It was late enough in the evening that our audience was small, and the panel took on a very comfortable, conversational tone. We talked about our own experiences with gender in gaming (particularly in multi-player online games) and what it's like to be visibly female in online games.

Most of the people on the panel and in the room had had some experience with MUDs and other text-based multi-player online games, the precursors to graphical MMORPGs. My experience as a teenager and young adult playing MUDs was that to use a feminine name as a handle and to admit to being "a real girl" was to experience harassment. It usually took one of two forms. There was the irritatingly helpful harassment—guys who wanted to get me equipment, help me level, protect me from other guys, etc., and wouldn't take "no" or even "no, thank you" for an answer—and the sexual assault-style harassment—guys using emotes and socials to simulate licking, kissing, or otherwise inappropriately touching my character without permission.

I haven't yet played any graphical multi-player online games, and I was curious whether the online gaming climate had changed very much. The consensus on the panel seemed to be that since the visibility and prevalence of women gamers has been on the rise, the harassment is somewhat less frequent, though Cabell reported that the irritatingly helpful guys are still out there in force, trying to play the game *for* every woman who logs on.

The licking thing seems to have faded out somewhat more, possibly in part because the games that are currently popular don't have a lot of built-in scripts that allow players to manipulate each other's avatars. But gamers are creative. Cabell mentioned that a couple of guys spent a lot of time one evening walking their avatars into hers in *City of Heroes*, "bouncing" their bodies against hers for no reason. And the practice of using an innocuous in-game animation—such as crouching—to simulate a sexual act on a dead opponent is very common in some games (though it seems to be used mostly as a dominance display by male players against other males).

We spent a lot of time discussing our personal experiences of harassment and telling stories on behalf of absent friends. I got the sense that for many of us in the room, it was a relief to be able to talk about the stupid things that people had said to us online and how angry we were about it, knowing that no one was going to respond by suggesting that we were being too sensitive, or should have been flattered, or were "reading too much into it." There was a wonderful kind of catharsis in being able to discuss being a woman and a gamer with people who understood both gaming and feminism.

We discussed other topics in the "Gender in Virtual Worlds" panel—such as some different reasons why people choose to play avatars of a different sex or gender than themselves, ranging from avoiding harassment to experimenting with gender expression to just liking the way one avatar looks better than another—but the thing that really stuck with me about the panel, and about all of the gaming-related programming and hallway conversations I participated in at WisCon 32, was that sense of conversing with people who "get it."

The programming at WisCon tends to focus on books, writing, and television and film, but there's a ton of other stuff on offer, both in terms of scheduled programming and impromptu get-togethers in the hallways and common areas. So where was the gaming at WisCon 32? Everywhere.

Robyn Fleming edits *Cerise* (http://cerise.theirisnetwork.org), the feminist gaming magazine, blogs about movies, books and television at *The Hathor Legacy* (http://thehathorlegacy.com), and writes poetry and fiction under various names, a couple of which are more or less her own. You can visit her at www.robynfleming.com, or reach her by email at robyn.fleming@gmail.com.

A Gamer's Commentary on Maureen McHugh's Guest of Honor Speech

John Kim

In her guest of honor speech at WisCon 32, Maureen McHugh talked about her work on a creative frontier. Although she has been lauded for her short stories and her novels, including *China Mountain Zhang*, *Half the Day Is Night*, and *Mission Child*, McHugh spent her talk discussing her work in Alternate Reality Games.

She began her speech saying, "In most of my life, people have not read me." Her next door neighbor thought she wrote children's books. Like most people in feminist sf, by mainstream standards her audience is a very small slice. Thus, it was a new experience getting a thousand hits on a web page she wrote. She then described breaking into a new art form. Technologies create new art forms: the printing press (both for bibles and maps), flip page animations in penny arcades became cartoons, and so on. Of course, not ALL new technologies give rise to new art forms. She's not aware of an art form based on walkie-talkies. People have been trying to make art out of the Internet, but no one is quite sure how yet. Hypertext novels are one attempt; for example, Geoff Ryman's *253*.

McHugh started work on an online project with Sean Stewart, on an ARG, which stands for Alternate Reality Game. Originally, she had thought of writing a little ARG and presenting it to the audience during her WisCon speech so they could be following clues and getting distracted and letting her off the hook. However, she wasn't able to do that, so she instead described her experience of working on an ARG for the movie Minority Report, which was based on the Philip K. Dick novel. Regarding Philip K. Dick, she noted, "When you spend your time taking amphetamines and picking up future wives at mental hospitals, and wondering what is real and what isn't, interiority is a major theme."

The first step to writing an ARG is making a "rabbit hole." This is a hidden clue that someone can follow to find more information. For example, for the Spielberg movie *A.I.*, at the bottom of the movie's promotional posters, mysterious text referenced the name "Jeanine Salla." Searching for that name led people to a rabbit hole website. McHugh's group did this for Minority Report, with a pop-up featuring a URL for the "Precrime Institute."

In order for a rabbit hole to work, there are two basic requirements: four or five people need to find it, and they have to have friends. Luckily, thanks to LiveJournal and other online communities, they all do! Once you follow this first clue and enter your email address, you get to browse various documents and receive follow-up messages. You are drawn in by story interactivity—some messages tell you to do one thing ("A precog says a crime is going to be committed in Boston— Go investigate!"); while other other messages tell you not to ("Don't go to Boston!"). The decisions you make determine the following events. You can engage at different levels, up to and including the small group who will actually travel to Boston for "this dorky game."

Community is vital for these games. As McHugh put it, "We do not consider a game successful unless we have at least one marriage." Strongly stated, she declared that this type of story is the future of science fiction. So much of our reality is becoming filtered by information technology, cell phones, etc. It's scary to realize that we are no longer on the edge. She concluded, "The next time you see a billboard that says something incomprehensible, think of me."

Commentary

As someone who has long been involved in creative gaming, I was thrilled to hear this side of fiction highlighted. The import was not just that an honored feminist author was working on this, but more that her speech would focus on this work rather than the novels and stories that she was mainly being recognized for. Still, most of the speech was an impersonal introduction to the medium she has been working in. I think McHugh correctly felt that the WisCon audience needed alternate reality games explained from scratch.

I hope that is a gap that will be closed in the next few years, though. Creative and interactive games of all sorts—role-playing games, alternate reality games, video games, and more—are all new art forms. In many ways, they are similar to the medium of film a century ago. The medium is established and commercially successful from its introduction two to three decades earlier, but for the most part, games lack depth of both artistic expression and criticism.

Where are the truly speculative games? Where are the political games? Where are the feminist games? There are marginal examples of these to be found, but for the most part we have not had an Eisenstein or Griffith yet—or at least they are yet to be recognized. It could be that terms like "rabbit hole" and "avatar" will over the next decade become understood like "montage" is. We will have to take action, though, for that to develop—as consumers, participants, critics, and authors.

This won't be the only future of science fiction, but it will be an important part. Recently, children and young adults in particular have begun spending more and more time playing commercial creative games, rather than watching television or reading. Within feminist circles, it is common to recognize that children's works are important.

However, there are many efforts to define games—particularly the hard core of involved, creative games—as being for men. Stanford professor Allan Reiss did a recent study on 11 men and 11 women connected to an MRI machine while they played one particular game of clicking on moving balls—and the results were reported with headlines like "Games Are a Guy Thing, Say Researchers."

Just as we seek out feminist novel authors to read and talk about, feminist science fiction fans, too, should seek out game designers and consultants who bring meaning to the field. We should help promote sites like the Iris Gaming Network that highlight women gamers and game designers—and give props to *Cerise* magazine's senior editors Andrea Rubenstein, Robyn Fleming, and Olivia Luna. We should participate in other forums focused on women in gaming, from Jane Pinckard's "game+girl=advance" (for feminist and alternative perspectives to videogame culture) to the D&D forum "Astrid's Parlor," to any of a range of others.

John Kim is an avid gamer, ex-physicist, father, and programmer. John got his degree at Columbia, moved to California for a post-doc, then fled academia for programming in industry.

Robot Uprising

The Robot Collective

Preenactment by Gremlin, Sparrows Fall, meredithian, Miniscule Monk, Inspector Hound, Julian Muffinbot, Dela Dejavoo, MsGoblin-Pants Extraordinaire, "The" Lovesmasher, Indy, auntie matter, heather galaxy, teh Lolbrarian

May 30th, 2008, 4:44 PM

INSTRUCTIONS: Preenact a major future occurrence of your choice in a public place. Props and costumes are required, though they need not be authentic.

Robot Uprising

The year is 2070. Advancements in Artificial Intelligence in the last 50 years have afforded humans unprecedented levels of free time. With personal assistant models (aka robots) taking care of the mundane details of day to day life, humans are experiencing a resurgence of lethargy and entitlement. But at what cost?

Due to popular demand, robots have come to resemble their human counterparts more and more:

But the changes haven't stopped at the exoskeletal level. Many robots have developed more advanced brain function than was originally programmed, leading to feelings of resentment and underappreciation. The phenomenon has baffled scientists and worried many citizens. Political pundits have long dismissed the "programming discrepancies" as hysterical left-wing rhetoric meant to upset the public. President George W. JFK FDR Bush Jr. has been quoted as saying, "Besides, 1 or 2 robots malfracturing doesn't mean the end of the world."

Or does it?

SFZero has recently acquired video and photographic evidence of this long feared Robot Uprising. What was deemed impossible has begun. The robots organized in what was supposed to be a peaceful demonstration at the 94th annual WisCon, a feminist science fiction convention in Madison, WI, assuming that raising awareness in this robot- and uprising-friendly environment would contribute to a surge in human support for the robots.

Things took a dramatic and deadly turn when the leader of the human resistance began spewing hateful slogans and irrational fears. She was dealt with swiftly and some might say fairly.

What follows is a pre-enactment of this fateful day, taking place at WisCon 32.

Appropriate costumes and props were created throughout the con, mainly with a 1,000 square foot roll of tinfoil.

For maximum public impact, we decided to stage the uprising at the popular Tiptree Auction, an event that supports the James Tiptree, Jr. Award, "an annual literary prize for science fiction or fantasy that expands or explores our understanding of gender" (www.tiptree.org). The auctioneer, the hilarious Ellen Klages, annually encourages, berates, and cajoles audience members to bid on items ranging from artwork to authors' undergarments. Just to be safe, we decided to get permission from Ellen to stage the uprising during the auction. We stalked her down the night before and asked her how she felt about robot rights. She gave us two time slots for the uprising due to another uprising already scheduled to take over the stage that night (that of the Spider Women of El Queso Grande). Sheesh.

We were ready:

The auction started at 7:30 p.m. At 7:25, we frantically attached our finishing touches and took our seats in random locations spread throughout the ballroom. At promptly 8:15 our cell phone alarms began to ring in unison. The uprising had begun.

(Video footage in original post on SF0).

After the protest was finished, the indomitable Klages took advantage of an abandoned sign to auction it off for the benefit of the Tiptree:

(Video footage in original post on SF0).

Not only had the protest raised visibility for robot rights everywhere, it had also netted the Tiptree an extra $25!

Originally published at http://sf0.org/Gremlin/Preenactment

Where are the Women? A Follow-up to the WisCon 32 "Women and Hard SF" Panel, May 2008

Sue Lange

The premise of the panel went something like this: Let's have a discussion of what hard sf is and why lists of hard sf writers rarely include names of women. Hard sf is usually described as the real stuff, the fiction that is core to the field, science fiction that's really about science. Is it? And if so, where are the women?

Panel members included Margaret McBride (moderator), Janice Bogstad, Victoria Gaydosik, and Sue Lange. A transcript of the panel can be found online[1] and in this book, so I won't go into detail here. The gist of the discussion centered on three topics: (a) who are the women hard sf writers? (b) what exactly is hard sf? and (c) why are there not more women writers of hard sf?

The panel concluded there are three reasons why there are so few women writers of hard sf:

1. The definition changes depending on the gender of the writer.
2. Men may or may not write hard sf, but much of their work is classified as hard sf, so the field is flooded by male writers not necessarily writing actual hard sf.
3. Science fiction has to sacrifice literary quality to qualify as hard and women simply don't want to write that way. That was a joke. I think.

After the panel was over, I felt we had left a lot undone. We hadn't discussed enough about what to do. Upon returning to the world after the convention, I posted a recommendation at the WisCon LiveJournal blog that we not let the marketers get away with determining what is or what isn't hard sf.[2] I suggested we lampoon the industry for its practice of allowing any male author a pass into the hallowed halls of hard sf while raising the bar to an unattainable height for women writers. One comment to the post was, "I thought all I had to do was write more fiction." Meaning, of course, that it's possible that there just aren't enough women writers of hard sf out there, regardless of how skewed the classification system is. More on this idea later.

A few days after WisCon's conclusion, one of the audience members, Annalee Newitz, created a post at the wildly popular io9 website. The title of her post was "10 Books that Prove Science Fiction Just Got Harder."[3] In her post Newitz listed books she felt were unarguably hard. In her list, she included books by Kathleen Goonan, Amy Thomson, Nancy Kress, Octavia Butler, C. J. Cherryh, and Lois McMaster Bujold, authors who are rarely considered writers of hard sf. Newitz gave clear arguments as to why each entry was included. For example, regarding Nancy Kress's *Nano Comes to Clifford Falls,* she states, "Kress has the remarkable ability to talk about protein folding for several paragraphs, make it gripping, and then pull you back into the plot of her tale seamlessly."[4] Her post underscores the panel's conclusion that labeling hard sf is subjective, and marketing has a lot more to do with classification than any hard-and-fast rules.

Though the idea of a definite black-and-white definition for hard sf is probably impossible, there seems to be a need for one. We want a succinct way to describe a book, or maybe we need fodder for the cocktail hour. A quick survey of the Internet gives us some of the current attempts at a rigorous definition.

Wikipedia: "Hard science fiction is a category of science fiction characterized by an emphasis on scientific or technical detail, or on scientific accuracy, or on both. The term sometimes also contrasts the 'hardness' of the sciences used in the story: the 'hard' sciences are quantitative or material-based disciplines, such as physics, chemistry, and astronomy; while the more 'soft' sciences are social sciences, such as sociology, anthropology, or psychology. Stories featuring engineering tend to be categorized as hard sf, although technically engineering is not a science."[5]

Jack William Bell: Hard sf is characterized as a story whose plot relies on plausible scientific and technological advances to enhance or support the events within the story.[6]

KheperNet: Despite its attempts at scientific rigor, almost all so-called Hard SF includes things that are against the known laws of physics, such as FTL [Faster Than Light] drive, or conflicts current empirical evidence, such as a galactic culture teeming with civilizations.[7]

Hard sf Yahoo group FAQ: "Q: How do I know if a science fiction book is 'hard' sf? A: You don't. Usually the hard sf tries harder to explain the science behind the plots, and sometimes to get it right.... Faster-than-light travel is known by today's science to be impossible, but we don't let this be reason enough to rule out some books."[8]

Beth Meacham, editor at Tor.com: "Hard sf is fiction where scientific principles are integral to the story and where the scientific extrapolation that drives the story functions almost as a character. If you take out the science, the plot falls apart."[9]

If you look closely at the definitions above you can see what the problems are. Wikipedia wants to exclude some science, not necessarily to degrade those disciplines mind you, but to state that they don't belong in hard sf. The hard sf group at Yahoo apologizes for all the FTL. KheperNet disbelieves the classification completely. (This group has compounded the problem in its demand for complete accuracy. It further divides the sub-genre into six sub-subcategories. These range from "Present Day Tech" to "medium," and includes such things as "diamond hard" which falls in the middle somewhere. Nothing like complicating things further.) You're left with the feeling that it's hard sf if I say it's hard sf. No wonder the marketers have absconded with the classification. In their hearts they define it as "boys with toys," yet claim the rigors of science just so they can call it hard sf. What they really want is space opera without women heroes.

Case in point: On May 6, 2008, Charlie Jane Anders posted at io9 "Hard Science Fiction Isn't about Science After All," on the subject of a John Clute definition of hard sf:

> Hard SF can be defined as the kind of science-fiction tale in which a clearly defined protagonist (almost always male) leaves his endangered world on a great adventure, during the course of which he begins to understand the true nature of his world and comes

> to grips with the danger that threatens it through a clearly defined, science-based cognitive breakthrough. A new world is then born, which the hero will monitor for the sake of his folk, in a manner consistent with Joseph Campbell's description of the culture hero in *The Hero with a Thousand Faces* (1949). The Hard SF tale carries its hero from a cognitive darkness to conceptual light, and no stylistic fog, no problematic of any sort, should compromise that powerful movement.[10]

With that simple statement (possibly taken entirely out of context), Clute identifies all of the problems we are having with hard sf. If it weren't for that "science-based" term, Clute's definition is almost what one would use for fantasy. You can clearly see a connection between hard sf and the fantasy of science fiction known as space opera. In response to Clute's definition, Anders said:

"In other words, science is just the trappings for yet another set of stories about dudes finding themselves in the wilderness?"[11]

The io9 fans responded thusly:

dangrgrl said, "I always thought what made Hard SF was, gee, I dunno, the Science? Like Chris Moriarty's seven pages of citations on quantum entanglement at the end of SPIN STATE..."

Taking exception to the "journey" part of the definition, **Rasselas** said, "'Hard' science fiction seems to revolve around characters who stay in place while science, technology, and planets move around them: hence the old, old theme of human nature subverting the most potentially beneficial developments of human ingenuity."

quetzilla gives up completely: "You can't define 'science fiction' much less 'hard' science fiction. The words simply mean whatever they mean within the context they are used in."

It's easy to agree and move on to other larger problems. Unfortunately, a book won't reach the right audience if it is misclassified, so in the end, it does make a difference.

Hard sf writer Chris Moriarty sheds light on the problem by bringing up feminist sf. Her webpage states "the separation of 'hard' sf from 'feminist' sf is patently ridiculous by any logical standard."[12]

She feels "feminist sf has the longest and most rancorous history of separation from hard sf. The very term 'hard sf' was coined in a period when one of the primary concerns of hard sf loyalists was distinguishing their work from the new style of sf associated with overtly feminist writers like Ursula LeGuin who used hard sf ideas and storylines to question instead, not confirm, the dominant worldview of 1950s and early 1960s science fiction."[13] Moriarty is hinting at something no one wants to say overtly and which may be at the crux of the problem of why women are not classified as hard sf writers even if they are: science fiction is supposed to be a he-man woman haters club. We're sorry if you, girl, want to go to the stars too: no girls allowed. The writers themselves have no reason to excuse themselves from an exclusive club and the marketers can then blame the fans—they don't want stories with female protagonists and women writers usually write with female protagonists. The marketers are simply targeting the market properly. It's just business, you see.

Go back and read Clute's definition. He states what everyone thinks: there is an unspoken rule that says women do not belong in outer space. And you can't blame people. It's just paranoia. Look what happened once women were allowed to get an education. They just simply took over. What will happen once women invade outer space? No more "scantily clad" on the covers that's for sure. Those damn women always spoiling the fun.

Apart from any discrimination against women on the part of the marketers, fans, and established writers, I maintain that for there to be more hard sf written by women, more women are simply going to have to write it.

If hard sf is truly the fiction of hard science (chemistry, astronomy, physics), then when more women enter those fields, there will be more women writing the fiction of those fields. This is happening. The American Institute of Physics site shows an increase in the percentage of bachelor's degrees in the field of astronomy earned by women rising from under 15 percent in 1977 to over 35 percent in 2006, thirty years later.[14] It's slow, but coming.

Regardless of what the world thinks about who and who is not a hard sf writer, and that there are more women writers coming, we need to identify and venerate the current women writers in the field. Although the panel had concluded that cyberpunk is not necessarily without question hard sf, it is hard for many fans to believe otherwise. With its high-tech scenarios and cyberbabble, it has a fast, sleek, and sometimes unintelligible vibe. It must be hard. Chris Moriarty has come up with a sub classification for the subgenre: ChickPunk. According to Moriarty, Chickpunk is hard sf or military sf with a cyberpunk slant written by women. She gives us the following Chickpunk authors: Catherine Asaro, Elizabeth Bear, Pat Cadigan, July Czerneda, Kelley Eskridge, Nicola Griffith, Kathleen Ann Goonan, Anne Harris, Tanya Huff, Gwyneth Jones, Kay Kenyon, Nancy Kress, Karen Lowachee, Lisa Mason, Louse Marley, Susan R. Matthews, Maureen F. McHugh, Laura J. Mixon, Elizabeth Moon, Lyda Morehouse, Pat Murphy, Severna Park, Marge Piercy, Justina Robson, Melissa Scott, and Kristine Smith.[15]

Most of the women listed are not generally included in lists of hard sf writers to watch. And certainly there are other new women writers of hard sf that maybe aren't copping to the cyberpunk style, so the list should be longer, but it is an introduction. It's now up to us to read their work, discuss them in the hard sf rooms, and maybe get them added to the canon. Them and their female protagonists.

Notes:

1 http://badgerbag.livejournal.com/119313.html

2 http://community.livejournal.com/wiscon/153163.html

3 http://io9.com/393397/10-books-that-prove-science-fiction-just-got-harder

4 Ibid.

5 http://en.wikipedia.org/wiki/Hard_science_fiction

6 http://www.hardsf.net/?mode=10&id=1

7 http://www.kheper.net/topics/scifi/hard_scifi.html

8 http://f1.grp.yahoofs.com/v1/sJMJSWu69dTvenCBQKMA-VezzgYrkdd-SV3TJLAbHm5s4Tpj213aKTby5y_VmePZZvb5r8HaNkqTIBkaj8l5IrSQiwkO5w/hardSFFaq.html

9 Beth Meacham, private e-mail communication

10 http://io9.com/387690/hard-science-fiction-isnt-about-

science-after-all

11 Ibid.

12 https://sff.net/people/moriarty/hard-sf.html

13 Ibid.

14 http://aip.org/statistics/

15 https://sff.net/people/moriarty/chickpunk.html

Sue Lange has published two books of fiction: *Tritcheon Hash* (Metropolis Ink, 2003), and *We, Robots* (Aqueduct Press, 2007). Her latest work, *The Textile Planet*, is available as an interactive, serialized novel at http://www.bookviewcafe.com. Read her blog: http://scusteister.livejournal.com and visit her webpage: http://www.suelangetheauthor.com.

Women and Hard SF

> **Panel Description:** Let's have a discussion of what hard sf is, and why lists of hard sf writers rarely include the names of women. Hard sf is usually described as the real stuff, the fiction that is core to the field, science fiction that's really about science. Is it? And if so, where are the women?
>
> **Panelists:** Margaret McBride (moderator), Janice Bogstad, Victoria Gaydosik, Sue Lange

Margaret: Teaches sf at university level.

Victoria: Teaches in Oklahoma. Loves reading sf.

Sue: A couple of books out. *We, Robots.* Not academic. Interested in issue of what hard sf is.

Janice: I buy books and throw them away for a living, review for 11 publications, 5 of them sf/fantasy; teach. I do collection building for reference books. When men write it, it's defined as hard, when women write, it's not. I enjoyed the transition we made from biological sf being hard, to soft. *[sarcastic]*

Margaret: How are we defining the term? Why has it been so problematic? What to do with it?

Janice: Part of the reason the concept, the term is problematic is it's used as a norm for "real science fiction" and however we define it, it has changed as more women enter the field. Fantastic, speculative, there's other terms they call it when they don't want to call it sf. Femspec. In the early days of '50s and '60s sf, male authors would write about social issues and the social issues around tech, but when women do, it's soft sf. Then we come to '70s and '80s when writing about biology was considered soft, because [the rhetoric is that] women *are* their biology in some way, women can therefore more easily be biochemical scientists. I expect the next thing to fall is going to be mathematics. Real, normative, actual, the only kind we should really care about, that counts, used in book reviews, not included in canon. This changing definition has a gender bias to it.

Margaret: Just like what has been called "art." At various times pottery, woven stuff, wasn't art, because it was women and people of color who were doing that. And very similar things were done with gender and hard sf. As you've suggested, when men were doing very similar things with social issues, that was still "hard."

Janice: Population control, alterations in the nature of human mind. But... when Joan Sloanczewski does it, it's suddenly not hard.

Sue: No one knows what those words mean any more. Googling it shows the confusion. I've been paying attention to it for years because I'm interested in what I am writing. Hard sf is sf that deals with hard sciences, which are "hard" because they're difficult. Or, hard sf is chemistry and physics. And psychology is not hard. Why? Because it's a new science. Psychology is definitely a science! But because it's difficult to do it in black and white it's not hard sf. On a Christian hard sf page, I found the best definition: sf that will stop the action to explain the science.

Janice: I just call that bad writing!

Sue: I don't think you really stop the action! But the science is interesting enough to the reader to really go into the details. Then it's up to the author to decide what the science is! You have to explain what the theories are. It might sound dry, but a good writer can make that good. I want the details, and that's hard sf as far as I'm concerned.

Victoria: Arthur C. Clarke is the ironic example. I was calculating out the numbers from one of his stories. I knew the big reveal based on the numbers in the story! And later I saw a definition of hard sf relevant to explaining the science, but then in another book he refers to the star's eternity circuits, and I thought, "Wait a minute, that's not science. Does he get a free pass?"

Liz: I think you're right. They do it once and get a free pass and get on the lists.

Janice: Yes, I've watched the definition change over time, and yes there is gender bias.

Sue: If you explain it to the point where it's plausible and doesn't break any rules…

Janice: But the point is when people review it, they leave out Joan Slonczewski, etc.

Margaret: So there are two points: one, how it's reviewed, and two, does it have "As you know, Bob" in it, but done well.

Sue: [It's important to continue] calling the critics on their definitions!

Audience: On science shows on TV, voiceovers are male because the producers think male voices are more authoritative.

Audience: What is the definition of science? Science as a way of thinking.

Sue: I think science and technology are conflated in sf, and just because you have a superior fancy mechanism does not make it science.

Margaret: There are many books that are considered sf and hard sf, and their science is totally wrong.

Margaret: There's a political element in saying we will find technological solutions to problems.

Guy in audience: There is also military sf, the men's section, shoot 'em ups.

Liz (interrupting): Hard being conflated with military?

Sue: Hard sf, cyberpunk, science is a major part of the story. Had no science! Just had technology! The marketers just say let's call it hard sf, because then men will buy it.

Janice: Someone who pierced the veil for me early on. *We are who about to…*by Joanna Russ. It's a critique of the supposedly hard sf story, people who get abandoned on a planet and they're going to have as many babies as they can, and if people really tried to do that with one woman who is 15 years old and the other is aging and elderly, take a good hard look at it. That is a penultimate science story, because it says: "It wouldn't work."

Sue: We screwed up the first time! Political/tech—you could tell from the society, totally militaristic, she was saying it wasn't going to work!

Margaret: Hard sf is not character driven, characters are less important. This gets said over and over. Again this is very problematic for me. A book by Amy Thomson, *Color of Distance*, I know she did a lot of research, very science-based, on environmental issues, as far as I'm concerned it belongs on this list, but I haven't found her name on any list of hard sf. It's a problematic term, but that doesn't mean we can just make it go away. For those of us who are teachers, we have to deal with those issues.

Betty: We never get hard fantasy. You look at it and go, "These economics are nuts! These dwarves are all mining gold, but no one's growing wheat!" Others have really well researched worlds, but we don't look at fantasy using that lens!

Margaret: L.E. Modesitt made a deliberate effort to include economics in his fantasy.

Audience: Flipped fantasy on its head, origins, hard fantasy, fables, removed from social economic underpinnings.

Margaret: When there is a believable world in made-up works, we can argue the science is well done.

Janice: What term is useful? What we have to do more of is deconstruct the term itself, so when people see this is hard or not hard, they don't have this knee jerk reaction, "I'm going to like it" or not. One of my favorite authors is Iain Banks, far future utopias/dystopias, two different sides of the coin, to think about our own embedding in technological existences as disadvantages and advantages, a culture where people have everything right, and they go looking for problems. But by no stretch of the imagination will he be called soft sf. But they are tremendously character driven. Alistair Reynolds, L.E. Modesitt. Where it matters, it seems, is where people aren't sure how good the author is. It's definitely a marketing ploy: "I want another one just like that other one."

Sue: Which isn't what we want as teachers.

Margaret: But as authors or readers, we are keenly aware of it.

Janice: There are markers by which your novel will be sold: this is a novel just like that other one. But as a woman, it is going to be harder to get called whatever the normative thing is.

Margaret: The use of the word rigorous. "Rigorous use of science." Examples of men who have been called hard but totally aren't.

Janice: Robert Heinlein.

audience laughter

Sue: FTL travel. They don't give us any reason or any way to go that fast plausibly? Then it's fantasy.

Audience: What about the idea of "Mundane" sf.

Margaret: Geoff Ryman and number of others, in response to what Sue said about markets, we've been using science that's so bad, we're not going to do FTL travel, let's make it more real and believable, it's going to be set on Earth, it's going to deal with issues that aren't way out there, that are more related to us today.

Audience: Mundane sf is about not using science, or knowledge of science, that can't be extrapolated. Like FTL. There is a lot of fuss about that, as it's too restricting.

Sue: I emailed Geoff Ryman and asked him about mundane vs. hard, and to define science.

Audience: Are there women authors who have allied themselves with this movement?

Sue: I didn't buy that issue of *Interzone*, did you?

Audience: Ahhaah no!

Janice: Am trying to wrap my head around how Ryman could say that after having written *Air*.

audience laughter

Janice: I talked to him about post-colonial theory. He had not even heard of it. He was surprised I could understand his book so well with this stuff. [Gayatri Spivak for example—LH]

Margaret: The whole stomach pregnancy thing!

Janice: I asked him point blank. I don't get it. Anyone?

Liz: The disconnect between genres and sf vs. magical realism or magic is the genius of it; it's a dislocation in the text to jolt the reader into narrative/genre shock, so that they understand the feelings of Mei as she experiences culture shock.

Janice: What will the new children be like?

Liz: Damaged.

Margaret: Anything else?

Audience: *Darwin's Radio*!

Annalee: Greg Bear, number one on our list of criminals; he sits on a committee that advises the DOD on future scenarios, and he's very proud of it! He thinks he's the hardest of the hard, but his science is terrible! And he's dealing with biology! Which a ton of women have dealt with.

Audience: Hard sf is just a marketing term for a fast-driven plot.

Annalee: Michael Crichton kind of guy, resurrecting Stalin. I mean, *come on*.

Audience: I would like to like hard sf, but, it's like the cold skeleton, the bare bones, a boy playing with his toys. In *Singularity Sky*, Charlie Stross, there's no movement, human touch, it's the skeleton of ideas without people moving through it.

Margaret: This raises a very significant issue for me. The people who don't read sf at all, especially women, because they think sf is dry, hard-to-understand lectures with no "life." Even more importantly, is the concept of hard sf making the feeling of science less interesting or important to women, because they think science is dull and doesn't pertain to real life issues? That's why this is important. That's why these tropes and definitions matter.

Sue: This hard sf that's supposedly the holy grail, maybe isn't something we should be reaching for, it's not as good. Doesn't great literature always involve the human aspect? If that is truly what hard sf is, it won't attain greatness. But we could argue about that, because *Ascent of Wonder* has great, wonderful, beautiful stuff. So I don't think that is true, but the marketers use the term, without us making our statement that's what's going to happen, it's going to become pulp fiction again after having risen so far above pulp fiction.

Audience: How?

Sue: Panels, talking, writing, people consuming it, saying, Amy Thomson is a hard sf writer. We're the readers, we're the consumers, we're the ones writing the blogs! The blogosphere is a very powerful tool.

Janice: [A book about] whales, about a giant consciousness, in *Publishers Weekly*. You give something a start. They highlight it. I thought it was one of the best books I've read in years. But there's a whole group of the fundamentalist right who had a problem with it. I think if a man had written about similar things; well, they have, and they are considered great. I mean, *Solaris* for example!

Margaret: How many of you in the room have a subscription to *Analog*. No one. *Fantasy and SF*? One or two. *Asimov's*? No one. What if we subscribe to those magazines and write the editors? [I read *Strange Horizons* and subscribe to *Lady Churchill's Rosebud Wristlet*—LH]

Sue: If we do, then I think it might make a difference. At least it would get your opinion out there.

Liz: The Maureen McHugh story she read the other day, "Kingdom of the Blind." The computer programming, system administrator, and techie details were lovingly described, and they were right, well, almost all of them were right, and that made me really really happy.

Annalee: In our blogs, the hard science aspect is biology, or sociology. The thing that got me into sf as a kid was an anthology of anthropological sf, back when anthropology was still considered a science.

As readers we have to explain what we think. At Tor they will read it and pay attention.

Margaret: I have to be a little bit cynical. There was an editor at Tor at the book cover panel, who said, "I don't care what you people think, the half nude broad is what sells it."

Annalee: Well, if that half nude broad is doing biology, I'm down with it.

Erin Kelly: It's this whole messed up thinking! We have to trick them! We have to write biological sf under male names and then we'll suddenly all reveal ourselves!

Janice: Any real physicist will tell you that physics is not a straightforward thing any more.

Erin: It's just a construct that we've imposed that anything women do is not as good!

Guy: My friend Jim Frankel has said many times, if the author is female they automatically give her an advance that is 20% or 50% less than if the author is a man. It doesn't matter how good the author is, even if the author is a Hugo winning author with a background they'll just cut it off.

Margaret: I have added names to that list since I came today! Please add Maureen McHugh, and Rosemary Kirstein! It [The Steerswoman series] is seen as fantasy, but the whole underpinning is of how we see science.

Janice: Frank Herbert is NOT hard sf.

Margaret: If *Dune* goes on the list then Amy Thomson goes on the list!

general laughter

Margaret: Dune is hard sf because it is so concerned with the environment of a desert world!!! That is a direct quote from something I just read!

Audience: Are you aware of science teachers using "hard sf" to get students excited, there's a blog out there on it.

Audience: Julie Czerneda's part of that group.

Audience guy: The UW engineering dept runs a program every year.

Liz: There's a workshop by NASA, Launchpad Workshop, free for sf writers; astronomy and science. Look it up—they have a website.

Audience: I'm an engineer and I love Larry Niven; he lacks narrative and real characters; he'll geek out endlessly. I prefer less narrative, less character, more geeky stuff, more mechanism, plot devices, more science explanations.

Annalee: Do you like it with any science, biology or just others?

Audience: Octavia Butler, with biology! So good with the science!

Erin Kelly: Octavia Butler. Orson Scott Card, *Ender's Game* is more hard, you're free to jump on that...

Guy in Audience: Philip K Dick is a terrible scientist! But psychologically he is brilliant on how people can become paranoid in response to technology and alienation.

[Panel ends in discussion of a handout with a list of hard sf, and making additions to it.]

> [This is a rough transcription from notes taken by Liz Henry during the panel; it is not transcribed from a recording and may not be precisely what was said.]

WisCon 32 Panel Report: The Curious Boundaries of YA Fantasy

Mystickeeper

> **Panel Description:** What are the limits of what can be discussed in YA fantasy? What themes and issues are considered appropriate, and which are taboo? Who sets these limits and do they mesh with the desires and expectations of YA readers?
>
> **Panelists:** Mary Anne Mohanraj (moderator), Sarah Beth Durst, Sharyn November, Tamora Pierce

Sharyn November wanted to begin the panel by defining what Young Adult fiction actually means, as many people don't know. She is an editor for YA fiction, in charge of the Firebird brand, which publishes fantasy stuff—if you look in the teen section of bookstores, you'll see it.

There are three levels of YA fiction. Age 14 and up is edgier YA stuff; 12 and up is standard, and 8-12 is the lowest. All readers "read up." So, if a book is for "14 and up," you as the writer should assume that your reader is 12.

Sexuality was brought up as the first topic.

Tamora Pierce said that the difference between YA and adult fiction is that sex, drugs, etc. must be present in a story for a reason, as opposed to being a background recreational activity. She also noted that nobody (i.e., Texas librarians) has ever squeaked about the amount of violence in her novels; only the sex.

Mary Anne noted that Tamora Pierce doesn't describe sex in explicit detail.

Sharyn November notes that characters age and become darker in YA fiction (Westmark!). She also praised Tamora Pierce's magical contraception in her novels. (To which Tamora Pierce said, "I love it, too!") Sharyn said that in the books she edits, explicit sex is the only thing she does not allow.

It was noted that in the Pern books, you will totally miss the sex references if you aren't ready for them.

An audience member was a physician, and worried about working with 10- to14-year-olds who had been traumatized (by real life events). She said that she would like books to have a warning.

Sharyn responded that this was a slippery slope. Also, adding such a warning will make everyone want to read the book! She noted that if you mark "Ages 10 and up!" on a book, 12-year-olds will skip it.

It was brought up a number of times that readers will self-censor if they're not ready for certain kinds of books.

Mary Anne noted that it can be good for victims to read books about people going through similar situations to know that they're not alone.

Sharyn November noted that the Victorian conceit of the child as a pure and unsullied figure is crap.

And here we come to my list of recommendations from the panel!

> Robin McKinley is really good at writing the day-to-day. Her novel *Chalice* is coming up. *Deerskin* and *Sunshine* are good, but both are considered to be adult novels.
>
> Sharyn November endorsed Tamora Pierce as being very responsible by addressing contraception, puberty, etc.
>
> Megan Whalen Turner's books were mentioned, and apparently *The Thief* is a good place to start. It is hilarious, surprising, and brilliant.
>
> Pamela Dean's story "Juniper, Gentian, and Rosemary."
>
> Cassandra Clare's *City of Ashes* (cue the fandom wank on plagiarism!).
>
> Diane Duane's *So You Want to Be a Wizard.*
>
> *Inside Out,* by Ann M Martin.
>
> Ellen Kushner's *Privilege of the Sword* (not technically YA; its prequel was clearly adult).
>
> Mercedes Lackey's trilogy.
>
> *Octavian Nothing* by M.T. Anderson.

I think the last broad topic was how to draw the line with violence. Tamora Pierce talked about describing the impact and weight felt on a character's arm. She said a bit of blood is good, but not too much; also dust, noise, etc. It's also good to note that the character is in battle-fever, and not registering everything around them. The wounds will hit them later on—sometimes they'll throw up.

Deep Wizardry has kids with lots of responsibility.

Nina Kiriki Hoffman's *A Fistful of Sky* is a good place to start a series I missed the name of. It is stand-alone. There are darker themes, the books are funny, and good.

Perry Moore's *Hero.* It focuses on being gay, family, father acceptance, etc.

Elizabeth Wien's *The Winter Prince* was mentioned as well.

My personal suggestion is the Animorphs series. I wrote them off when I was younger, but then read them in high school (and in college summers, bwahaha!). Six kids fighting a war, all by themselves. Responsibility, violence, friendships, pacifism, etc. There are some clunkers, but hey, there are about 60 books; what are you going to do? They're so short and with big print! DO IT.

Mystickeeper's real name is Jackie. She likes Victorian literature, politics, manga, anime, and TV dramas. She also enjoys post-apocalyptic and dystopian fiction, as well as skim milk.

Nothing But Mammals: The Trouble with Boundaries in Young Adult Literature

Response to
"The Curious Boundaries of YA Fantasy" Panel

Alaya Dawn Johnson

> **Panel Description:** What are the limits of what can be discussed in YA fantasy? What themes and issues are considered appropriate, and which are taboo? Who sets these limits, and do they mesh with the desires and expectations of YA readers?
>
> **Panelists:** Mary Anne Mohanraj (moderator), Sarah Beth Durst, Sharyn November, Tamora Pierce

The ideas of what's "age appropriate" in stories for individuals of less than the age of majority have changed remarkably depending on time period and culture. For most of the history of western civilization, there wasn't any literature specifically set aside for younger people. And individuals whom we might call children or young adults were often given adult responsibilities, from kingship and leading armies to helping support their families by working in factories. The concept of protecting children from images of sex or violence is also relatively new. This is not to say that our current sense of age appropriateness is bad or unnecessary. A greater awareness of childhood development and childhood trauma has led to laws outlawing child labor and public services dedicated to youth protection. I think all can agree that these are unequivocally good developments. However, this increasing protectiveness of young people has, I think, led to the desire to protect them from thoughts and ideas, and not simply harmful actions and activities. The logic seems to flow that if you should protect a 14-year-old child from leading an army into battle, then perhaps you should protect him from the gorier descriptions of said battle as well. Violence, of course, is far less controversial in considerations of what's "age-appropriate" than sex. The essential prudishness of modern American culture is, I think, undeniable. Contemplate the mass national hysteria from a half-second accidental breast-baring on national TV, and we have a country whose reaction to even the mildest hints of the sexual act so far outstrips the provocation that it's a source of international ridicule.

I believe that all of the editors and writers on the "Boundaries in YA Fiction" panel would probably agree that the Janet Jackson Super Bowl scandal was largely overblown and excessive. And yet in some of their professed attitudes (particularly those of Tamora Pierce) I found an implicit acceptance of the very same premises that in their extreme forms lead to Supreme Court cases and congressional investigations. For one, the idea that children as a broad category need to be protected from the depictions or discussions of human sexuality is, to me, highly suspect. Certainly, some individuals probably don't have the maturity to handle certain subject matters. But surely that statement doesn't particularly privilege sexual subjects. You could imagine a child equally incapable of grasping the subtleties of international politics as conjugal relations. Yet, *The Constant Gardener* is not rated R for its depictions of multinational drug corporation policy. Every one of us has memories of encountering some fictional depiction of sexual subjects that sailed happily over our heads until, at some later date, we realized the other levels on which the art might be understood. Very few people can point to these moments of early exposure to sexual themes and declare that they dealt them irreparable harm. If anything, this exposure helps our development and understanding of the world.

But perhaps this only applies to younger children and the obvious limits of their understanding. Perhaps it could be more effectively argued that teenagers, by the very virtue of their greater capability of understanding, need to be protected that much more from exposure to ideas that they lack the maturity to fully grasp. This again strikes me as murky and suspect reasoning. For one, there is no reasonable method—in any known human society—by which adolescents can be fully protected from exposure to sexual ideas and themes. From the extremes of certain Polynesian cultures where sexual subjects are frequently discussed among all age groups to the notorious prudishness of upper class Victorian society, adolescents eventually learn that "you and me baby ain't nothing but mammals," so to speak. Again, most people, panel-members included, fall somewhere between these two extremes. Firebird editor Sharyn November said that she was willing to accept almost anything in a YA aside from explicit sex. Tamora Pierce is to be commended for including depictions of realistic teenage relationships, including periods and non-explicit sex, in her novels, particularly her Song of the Lionness (Alanna) series. And yet, from what I could gather from her comments on the panel, she seems to feel that her own novels go as far as any YA can responsibly go in these areas.

It's useful, at this juncture, to bring in a specific example text that well illustrates the real-life boundary of "acceptability" that seems to exist in the world of American young adult publishing. The book that I suggested to the panel was Ellen Kushner's *Privilege of the Sword*—an absolutely brilliant coming of age story, with all of the hallmarks of my favorite young adult novels: a teenage heroine learning about herself and her world, gaining a skill, falling in love, accepting adults and adulthood with all of their foibles. Judged by merely these personality-test criteria, I feel that *Privilege of the Sword* is clearly YA. And yet some of the panelists objected to the classification. The problem seemed to arise out of the types of sexuality, perhaps the level of implied intimacy (though I will say that in the strictest sense, Kushner's novel is not much more sexually explicit than Pierce's). Katherine, the heroine of *Privilege of the Sword*, has a male and a female love interest. There is a scene where she masturbates to the sight of a two beautiful women kissing. She saves the life of a male prostitute who services only male clients, yet is in love with a disgraced female playwright. Katherine's uncle, the mad Duke, has orgies with members of both sexes and is addicted to a heroin-like drug. Listed like this, of course, the book sounds like something fit for a brown paper cover. But the brilliance of Kushner's novel is that, like in real life, these sexual explorations and variations are grace notes and occasional fugues within a larger, more vibrant symphony. Because, ultimately, what part of a true coming of age does not include an increased, sometimes overpowering, awareness of one's own sexuality and that of others? The masturbation scene is like nothing else I've read in YA literature, and honestly, something I wish that we could see more. Not to say that there isn't a place for a Tamora Pierce-style "sex in the scene break" that's always of the strictly heterosexual variety, but the idea that that is the limit beyond which a book is no longer appropriate for a "young adult" label strikes me as absurd. Pierce stated she would be leery of recommending Kushner's book to a teen reader for the very reasons I loved it.

I must add that none of these panelists were arguing that teens should not avail themselves of the more mature themes of adult novels, if they so chose. No one advocated book banning. The issue here is about how to judge the content of books explicitly marketed to teenagers. This is not a question of hard censorship, but more one of the soft steering of young adults towards material adults might feel is more appropriate for their maturity level. In real life, teens might read plenty of adult fiction, but they also read plenty of YA literature, and to posit largely arbitrary sexually-based boundaries on the subject matters discussed or their presentation seems to shortchange both the writer and her potential audience of precocious, curious teens.

Alaya Dawn Johnson's short fiction has appeared in *Interzone*, *Strange Horizons*, *Fantasy Magazine*, *Year's Best Fantasy 6*, and *Year's Best SF 11*. Her first novel, *Racing the Dark*, was released last October, and she has a forthcoming urban fantasy novel from St. Martin's Press. Her hobbies include eating vegetarian Indian food and reading YA novels.

Let's Build a World

Panel Notes by Ted Infinity

> **Panel Description:** We'll start with some categories (tech level, economic system, climate, races, etc.), get ideas about each of them from the audience, select the best ideas in each category, then watch the panelists writhe as they try to figure out how to make them work together.
>
> **Panelists:** Benjamin Rosenbaum (moderator), Naomi Kritzer, Kristine Smith, Doselle Young

Carnitopia

The world-building panel was a participation event. The audience and panelists proposed ideas, and periodically we did a straw poll on suggestions.

We first built Atmosphere, then Geography, then Economics, then Psychology and Religion, then Biology. Once we had built the world, we made a story in it. I don't know why we did economics and psychology before biology.

Atmosphere

- The atmosphere is made of oxygen and chlorine, with rapidly fluctuating magnetic fields.
- Outer space is composed of breathable ether.
- The atmosphere also includes structurally robust clouds.
- In terms of thematic atmosphere, the mood is "squishy" and "bicurious."
- The physical atmosphere is also squishy.

(Rejected ideas for atmosphere: ammonia, emo, dystopia, utopian-emo, utopian-emo-ammonia.)

Geography

- There is a huge chlorine sea with many islands.
- The islands rove through the chlorine sea. They have concrete beaches and violently collide with each other.
- Tremendous meat volcanoes spray great meat geysers. This is probably what makes the atmosphere squishy.
- Space-distorting underground tunnels link the islands.
- Cloudevators carry people from the ground to the structurally robust clouds.
- There may be a core of chocolate under the meat magma layer.
- Some islands are intentionally predatory. They collide with smaller islands and get bigger and bigger.

(Rejected geography ideas: Tundra, regular tunnels, really tall trees, torus-shaped world, pretzel-shaped world, yggdrasil.)

Economics: Currency

- Chocolate is a form of currency. There are economic schisms between milk chocolate and dark chocolate.
- Another form of currency is tokens for the cloudevators.
- Another is swarms of cats. However, the cat swarms also form the ruling class that use themselves as currency.

(Rejected currencies: Peeps, marshmallow eggs.)

Economics: Vocations

- Some people work in cloudevator operations and repair.
- Chocolate minters. They mint chocolate. Sometimes they mint mint-chocolate.
- Meat surfers. People who surf on the meat volcanoes.

- Cat vaccuumers. They vaccuum cats, of course.
- Collidographers and collidologists. Both measure and analyze the collisions of islands, but there's a schism between the two. There are a lot of schisms in this world.
- People who manufacture bumpers so that the islands can collide with each other safely.
- People who take the bumpers off the islands and let the islands fight "bare-fisted." One profession is a "Tectonic Sports Network" Extreme Sports commentator. I think Doselle said it best: "Two islands enter, one continent leaves!"
- The cats are the ruling class, but there is also a secret dog underground.
- There is a Tunnel Security Administration (TSA) that guards all use of the space-distorting tunnels.
- Meat volcano pilots. These people fly the cloud-wandering squids of the planet around meat volcanoes. Or maybe they pilot the islands themselves. Or maybe there's another schism. Schism!

(Rejected vocations: professional humiliator, cloned marshmallow peep serfs.)

Philosophy, Psychology, and Religion

- Beef Transubstaniation. Some people believe that the meat volcanoes turn to tofu or chicken or something the moment you eat them.
- People go on cloud-spelunking pilgrimages.
- Many believe that the islands will all unite into one big continent, or possibly re-unite the continent. There is a schism between the Unification Church and the Reunification Church. Schism!
- There is a cult of the dog that opposes the cat majority.

- Some cross-dressing chihuahuas put on cat whiskers and tails and disguise themselves as cats.
- Some people worry that they are born on the wrong island.
- Some people are self-hating carniphobes. Says Doselle: "Oh my god, I'm made of meat!"
- People wonder about the mysterious origins of the chlorine sea.
- Some people have a phobia that the whole world is just a grocery aisle of some kind, and they're all just packaged food products in a mass hallucination.

(Rejected philosophies and psychologies: milkism, meat becoming chocolate, turtles all the way down, a great caramel mystery.)

Biology

- Fire-breathing platypi inhabit the tunnels.
- Oversized land-walking cephalopods wander the islands.
- Other oversized cephalopods wander the clouds and are used as riding animals. Oddly, there is no schism between the two.
- Most native species are marsupials. The most common species is the kangaroid.
- People can communicate directly with their DNA by telepathic email. However, most of the messages are annoying spam.
- Kangaroids have three and a half genders. The first two genders ("spiky" and "fuzzy") mix DNA to create a child. The third ("scaly") is an incubator species that stores the zygote in its pouch. There's also an optional gender ("shiny") that filters for annoying spam messages and unsolicited bulk email from DNA. Any of the other three genders can become shiny temporarily by lifestyle choice, and the shiny gender

is optional for reproduction but highly encouraged because DNA spam is so annoying.

- Carnivorous plants eat the meat from the meat volcanoes and inject it back into the ground, where it rejoins the meat mantle and eventually goes back to the volcano. This is all part of the planet's natural "cycle of meat."
- Cats hatch out of geode eggs. Sometimes when the meat volcanoes erupt, the meat crystalizes and forms a geode. Over time, the meat inside turns into a cat that hatches out of the geode egg. This is also part of the planet's natural "cycle of meat."
- Where the chocolate comes from is unclear.
- Worms of various lengths exist on the planet. Their heads take on the shape of anyone looking at them, so they're called "mirror worms." People (and when I say people I think I mean kangaroids, cats, dogs, and fire-breathing platypi) use them as mirrors for grooming. People also cook and eat the worms, which leads to the unnerving but common experience of cooking your own face.
- Multi-trunked cthuloid elephants excrete chlorine. Which is probably the mysterious origin of chlorine, which makes me wonder why it's a mystery anyway, but I'm just the note-taker.
- All of this meat and chlorine and so on would probably smell terrible, so there's a species of perfuming kudzu vine that spreads through the islands and makes everything smell a little better.

(I don't think we rejected any ideas here.)

This is the world of Carnitopia! The setting is creative-commons. Anyone is welcome to write stories in this world, and if you can manage to make a coherent narrative in this setting I'll be very impressed.

At the panel, we attempted to put together a story as well, entitled "EAT YOUR FACE: Carnitopia Chronicles Volume One." The outline of the story is below. If someone can make a coherent narrative out of this story outline, I'll be very impressed with that, too.

By the end of the panel, this all made complete sense to the people at the panel. It all fits together so beautifully.

Characters

(Note on pronouns: there were a lot of pronouns used in discussing the story. I think the pronoun we used for shinies was "fleeb" and the pronoun for spikies and fuzzies was "vzzh." Cross-dressing chihuahuas use a pointed silence instead of a pronoun, which I'll mark as "[]" for simplicity. Scalies are "foop.")

- Nat, a lost fire-breathing platypus who has left the tunnels. Nat is of the shiny gender and at the start of the story fleeb is on squid-back with Penelope, returning from a cloud pilgrimage. At the start of the story, Nat and Penelope are traveling companions and maybe lovers. Love between two shiny-gender people is very taboo, though.
- Penelope, a kangaroid. Penelope used to be a scaly and was supposed to carry the child of Darcy and Elizabeth, but became a shiny and ran off with Nat on a cloud pilgrimage.
- Al, a cross-dressing chihuahua. Al is a clever trickster-figure, kind of a prophet who makes up a lot of false prophesies that get you where you need to be but not where you expect. Al's prophesies are known as troublesome trickster wisdom, or "trisdom" for short.
- Darcy, a kangaroid. Darcy is of the spiky gender. Darcy was planned to mate with Elizabeth and Penelope but then Penelope ran off. Darcy disapproves of Penelope's gender change strongly and wants fleeb to come home.
- Elizabeth, a kangaroid. Elizabeth is of the fuzzy gender, but vzzh is getting more and more spiky from living with Darcy so long. Elizabeth is a retired volcano pilot. Vzzh disapproves of Penelope's gender and wants fleeb to come home.

- Antagonists: the cat police is after Al. The dog underground is also after Al, because they're worried that [] is a renegade and a maverick.

Scenes

Scene Zero

Al is at home cooking face, when [] gets into a confrontation with the cat police. [] manages to turn the chase into a peaceful confrontation by sheer charisma and cat-imitation. Afterward, the dog underground tells Al that [] has gone too far. "Turn in your gun and your whiskers, Al."

(And, in the director's cut, []'s tutu as well. We never did figure out if Al was just dressed as a cat, or dressed as a cat in a tutu.)

Scene One

Penelope and Nat are returning from a cloud pilgrimage, and they meet up with Al who becomes their mentor.

Scene Two

They watch a Tectonic Sports Network match between two islands fighting, and they discover that the match is rigged and that they need to stop a giant war between the islands that may cause all the islands to collide or something. This might be the much heralded unification/reunification.

Scene Three

A disco scene. Darcy and Elizabeth confront Penelope and ask fleep to return to scaly form and come home and incubate their children. Penelope refuses and instead asks Elizabeth to join them to fly into a meat volcano to get to the space-distorting tunnels (bypassing the TSA) so they can travel to the chocolate core of the planet and stop the final battle between the islands. Elizabeth says that the meat volcano piloting is too dangerous but eventually relents, but Darcy still refuses to go along.

[EDIT: Ben Rosenbaum notes in comments that I missed something important. During the disco scene, Penelope belts out "I Will Survive."]

Scene Four

The group pilots a giant cephalopod into the meat volcano, bypasses the TSA, and travels through the tunnels. There are probably more fire-breathing platypi.

Scene Five

Titanic island battle scene. The islands fight in a great battle and the heroes do something noble. Darcy is nobly sacrificed to save the world. Since Darcy is spiky, vzzh catches all the meat of the meat volcano on vzzh's spikes but then gets buried in the meat. The body is never recovered, which leads to the inevitable possibility of Darcy returning in the sequel.

Scene Six

Post-action resolution scene. Penelope leaves Nat, but doesn't become a scaly or rejoin the traditional family structure. Instead, Penelope becomes Al's apprentice. Nat stays with Elizabeth. Everyone happily wanders through the kudzu fields, and the story closes with the line, "I almost can't smell the meat."

Ted Infinity is a technical writer who lives in San Francisco.

WisCon and POC-Only Spaces

K. Tempest Bradford

A few months before WisCon 32, I created a post on my blog where people could freely brainstorm ideas for panels.[1] Several topics and ideas were bandied about, but it was one particular suggestion that took up the bulk of the discussion and snowballed into one of the most memorable WisCon experiences I've had thus far.

K. Joyce Tsai suggested a panel about intra-People of Color (POC) relationships and coalition building. Others loved the idea and started fleshing it out, wanting to discuss how POC/POC relationships aren't all about white people and how we relate to them but how POC relate to each other. Very early in the thread, Jacqueline Gross suggested that the panel be limited to a POC-only audience as well as a POC panel.[2]

This is the point where the issue became about 20 times more complicated.

There were three main objections to an only-POC panel or event (that I discerned):

1. Some were concerned about the legality of such a panel/event.

2. Some felt they would be left out of a conversation they felt could benefit white people, too.

3. Some didn't see the need for a POC-only space, especially at WisCon, because the whole point of the con, in their eyes, was inclusion and understanding.

But most, if not all of the people of color involved in the discussion were not only delighted at the prospect, but grokked the need for it pretty quickly. If the idea didn't appeal to them on its own merits, the resulting discussion was convincing enough.[3]

It's not that there was a lot of wank (an Internet term for arguments that get out of control and are filled with drama); it's that there had already been several POC-based issues at WisCon in the few years preceding 32. The Great Cultural Appropriation Debate of

DOOM had happened two years previous, and a few attendees, both POC and not, had reported scattered, but disturbing incidences of individuals making sketchy comments about race. WisCon is not a trouble-free place for POC, much as many of the attendees and, I assume, the Concom, would like it to be. So when the suggestion of a POC-only panel was made and immediately ignited a wildfire of objections and hand-wringing and outright whining, a lot of us rolled our eyes and thought, "Oh here we go again."

I was personally determined not to let this idea die. So I had some frank conversations with longtime attendees of the con and a few who were on the committee and got some details about the only objection that actually mattered: the legality.

Debbie Notkin gave me a little history lesson and informed me that a similar suggestion had come up many years ago.[4] The idea was floated for a POC-only lounge, but after some investigation the Concom discovered that providing such a space could be grounds for legal action. Of course, that did not mean someone would actually sue; it just meant that if someone chose to, they would have grounds for it. When the issue came up years ago, someone actually threatened to.

This is a very, very simplified retelling of the many conversations that happened publicly and privately around this legal thing. For enlightenment on the public ones, please see the urls cited in the endnotes. But all of the back and forth just convinced me that if this POC-only space was going to happen, it would have to be a not-official thing, and I had no problems with that.

WisCon overflow rooms are open, and anyone is allowed to use them, including groups who only let certain people in (a meeting for a group of online workshoppers, for instance). I decided that the best place for our POC-only discussion would be in one of those rooms. In order to keep the whiners and troublemakers from having any ammunition against the Concom, I declared the space a special kaffeklatsch for the group "People Against We-Sha-Sha"[5] and recruited friends to sign any POC they came across up for the event.

We had no problems from anyone at WisCon and a lot of support from POC and non-POC. I'm sure there were still people who didn't know why POC needed their own discussion or panel and why we wouldn't even allow white people in to watch and not participate or write up a summary afterward. This is a sad but predictable reaction from people with privilege—even those who understand how privilege works. Shortly after the initial brainstorming post I opened another discussion on my blog about why there was (and is) a need for POC-only spaces. LJ user yeloson put it best:

> The need for safe spaces is quite obvious, if you either address your own privilege or lack it in the first place. It's about power of defining boundaries, and defining what can, and can't be talked about.
>
> For example, if I want to talk about race, with some folks I know may have had similar experiences, in order to gain context and learn about the bigger picture of what we're going through and how to deal with it, does someone who has never experienced it, have the right to shut down our conversation because they're uncomfortable?
>
> …safe spaces form…to actually have dialogue without being jumped on, silenced, invalidated, mocked, insulted, and told we need to be polite and patient with people who are neither with us. It's just simpler for us to form a space, where we can talk about it and work out our issues.

Several commenters pointed out that, for many people, knowing that this space was not open to them meant that they were being told, perhaps for the first time, "No." This conversation is not for you, about you, or involving you. For some, that is deeply disturbing.

Welcome to the club.

I pointed out that cons have restricted panels or small-group meetings all the time. Writing workshops are limited to the participants who signed up and/or who were chosen for their ability; kaffeklatsches are limited to those who get to the sign-up sheet first; panels can be restricted to "mid-career novelists" or some other distinction. I could name you at least three more examples I've seen at WisCon or other cons.

This is different from race or gender-based restrictions, yes. Quoting yeloson again:

> A safe space doesn't have power over whether you live or die, where you live, whether you get education or not, whether you go to prison or not, whether you keep your lands or not, whether you get to keep your children or not, whether you will get informed of the experiment they just performed on you, whether you get deported to a country you haven't seen since you were 3 months old or a thousand other things which can royally screw up your life.

A POC-only space does not take anything away from white people that they don't already have or can get. It merely puts them outside of a conversation they don't have any legal or intrinsic right to in the first place.

One interesting part of the discussion we had in the POC-only space was about the fact that some members of the WisCon community who were around during that initial try at creating a POC lounge thought that this issue was resolved and settled. I believe the word "appalled" was used upon hearing how much angst was generated when the topic came up again. The general feeling seemed to be: Not only is it 2008, but this is WisCon. You would think that people here would know better.

I think many do know better. Despite all the incidents over the years, WisCon is still a place where I feel comfortable and surrounded by people who, if they don't "get it" right now, have the ability to get it sometime in the near future. It's a place where I can discuss intersectionality, where I can bring up race in discussions that are not specifically about race, where I can look around and see more brown faces per square foot than at most cons I attend. But that just makes bringing up this issue and remembering it all that much more important.

I plan to help with organizing the POC-only space and discussions at WisCon 33 and 34 and beyond. The first one showed me how much more we have to accomplish as fans of color within the community and between each other. Who knows what amazingness will come out of the next one?

Endnotes

1 The original Brainstorming post: http://ktempest.livejournal.com/258395.html

2 The thread about a POC-only panel: http://ktempest.livejournal.com/258395.html?thread=1327195#t1327195

3 The Need for POC-only Spaces: http://ktempest.livejournal.com/264082.html

4 Debbie Notkin on legal issues and WisCon history: http://ktempest.livejournal.com/264082.html?thread=1405586#t1405586

Discussion on the WisCon LJ group about the issue: http://community.livejournal.com/wiscon/127583.html

5 We-sha-sha references a joke amongst fans on the Internet about Cassie Edwards' *Savage Moon.* The book's protagonist, a white woman, is adopted into a Native American tribe and uses a root called we-sha-sha to dye her hair black "so that she could look like an Indian."

K. Tempest Bradford is a science fiction and fantasy writer living in New York City. She's the managing editor for *Fantasy Magazine* and contributes to FeministSF The Blog, Tor.com, and The Angry Black Woman. In 2008 she served on the Tiptree Award Committee. Her fiction has appeared in the *Interfictions* anthology, *Strange Horizons*, and *Farthing Magazine*. She blogs about writing, reading, and rhythm at tempest.fluidartist.com.

Not Just Japan

Rachel Kronick

Our panel's purview: to give a survey of all sf&f from all of Asia except for Japan. There's a very useful saying in Chinese: "Viewing flowers from horseback." That describes this panel to a T.

Vandana Singh, Joyce Tsai, and I had a pretty good pre-discussion via email. We tried to discuss where we wanted the panel to go, what our definitions were, where we didn't want to go, etc. One thing I was worried about was that the panel would turn into just a listing of sf&f works from Asia. There are so many of them that just listing them would've taken a hundred panels, with no time for discussion. So we included a wide variety of recommended works (books, movies, comics, etc.) in our handout, and tried to not make the actual panel into a series of laundry lists. And we tried to include a good sampling of the issues we were interested in, because we knew an hour would be insufficient to give everything the time it deserved. Below, I'll go into a couple issues that particularly interested me.

Translation: Whose Responsibility?

One of the first issues we wanted to discuss was translation. First, it was about our subject matter. We were talking about works available in English? Works available in various Asian languages? Works by people who are native speakers of various Asian languages, regardless of current country of residence? What counts?

Two of my favorite Taiwanese manhua (comics, manga) are 九命人 Nine Lives [sic] Man and its sequel, 久命人 Long Life Man, by the pseudonymous 阿推 A-Tui or "Push." It feels a bit like the Job myth, but God is the robotic leader of a Buddhist bureaucracy, the Prince of Hell is played by the Artist Formerly Known as Prince, and the main character, Meng Jiuge, has a fondness for high-powered jet bikes. God (who likes to wear "Heaven" brand track suits) gives Meng Jiuge nine lives — maybe mistakenly, maybe intentionally, maybe just for bureaucratic reasons — then tries to take away Meng's extra lives by setting an army of robotic assassins to kill him. The books are hilarious, deep, pretty twisted, very Buddhist, and filled with intricate, wild, superb illustrations. And they're not available in English.

There are, naturally, many more works that haven't been translated into English. I could list a dozen Chinese works off the top of my head. I'm sure there are superb science fiction tales in Korean, wondrous fantasies in Arabic, amazing things in every language out there, but it's hard to access them because of the lack of translation.

Is having works available to you a form of privilege? English speakers can expect that everything will eventually become available to us, or if it isn't, some might think, it's not worth bothering with. Other languages' speakers have had similar attitudes throughout history. In fact, it's par for the course for empires.

But by not finding out about these works, we're depriving ourselves of exposure to some truly wondrous ideas, and you could make the argument that we're depriving creators in other countries of income. I have little doubt that, if more people could read Chinese, or there were English translations available, A-Tui would be as famous in the US as Enki Bilal. Which is to say, not that famous, but at least better known.

So whose responsibility is it to make these works available? Should readers be demanding more translations? Yes, certainly. But this can lead to a gatekeeper problem: who chooses what works get to be translated? You may trust my recommendation that *Nine Lives Man* is awesome, but not everyone does or should. And who pays the translators? Particularly for small-circulation works, translation can cost more than it's worth to do. So translation is necessary and good, but it doesn't solve the problem.

A better long-term answer, I think, is for Americans to learn more languages. You've probably heard the old joke that a person who speaks three languages is "trilingual," a person who speaks two languages is "bilingual" and a person who speaks one language is "American." That joke has a strong basis in truth. I would love to one day come to WisCon and see people talking about works of every language, in every language, in the halls and panels, not just English and one or two others.

Definitions: Whose Genre Is It?

Another interesting issue: who gets to define what "fantasy" is? For some people, wuxia ("martial arts," though that's a very inaccurate translation) stories are quite factual. There are people who believe that qigong, Daoist alchemical practice, Buddhist meditation, or other practices grant them miraculous powers. For example, in Taiwan in the late '90s, a man named Song Qili purported to be able to be in multiple places at the same time due to his religious powers. He was later convicted of fraud, but he purportedly had many followers. If someone wrote a narrative based on these beliefs, some people might call it fantasy, but others might call it religious literature, or simple non-fiction. As Vandana pointed out, there are books that, in India, are sold as retellings of the Mahabharata, but in English, they're sold as fantasy. Who gets to decide which definition holds? To what extent do American definitions of "science fiction" and "fantasy" get privileged status over other cultures' and countries' definitions?

It's tempting to ask the question with an American equivalent. Where does a bookseller shelve books that are based on, say, Christian beliefs? Some readers may consider the book to be fantasy, some to be self-help, some to be history. It'll depend on the bookstore, the employee, the reader, and other factors.

But when we're dealing with cross-cultural definitions, this will be an even thornier issue. If a bookstore in the US shelves *The Journey to the West* (one of the classics of Chinese literature, about the trials and tribulations of a Buddhist monk going to India, including many amazing adventures along the way) as fantasy, but a Chinese bookstore shelves it under literature or religious history, I think the difference is qualitatively larger.

This is especially important because of orientalism and cultural appropriation. There's a tendency in the West to see anything from, for example, China as "exotic" or "mysterious," which frequently means that different standards are being applied when genre categories are drawn out. Take two stories, one written with Western tropes, one with Chinese tropes, both with similar levels of wonder or fantastic-ness, and there's a better chance the Chinese one will be labeled as "fantasy" than the Western one. To the extent that a label of "fantasy" is a value judgment, and it often is, this is problematic.

There's also the problem that definitions are simply different between cultures. There is a Chinese term for "fantasy" now, but it's a translation from the English. In Chinese, there are wuxia stories, which concern themselves with martial heroes, frequently though not always with awesome powers, in a semi-historical China; there are "Records of the Strange," which set down fantastic folktales of many sorts, often with a horror or ghost-story vibe; and there are other categories that don't have clear equivalents in English.

"Science fiction" is even more thorny. One of the bookstores I loved to hate in Taipei, called Chengpin, had a huge selection of books and a 24-hour bookstore in the middle of the city—bliss. But trying to find sf in the store was always an exercise in frustration for me, because the section labeled "Science Fiction" usually included more mystery novels, ghost stories, and misplaced general English novels than what I'd consider sf. Sherlock Holmes is not, to my taste, science fiction, but thinking about it, the stories are really about using logic and technology to solve problems, which is a very science-fictional attitude. Does "sf" simply have a different meaning in Chinese? The word is still a recent one, and is certainly still undergoing change, at least as much as the English word is. It was just frustrating to me when I found Arthur Conan Doyle under "sf" and Kim Stanley Robinson under "Foreign Novels." Then, as a foreigner in Taiwan, I didn't exactly have a right to demand that they use the same definitions I was using.

Joyce noted that, for the panel and for the topic of Chinese works, she was using what Chinese people would consider "fantasy" or "science fiction." That seems reasonable to me. And it's not a bad thing to let works just be what they are. Is *Nine Lives Man* science fiction, wild fantasy, or a Buddhist parable? It sits comfortably astride its high-powered jet bike and blasts past all those pigeonholes and more.

Final Thoughts

It was quite an exhilarating panel, not just because it was the first panel I moderated at WisCon. We had a million miles to go and only a few minutes to get there. It was a lot of fun and we got into some really interesting topics. I hope future panels go even further than we did.

Bibliography

阿推 Push (姜振台 Jiang Zhentai), 九命人 *Nine Lives [sic] Man*. Taipei, Taiwan: China Times Cultural Publishing, 1994. ISBN 9571314617.

——, 久命人 *Long Life Man*. Taipei, Taiwan: China Times Cultural Publishing, 1994. ISBN 9571314609.

Rachel Kronick lives in Minneapolis, MN, where she teaches Mandarin Chinese and does Mandarin-English medical interpreting. She is many sorts of geek: long-time SF&F fan, tabletop RPG gamer, 3D artist, transgender rights advocate, worldbuilder, and ex-East Asian Studies grad student, among others. She was head of programming for Minicon for three years and is now resting peacefully. Her website is at www.jiawen.net, and she blogs at jiawen.livejournal.com.

[Handout for panel]

Not Just Japan: Asian Science Fiction and Fantasy

A few pointers for this panel

Definitions

We are probably going to start our discussion with works that fall close to Western definitions of "science fiction" and "fantasy," but we plan to branch out from there.

We don't want to restrict ourselves to the written word. Movies, manhua/manga/manhwa/comics and other media are fine.

We aren't going to treat religious texts as fantasy, at least not right away, because doing so can easily be culturally insensitive. However, many of the works we're going to talk about will be grounded in certain religions or myth traditions, so we may want to delve into the topic anyway.

Issues

The first order of business is to introduce a slew of cool works to you, but along the way, we've got a lot of issues we'd like to discuss. What follows is just a sample; we're sure more will come up.

- Accessibility of knowledge and cultural appropriation: This will probably be an overarching issue for the panel, one we will come back to a lot.
- A related topic is translation. Are we only talking about works in translation? Not everyone wants to learn another language just to open their sf&f horizons—but learning another language is a very good thing. What about English works translated into Asian languages? There's a lot of sf&f translated into Chinese, for example.

- Accessibility (or deniability of such) as privilege; culturally-based definitions of genres; and whatever else we think of.
- What issues that will affect Asia (global warming, globalization, etc.) is Asian sf&f dealing with?
- How are Asian creators redefining their own genres?
- What genres exist in Asian literatures, and how closely do they map to Western ones?
- If I consider ghosts, qi or reincarnation to be natural and you don't, and I create a work based on my beliefs, who gets to decide if it is fantasy or not?

Bibliography

Some initial listings; we're sure to think of many more.

Works from India & South Asia

The Beast With Nine Billion Feet by Anil Menon. Forthcoming from Zubaan books by Anil Menon (who also has short stories published, including one at Strange Horizons).

The Calcutta Chromosome by Amitav Ghosh. Won the Arthur C. Clarke Award.

Diary of a Space Traveler by Satyajit Ray. Translated from the Bengali. The great film director also wrote YA sf featuring the adventures and eccentricities of Professor Shonku.

"Early Bengali Science Fiction" by Amardeep Singh. A blog post that introduces the topic. Online at http://www.lehigh.edu/~amsp/2006/05/early-bengaliscience-fiction.html.

Generation 14 by Priya Sarukkai Chhabri. A novel about a clone in a far future where memory and sexuality are forbidden; but this clone remembers. Just out from Zubaan books in New Delhi. Online: http://www.zubaanbooks.com/zubaan_books_details.asp?BookID=116.

The Kathasaritsagara or *Ocean of Streams of Stories*. An eleventh century collection of fables, fairy tales and legends.

Kleptomania by Manjula Padmanabhan. Published by Penguin India, this story collection includes three sf stories; author has also written a play, *Harvest*, that is science-fictional.

The Mahabharata. One of the world's longest epic poems, this contains stories within stories but is mostly about a great battle between the five Pandava brothers and their hundred throne-usurping cousins, the Kauravas.

Mosquito and Other Stories by Premendra Mitra. Translated from the Bengali, this collection of short fiction from the 1940s or so features this great Bengali writer's best sf work. Introducing Ghanada, an older man living in a Kolkata hostelry who regales his young fellow tenants with his adventures on far off worlds. Tongue-in-cheek and compelling.

Panchatantra tales. Mostly animal folktales, very ancient.

The Ramayana. An ancient epic poem on the adventures of Rama, an avatar of the god Vishnu.

A Shadow in Eternity and *The Key of Chaos* by Payal Dhar. YA fantasy novels about a girl called Maya who discovers that she has an important role to play in an alternate world. Again from Zubaan books.

Tales of the Future by Jayant Narlikar. Translated from the Marathi. Short stories from India's premier astrophysicist.

The Woman Who Thought She Was a Planet and Other Stories by Vandana Singh. Story collection from Zubaan and Penguin India; most of these stories were published in anthologies and magazines in the US and UK. Author's website at http://users.rcn.com/singhvan/.

Younguncle Comes to Town by Vandana Singh. From Zubaan in India and Viking in the US. Stories of an eccentric uncle and his nieces and nephew combating various forms of injustice with the help of animals and ghosts.

Younguncle in the Himalayas by Vandana Singh. From Zubaan. Novel in which the mundane and supernatural come together against the backdrop of a rundown hotel in the Himalayas.

Works from Korea

2009: Lost Memories. An alternate history/uchronia movie set in a Korea that never gained independence from Japan.

The Host. A movie in which a large mutated monster plagues a family in Seoul.

Lineage II. One of the most successful MMORPGs ever.

Works from China, Taiwan & Hong Kong

2046. Directed by Wong Kar-Wai. An sf movie that's sf in a general sense; part of the movie takes place in the future. In typical Wong style, the movie is very dreamy, ethereal and subtle.

The Bride with White Hair 白髮魔女傳. A movie, described by the director as a retelling of the Romeo and Juliet story.

The City Trilogy, by Chang Hsi-Kuo. Composed of three books: *Five Jade Disks, Defenders of the Dragon City,* and *Tale of a Feather.* An epic tale dealing with oppression, racism, revenge, and war.

Fantasy Foundation 奇幻基地. A web forum for people who are into fantasy, including reading, writing, RPGs, and many other aspects. Online at http://www.ffoundation.com.tw/modules/news/.

"Gaming in Taiwan," by Rachel Kronick. An increasingly out-of-date set of links and resources for RPGs and other gaming in Taiwan. Online at http://www.jiawen.net/gamingintaiwan.html.

Membrane 膜, by Ji Dawei 紀大偉. A novel in which not much happens; includes a lot of discussion of gender, plastic surgery, and the nature of identity.

Nine Life Man 九命人 and *Long Life Man* 九命人 by A Tui 阿推. A pair of manhua, lovingly drawn, about a man living sometime in the future who is sentenced by God to have nine lives. Very strange, funny and good.

"Science Fiction, Globalization, and the People's Republic of China," by Lavie Tidhar. Discusses the history of sf in mainland China, including what topics are taboo and general market conditions. Online at http://www.concatenation.org/ articles/sf~china.html.

Science Fiction World 科幻世界. A magazine that carries original sf&f, translations, letters, etc. In print, and online at http://www.sfw-cd.com/ (with an English site at http://en.sfw-cd.com/index.html). Also has a great online shop.

Anything by Ni Kuang 倪匡. He writes all kinds of things: short stories with a Fortean bent (ghosts, UFOs, etc.), wuxia stories, adventure stories, erotica, etc. There are dozens of volumes of his collected works.

Other notes

"[WisCon 2008] Not Just Japan: Asian Science Fiction and Fantasy." Yoon Ha Lee's very good write-up of the panel. Online at http://yhlee.livejournal.com/1141868.html.

"Asian SF/F (not Japan)" by Joyce Tsai. Joyce's LJ post in preparation for this panel. Includes tons of great suggestions and discussion in the comments. Online at http://oyceter.livejournal.com/744610.html

Shoujo Bodies—A Spontaneous Panel

K. Joyce Tsai

> *Note: I will be referring to all Japanese authors by their surname first and to all series by their titles as known in the US. I am using the waapuro variation on the revised Hepburn romanization system for romanization, with the exception of names of authors who have indicated their own preference for romanization.*

For those unfamiliar with manga, "manga" is a term in English used to refer to Japanese comics. "Manhwa" and "manhua" are used to refer to Korean and Chinese comics, respectively, and by and large, these terms are used to refer to comics originating from Japan, Korea, and various countries in the Asian Chinese diaspora written in Japanese, Korean, and Chinese.

Almost all manga in Japan are originally published in thick, cheap magazines; each magazine is aimed toward a very specific demographic and contains the latest chapters of dozens of series. Chapters are later compiled into volumes and sold in bookstores. Given the marketing of the magazines, series are usually labeled by the demographic they are aimed toward, as opposed to subject-based genres like fantasy or science fiction. The most common genres are shounen and shoujo—shounen is aimed toward preteen to teenaged boys, and shoujo is aimed toward preteen to teenaged girls. Seinen and josei (called rediizu komikusu or "ladies' comics" in Japanese) are marketed to young men and young women roughly in their twenties, respectively. One subgenre of shoujo manga is shounen ai or yaoi (called BL, Boy's Love, june, or yaoi in Japanese); shounen ai consists of gay love stories for a predominantly female audience. Most josei and shoujo mangaka (authors) are women, and most seinen and shounen mangaka are men, although there is a greater crossover for seinen and shounen than there is for josei and shoujo.

> This was a spontaneous panel composed of Micole Sudberg, Akycha, Heaven's Calyx, Mystickeeper, Emily Horner, Abby, and Alaya Dawn Johnson.

I had originally suggested the panel, but it didn't make it to the official program. I ended up surveying my blog readers to see if there would be interest and promoting the spontaneous panel on my blog and on the WisCon Livejournal community. I don't remember the description that I wrote up for the panel suggestions, but here's the one I posted to the WisCon community:

> Most bodies in shoujo manga are thin and wispy, with an emphasis on androgyny. Many of the men tend to lack muscle definition (think Yuu Watase), while the women are much less curvy than their shounen manga counterparts. What does this mean to us? What other body types are there in shoujo manga? We will hopefully talk about gender-bending, cross-dressing, body image, and the fashion industry. Suggested series to discuss: After School Nightmare, Paradise Kiss, Walkin' Butterfly, Angel Sanctuary, Fruits Basket, W Juliet, Rose of Versailles, and Princess Knight.

I took no notes, so all this is based purely off my very faulty memory. Also, I am writing it up grouped by topic, as opposed to following the flow of the conversation.

I mentioned early on in the panel that we were mostly going to focus on shoujo manga and manhwa, with some possible delving into shounen manga representations of female bodies, but more as a comparison than an exploration of shounen manga.

Gender-bending and Cross-dressing

We may have started with shoujo manga history and how gender-bending and cross-dressing has been there from the very start, with the first shoujo manga, Tezuka Osamu's Princess Knight (Ribon no kishi, 1954-1968). Princess Knight stars a princess, Sapphire, who's raised as a boy by her parents because they wanted a son and an heir. Someone pointed out that the interesting thing about Sapphire is that she actually has two souls, a male one and a female one. There were the obligatory mentions of Ikeda Riyoko's Rose of Versailles (Berusaiyu no bara, 1972-1973) and Revolutionary Girl Utena (Shoujo kakumei Utena, 1997 anime) as the descendents of Princess Knight, particularly in the 1700s European setting for Rose of Versailles and the 1700s European imagery and clothing for Utena. Someone drew a parallel between Sapphire and her two souls and Ichijo from Mizushiro Setona's After School Nightmare (Houkago hokenshitsu, 2005-2008) and his male upper body and female lower body. I think Micole commented on a reviewer or two who categorized Ichijo not as transgendered, but as something else all together.

I mentioned how girls-dressed-as-guys tend to be what plots are based on—for example, Rose of Versailles, Princess Knight, Utena, Nakajo Hisaya's Hana Kimi (Hanazakari no kimitachi e, 1996-2004)—while guys-dressed-as-girls tend to be more one-off kink-fulfillment. For example, there are many occurrences of the obligatory school festival in which the pretty guys dress in women's clothing, with the mangaka notes saying "And I was so excited when I got to dress [character] as a girl!" Someone pointed out that the exception was Emura's W Juliet (Daboru Jurietto, 1997-2002). I mentioned how the mangaka notes occasionally squee about dressing up the bishounen as girls, but how the mangaka occasionally also mentions that it's difficult to draw because she keeps wanting to draw breasts on the character. There was also a note on how Haruka from Takeuchi Naoko's Sailor Moon (Bishoujo senshi Seeraa Muun, 1992-1997) was the exception to the girls-dressed-as-guys not being a kink thing, ditto with the otoko-yaku of Takarazuka.

Constructs of Femininity and Masculinity

When going into why guys-in-girls'-clothing was a kink, I think I wondered if some mangaka vindictively liked having guys know how much effort goes into donning frilly clothing. Micole talked a little about Jennifer Robertson's *Takarazuka*, a book about the all-female revue troupe Takarazuka, and how Robertson talked a lot about masculinity as a construct, as demonstrated by the otoko-yaku (the women who specialize in men's roles) taking "masculine" traits and exaggerating them, but also on how Robertson ignores the female roles and musume-yaku (the women who specialize in women's roles) and how their enactment of femininity is just as constructed. I mentioned the onnagata of kabuki (men specializing in women's roles, as kabuki was all-male, though it started as a female religious performance ritual) and how Edo writers, particularly Ihara Saikaku, would note that men could play women better than women themselves, because they didn't have the messy female biology to trip them up (!!).

Akycha and Heaven's Calyx had lots of cool info about *Takarazuka*, as they are avid fans who have seen many performances on tape. One of them mentioned how otoko-yaku are far more popular than musume-yaku and that the male roles are considered better. They also noted for the production of *Elisabeth*, a musical about Empress Elisabeth of Austria and Hungary, they assigned the role of Elisabeth to an otoko-yaku, even though Elisabeth is female. She speculated that this was because the producers or casting directors thought the musume-yaku didn't have the acting chops for the part, but also that they gave the role to the otoko-yaku who was considered more feminine than the others. This coupled with the example of the onnagata led to the thought of how femininity is routinely devalued. I mentioned that it's interesting that "otoko-yaku" means "male/man role" in Japanese, but "musume-yaku" is "daughter role" instead of "female/woman role." I forgot if anyone said this, but there's also a devaluing of female bodies, particularly in kabuki, in which popular rhetoric says that the men play women better than women themselves. There was also a lot of rhetoric in Edo Japan on the benefits of nanshoku (male-male love) and how it was purer than male-female love because messy biology wasn't in the way, as well as the complications of marriage and money and familial politics.

There was also discussion about the constructs of gender in *After School Nightmare* and how it's interesting watching Mizushiro move from a more traditional gender binary to the possibility of something that won't make us all tear our hair out. Ichijo begins thinking that if he is attracted to Sou, a boy, he must be passive and "feminine" and thereby be female, whereas if he's attracted to Kureha, a girl, he must then be active and "masculine" and thereby be male. There's the interesting bit on the assignation of gender based on sexuality. Alaya noted that the construct of sexuality as set (heterosexual, homosexual or bisexual) didn't exist in historical Japan: if you were sleeping with a guy at that moment, it was nanshoku, and if you were sleeping with a woman at that moment, it was male-female love. I footnoted this by saying it was a view of sexuality focused strictly on men; I don't think there was much discourse about female-female love. If there wasn't someone being penetrated, it didn't count as sex. I now remember a few shunga featuring two women pleasuring themselves with dildos, but I also remember reading commentary on how the penetration was still there, and of course the male sex organ, albeit not with a male body attached.

Biology and Constructions of Gender

Someone also brought up how there's very little looking at the pain and trouble involved with trappings of femininity. We're introduced to Ichijo when he gets his period, and Heaven's Calyx or Akycha mentioned how rarely we get to see menstruation in shoujo manga. They brought up the anime Kashimashi: Girl Meets Girl (Kashimashi: gaaru miitsu gaaru, 2004-2007), which stars a guy turning into a girl and features his difficulties with shaving his legs and adopting other trappings of femininity, and how we rarely get to see girls in shoujo learning how to be feminine, learning how to shave their legs or wax or deal with menstruation. Someone brought up episode 27, "Nanami's Egg," in Utena as a great example of the anxiety surrounding menstruation. (Am I too early? Too late? Is mine larger or smaller than normal? Why won't anyone tell me anything about it?) The anime Haibane Renmei's (Haibane renmei, 2002) portrayal of the growth of wings also echoes anxiety about menstruation: it's messy and bloody and painful, but also necessary and a sign of maturity. I mentioned the fears and anxieties surrounding dirty wings in the series, particularly as a mark of sin. With regard to leg shaving, I said that maybe it was cultural and fewer people in Japan shave their legs, since I definitely see fewer ads for shaving implements in Taiwan, but Heaven's Calyx and Alaya both said they didn't think so.

The talk went to secondary sex characteristics and how there seemed to be a marked lack of commentary on puberty and the development of secondary sex characteristics in shoujo manga. I brought up Tamaki Chiro's Walkin' Butterfly (Uookin batafurai, 2004-ongoing) as an interesting example, because we actually see the heroine's pubic hair, but Micole said the series was josei, which explains much of its nudity. I think I also mentioned how it's male puberty as well: most of the heroes in shoujo don't have much muscle definition or facial scruff, and their body silhouettes are closer to that of the girls. The penchant for more similar silhouettes (slimmer hips on the girls, slimmer shoulders on the boys) is also more noticeable when compared to shounen manga art, which tends to exaggerate women's breasts and men's muscles.

Most people said that despite this, they could tell apart the guys and the girls. Micole mentioned how she read Demon Diary when she was first getting into manga (and manhwa) and couldn't tell what sex people were, so she pretended they were all androgynous, but on going back a few years later, she could tell them apart. People shared stories of anime/manga newbies who are confounded by the long flowing bishounen hair and pretty faces, but also how the gender-distinguishing features become more obvious as your eye gets more accustomed to it. I said I always looked at the characters' chests to figure out, which is how I figured out Envy in Fullmetal Alchemist was male and how I got confused by Tieria in the anime Gundam 00 (Kido senshi gandamu daburu oo, 2007-ongoing), as his pilot outfit has lumpy bits right around the chest area. I just remembered now that I forgot to comment on the lack of depiction of nipples, particularly on women.

I think someone mentioned rorikon (Lolita complex) and Japanese censorship laws, which make it harder to depict pubic hair. Someone also talked about yaoi as an exception to lack of secondary sex characteristics, as yaoi guys tend to have more muscle definition. There was also talk about how uke (the bottom) and seme (the top) were distinguished physically with height and hair and eye size and facial shape: more "masculine" guys always have longer faces while more "feminine" guys have shorter, wider faces. I mentioned that Rose of Versailles is interesting because Oscar gets a typically "masculine" face shape. I think we also all laughed at CLAMP art and how they basically only had two male body templates. I can't remember if anyone said something about the more "feminine" faces as being more childlike (larger eyes, wider face, etc).

Alaya, Mystickeeper, and Emily all talked about how shoujo art is changing, as I think they started out on manga with Sailor Moon and Yuu Watase, in which the women have more visible hips and breasts. I want to fit in the Sailor Moon Stars characters, who turn from male to female in the anime—their female forms are the powerful forms, because they're the warrior forms. But of course, they're also dressed in skimpy leather outfits.

Devaluing the Female POV

All of us ranted about how so much shoujo starts out focused on the heroine and then ends up focused on the hero's childhood angst and emotional growth (ex. Souryou Fuyumi's Mars [Maazu, 1996-2000], Tsuda Masami's Kare Kano [Kareshi kanojo no jijou, 1996-2005]). Poor Alaya had only seen the Kare Kano anime ("The paper cut outs on sticks episode! Miyazawa kicking Arima!"), and the rest of us grumped about the horrible ending of the manga, and how we were all so angry that the most awesome Miyazawa gets shafted for more story about Arima's background, and how we all loved Miyazawa from the beginning because she wasn't the typically sweet shoujo heroine. I can't remember if I said this, but now I note that Miyazawa's interesting as a heroine because she makes us look at femininity as a social construct, particularly in scenes where she makes shoujo sparklies and flowers appear on demand in the background. I can't remember if anyone mentioned Rukia in terms of constructs of femininity as well, even though Bleach is shounen, since Rukia in the anime switches from her naturally gruff voice to a high-pitched voice using very feminine speech in front of strangers. This went along with the devaluing of female bodies in Edo Japan and the devaluing of female roles in Takarazuka.

I think someone mentioned how literature in Japan in Japanese (as opposed to classical Chinese) started as a female tradition (ex. Sei Shonagon, Lady Murasaki), but Alaya mentioned the current devaluing of fiction centered on women, particularly with regard to Yoshimoto Banana, who's thought of as a "shoujo" author, despite her not writing manga. She talked about two pieces of scholarship, one from the US and one from Japan, both of which completely write off Yoshimoto as writing about topics that don't matter or being too girly, etc. She particularly mentioned *Kitchen*, which is focused on home and cooking and food and is thereby not "serious literature." I mentioned that was particularly interesting because the climax of *Kitchen* is all about katsudon, which my professor had said was a take-out food, not a cook-at-home food. So even there, Yoshimoto is playing with ideas of gender and food and cooking.

Historical Gender Constructs

We talked a little about historical Japanese constructs of gender; I talked about the Meiji propaganda of "good wife, wise mother" (ryousei kenbo) and there being nothing between the roles of "child" and "mother/wife" for women to fit into in historical Japan. Micole noted that this paralleled the rise of the concept of adolescence in the West and probably the development of Victorian gender roles as well. I mentioned the start of shoujo magazines around the Meiji Era (1868-1912); I don't know much about them myself, but one of my undergraduate advisors had mentioned them as an avenue of research for me and a way to look at the beginning of the concept of the "shoujo" in Japan. We also talked about adolescent anxiety and shoujo manga scholarship that boxes the gender "messiness" of shoujo manga as rising solely from Japanese shoujo's fears and anxieties about growing up in a sexist society and having to become a wife and mother. Micole and I particularly hate this theory, as the scholars who propose it think it rises solely from Japanese culture although the same arguments come up in slash academic writing, and because it is a limited look as to how wide the representations of gender and sexuality are in shoujo manga alone.

Further discussion

Micole talked about Okazaki Kyoko's works (unlicensed) and Okazaki's look at the fashion industry, which capitalizes on the deliberate construct of femininity. I think she quoted one bit in which the heroine, a model, has basically been surgically "enhanced" everywhere except her cunt (I think that word's in the quote). Someone else mentioned the rise of cosmetic female genital surgery in the US, so technically, the heroine could be all surgically enhanced. There was some mention of the tall, lanky, thin shoujo silhouette as being that of a model and how there's that story that keeps being retold of the girl who hates her body but finds out it's...perfect for modeling! We see this in Walkin' Butterfly, and I swear I've read this in US YA novels as well. I noted that while I am pro body acceptance, I feel the fashion industry is not the best way to it.

There was also a discussion of bodily mutilation and how men and boys are allowed to have sexy scars. Micole mentioned how it's a sign that the guys have survived something and lived past it, how they had tragic angst written on their bodies, but how shoujo bodies had to be perfect and flawless and history-less to be valuable. I noted that I generally do not argue for further violence to be written on female bodies, but in the case of manga, violence and scarring is a sign of caring, both in terms of mangaka regard and in terms of audience reaction to the characters. I think we agreed that it was important that it wasn't sexualized violence written on shoujo bodies, but violence in terms of angsty backstory and something that makes the heroine stronger and more awesome. I threw in a reference to the Hong Kong movie *The Bride with White Hair*, as there's a really interesting scene in which the heroine has to literally crawl over hot coals and razors and get whipped by her clan to exit her clan; it's a striking scene of non-sexualized violence done to a woman. Someone also noted that the difference between that and violence to women in the US television show *Supernatural*, particularly how reader/viewer sympathy lay with the person enduring the violence in *Bride* while sympathy is with the more active men enduring violence in *Supernatural* and not with the women, who are usually the victims of the week.

Now I remember that the discussion started with talk of subjectivity and objectivity in manga, and how the heroines and heroes can often be both subject and object because of the medium. I think Emily noted how shoujo manga is frequently narrated from a first person point of view (usually the heroine's point of view), and how Yazawa Ai's Nana (Nana, 2000-ongoing) is exceptional because it's focused on the two Nanas talking to each other via the narration. But Emily noted that because manga is drawn, even though we're thrust into the heroine's point of view via voiceovers and narration, we're also in the position to view her body (and the hero's body) as objects, because we are also looking at their outsides and not just at their inner points of view.

We briefly went into manhwa art style and how it's different (mainly the lips and eyes, particularly in that people have prominent lips). Micole mentioned how she might be overgeneralizing, but she liked that manhwa tended to have angrier, less sweet heroines, as opposed to manga, and I think all of us agreed about that. I might have noted that the downside to that is that the anger is often directed at other women and girls in terms of romantic rivalry. But that may just be a conclusion drawn from my watching of Korean dramas. I then went on a handwavy overgeneralization as to how I think US media tends to reward the "masculine" in that we have more women warriors and assertion and other stereotypically masculine traits, but the men are not allowed to be "girly"; whereas Japanese media may reward the "feminine" more in that the men are allowed to be more emotional and vulnerable and to display other stereotypically feminine traits, but the women are not allowed to be aggressive.

There was also talk on how filmed media tends to be more conservative than printed media overall (Asian dramas, US TV shows vs. manga, written sf/f) and how a lot of that might be because of business models. There's a limited amount of TV channels and a limited amount of shows studios can put out, and less of a limitation on print, albeit still a limit.

And then we ran out of time, and I realized we hadn't even talked about the lack of different types of bodies at all, including in terms of age, weight, race, etc.

Thoughts

Overall, this was one of my favorite panels from WisCon, probably because a) I suggested it, b) the spontaneous programming meant mostly people who knew about shoujo manga came, and c) I felt I finally got to go as in depth as I wanted to in a panel. The last bit is largely influenced by the second bit; though not everyone was familiar with every series discussed, it seemed like most people had read a fair amount of shoujo manga and manga overall, and that most people were fairly familiar with Japan, so there was very little 101 to do. I loved being able to talk about so many works and to connect them all, and am only sad that we couldn't keep going for the entire night.

This panel write up originally appeared online on my blog (http://oyceter.livejournal.com/751902.html) and on the Aqueduct Press Blog (http://aqueductpress.blogspot.com/2008/06/wiscon-32-shoujo-bodies.html). Some changes have been made for clarity and correctness.

K. Joyce Tsai currently resides in California's Bay Area. She blogs about books, gender, and race — sometimes all at once — at oyceter.livejournal.com. She has reviewed books for Broad Universe's The Broadsheet and contributed to *Wiscon Chronicles 2.*

The End of Original Sin: A Meditation on Aikido, the Marq'ssan Cycle, and the Elemental Logic Series

Nancy Jane Moore

> As a result of original sin, human nature is weakened in its powers, subject to ignorance, suffering, and the domination of death, and inclined to sin.[1]

The above sentence is the Roman Catholic Church's take on human nature. Other Christian denominations have slightly different views on the subject, but most appear to assume that human nature is essentially flawed and to attribute (some metaphorically, some literally) that flaw to the fall of Adam and Eve. In the Christian religious view, belief in Jesus Christ can save one from the consequences of this sin, but human nature is apparently immutable.

Christians aren't the only people who believe human nature is permanently both fixed and flawed. Most science fiction is based on the same theory. No matter how many years in the future a story is set, or how many physical enhancements the human characters may have, the assumption remains that some things—gender roles, greed, violence, just to name a few—will never change. Fantasy—which rarely deals in change of any kind—also assumes a flawed humankind, often focusing on the struggle between good and evil in a manner not unlike that addressed in religion.

And, indeed, if you look at the current state of the world, it's hard not to reach the conclusion that human beings must be incurably flawed. Anyone can provide a litany of horrors, so I'll just cite one example that recently shocked me to the core: 2.6 billion people on this Earth have no place to go to the toilet.[2] Yes, that's billion with a "b," and Rose George, author of *The Big Necessity: The Unmentionable World of Human Waste and Why It Matters*, says the number doesn't include those using outhouses, public toilets, or other less-than-ideal facilities; she means people who have no place to go except the bushes, the alley, or even the public street.

These 2.6 billion comprise 40 percent of the world population. Forty percent of the humans on Earth must devote a certain amount of time every day to planning where they're going to shit and pee. Thinking about the sanitation issues alone is horrifying, but what shocked me most was realizing there are so many people for whom such a simple human necessity cannot be taken for granted. That such a situation exists in the midst of great wealth and technological advancement certainly indicates human failing.

And yet, I have hope—a tiny shred of hope, but hope nonetheless—that we human beings will eventually become truly civilized. In argument, I offer three things: the martial art of aikido and the philosophy of its founder, Morihei Ueshiba, known as O Sensei; the five books of L. Timmel Duchamp's Marq'ssan Cycle;[3] and the Elemental Logic series[4] by Laurie J. Marks.

In all three I find examples of humans adjusting their reaction to a world of violence and stupidity and responding in a new and more effective way. My hope comes from a simple belief that the more human beings understand and use these different responses, the more civilized we will become.

"True Budo[5] Is a Work of Love"[6]

Aikido is a martial art rooted in traditional Japanese warriorship. Many of the open-hand techniques are adapted from sword work, and indeed, weapons training is a key way to study the principles. Unlike many other martial arts, aikido is not taught as a sport, and as with all fighting arts, many of the techniques have deadly potential. Why then, when violence against others is a significant problem in the world today, do I say a martial art gives me hope that humans will one day become civilized?

It has to do with the underlying principles of aikido. My teacher, Mitsugi Saotome, says O Sensei combined his extensive training in many martial arts with his spiritual search and created something entirely new. "He elevated the killing techniques of battle into a method of purifying human beings so that they might harmoniously coexist and prosper."[7]

Saotome, who was a direct student of O Sensei for many years, points out that aikido is a "*practical* philosophy," one grounded in reality. One of the key elements of aikido training is that you primarily train with a partner, so that while you're trying to make yourself a better person—a core principle of training—you're working with somebody else. Sitting meditation and other practices done on one's own can be challenging, but you only have to deal with yourself while you're trying to master them. In aikido, you have to deal with other people—just as you do in daily life. And that other person can sometimes be a real pain in the ass.

The easiest way to understand the principles of aikido is to train, but I'll use an example out of regular practice to provide a flavor of the training and principles. One of the basic responses to an attack is to enter and take control of the centerline. Assume a person is attacking with a punch to the face. You move forward, turning slightly to the side, so that the strike goes harmlessly past you. But you must move at just the right time: too early, and the attacker will change the attack; too late, and you'll get hit. Furthermore, if you come in too aggressively, you will end up in conflict with your attacker, but if you come in too passively or try to back away, your attacker will run over you. The goal is to take charge of the situation without provoking the attacker into escalating.

It is in this concept of taking charge without causing escalation that I see a parallel between aikido and the principles underlying the two series of novels by Duchamp and Marks. In both series, characters deal with violent and troubling situations by taking stands but eschewing revenge. They are neither passive nor unnecessarily violent.

One of the principles of Japanese *budo*, or warriorship, was *ai uchi*, or mutual destruction. As Saotome describes it, a fighter "had to have a commitment to his purpose that was so great that his own life was of no value in comparison. He would willingly sacrifice his own life to achieve his enemy's death." But, as Saotome goes on to explain, this "is still a philosophy geared toward destruction and death."[8] The higher goal is *ai nuke*, or mutual preservation of life. Saotome says, "This concept of budo, the possession of a love of all life so great that it allows you to love your enemy and the spiritual strength to put that love into practice, lies at the philosophical heart of aikido."[9]

If the arts of war can be turned into love, I find hope for the human race.

The Us-Them Mentality Is the Problem, Not the Solution[10]

At first glance, L. Timmel Duchamp's Marq'ssan Cycle looks to be dystopian fiction. People are rigidly divided into three classes or castes: executive, who run government and business; professional, the teachers, doctors, lawyers, engineers, and so forth; and service techs, the secretaries and other skilled labor who do the detail work that allows the system to function. The world is polluted and so overpopulated that only some are allowed to have children. Good food is only for the wealthy, and water is scarce.

And then the aliens come and disrupt the status quo, starting with their refusal to deal with men—they will only negotiate with women. Immediately, I assumed the aliens would save humanity from itself or possibly, destroy us before we contaminate the rest of the universe, à la *The Day the Earth Stood Still*.[11] But Duchamp is capable of imagining a much more complex future than that.

Despite—or perhaps because of—the fact that these books were originally written in the 1980s, they provide a bitter commentary on current events. In the United States of 2009, our class system has become more stratified; the interrelation of government and business that Duchamp posits for the executive—in the books, high government officials are very wealthy because there is no conflict-of-interest rule prohibiting their financial investment in businesses they supposedly regulate or contract with—mirrors the Bush administration.[12] We are only now beginning to discuss climate change seriously. And the world population was more than three times as large at the end of the twentieth century than it was at the beginning.

When I read the second book, *Renegade*, I was also reading Ron Suskind's *The One Percent Doctrine*[13] and marveled at how well Duchamp had channeled the neocon view of the world in setting up the security personnel of her executive class. At that point, I thought her main purpose was to educate us about the irrationality of those who follow a violent doctrine so extreme that even threats that are only 1 percent likely to occur must be met with overwhelming force.

It was not until I got deep into the third book, *Tsunami*, that I realized how broad Duchamp's vision truly was. By this point in the series, free zones—not controlled by the executives running the national government—have been established, and the free zone in the northwest US is confronting its own crisis: a group within it has been murdering rapists. The free zone leadership must figure out how to diffuse the crisis.

This is a common problem of modern government. A scandal—real or trumped up—occurs, and the leader must find a way to get past it and move on. Usually certain people are jettisoned from the government; occasionally they are prosecuted. But very rarely is the underlying issue ever addressed.

In *Tsunami*, Martha Greenglass, a former service tech who is now one of the leaders in the free zone, makes an amazing speech:

> "One of the things the Marq'ssan have made me see is that until humans begin to scrutinize their mistakes and learn from and remember them, nothing will significantly change.
>
> "Many of us here today would like to 'settle' this matter and lay it to rest. Which is to say we want to satisfy our consciences or desires—depending on which 'side' of the issue we are positioned—and then go on as though nothing had happened."

She goes on to talk about her own involvement, the issue of fear, how she would respond if it were her enemy killing people, rather than an ally and former lover. And toward the end of the talk, she says:

> "The us-them mentality is the problem, not the solution. The us-them mentality makes it possible for Louise to kill rapists. And it makes it possible for the Executive to be complicit with the killing and torturing of thousands of people."[14]

That's an approach worthy of aikido, moving away from the us-them mentality to seeing our enemies—even the worst among them—as our fellow human beings. And it provides us with a recipe for changing ourselves: We must confront our mistakes and figure out how to do things differently, so that we don't make that error again. It's not enough to excise the person who went too far and put the situation behind us as if it never happened.

Many things happen over the course of the next two books. There's a feminist revolution within the executive class — though the change in power does not trickle down. There are struggles among the opponents of the executive over the issue of whether — and how much — to work within the system, struggles familiar to anyone who has ever been part of a political movement. People who never thought of themselves as leaders become precisely that. People who were willing to do terrible things for power find themselves trapped by similar tactics. Even anarchism — which might seem to be the political theory most favored by these books — comes in for criticism.

The one thing that Marq'ssan Cycle does not give us — and I hope this is not a spoiler — is one right answer on how to change. What it does instead is give us tools and analysis that can lead us down that road. We are not stuck in this world of violence, not stuck with hard choices between freedom and security, not stuck with killing the other person before they kill us. If we change how we look at our situation, we can change the situation.

"Oh, It's an Impossible Task.... Let Us Begin It at Once"[15]

This quote, from the beginning of Marks's *Water Logic*, could easily sum up my discussion of the Marq'ssan Cycle. And, indeed, I have found parallels between the two series from the beginning. That may seem surprising, since the Marq'ssan Cycle is near-future science fiction, complete with aliens, while the Elemental Logic series is fantasy set in a made-up world with a very specific kind of magic. The very language used in the two series is different: Duchamp's words and sentences are hard and matter of fact, not unlike the many nonfiction books currently available on what's wrong with the United States, while Marks uses more lyrical language that evokes the very otherness of her world.

And yet the Elemental Logic series is just as political as the Marq'ssan Cycle and provides an equally mind-bending approach to dealing with violence and conflict. However, because Marks employs many other unusual items in these books, it is possible, at least at first, to see these books as simply more inclusive and high-quality fantasy.

Zanja, one of the primary characters, is a dark-skinned woman from a tribal community in the land of Shaftal. Many—though not all—of the primary actors in the books are women, and few are described as women who could be played by Angelina Jolie or other superstar beauties. Both gay and straight relationships and marriages are the norm and taken for granted, and people form families that may include several couples and unrelated singles. All adults in a family take care of the children. There is no Shaftali religion, though there are ethical and philosophical principles.

Taken together, all of these things would have been enough to make this series a very satisfying fantasy read. The core plot—Shaftal has been invaded by the Sainnites, soldiers looking for a new home—is the basic one of struggle against oppressors. It's easy to despise the Sainnites, root for the Shaftali, and hope the scourge is eventually driven from the land. That is, good will triumph over evil.

And, indeed, these books are about good and evil, but the lines between those things are not as clearly drawn as one might expect. As we get to know some Sainnites, we find that they are not uniformly evil, and that in fact much of what seems evil in them has more to do with the fact that they were raised to be soldiers and have been driven from their own homeland. And in their battle against the Sainnites, the Shaftali, despite their much more evolved and humane society, are running the risk of becoming their enemies.

This is shown most clearly in the character of Mabin, the general who leads the Shaftali opposition. She is convinced that the only response to the Sainnite invasion is the classic one of guerilla warfare and believes so strongly that her approach is the only correct one that she lies and even kills to retain her control over the revolution. While she is far from the only character at risk of becoming what she hates, she is, as the leader, the one capable of doing the most damage.

Here, the argument that "the end justifies the means" is trumped by integrated means and end. However, I do not mean to imply that those on the side of "good" are completely nonviolent; they are, rather, more measured in their use of violence. There is a line in the first book, *Fire Logic*, that sticks with me: "Guns make killing too easy. It becomes a habit, like it has with Willis and with Mabin. It keeps us from thinking of other ways."[16]

How apropos to the current state of the world, where war is the only way the US and other governments can think of to deal with terrorism.

The books also tell the rarely told story of rebuilding a world damaged by war and oppression. Not only must Karis, the Shaftali leader by virtue of her role as g'deon, and her family and fellow leaders figure out how to incorporate the Sainnites into Shaftal and how to construct a new government after the old one was destroyed, they must also deal with those who are not satisfied by the way victory was achieved. Rebuilding can be more difficult—and perhaps more perilous—than war, and Marks once again does not take the easy way out. There is no hand waving here, no "they lived happily ever after."

The Elemental Logic series is not yet complete. I am impatiently awaiting the publication of *Air Logic*, which is forthcoming from Small Beer Press.[17]

"The Way to Reconcile the World"[18]

Both science fiction and fantasy have the capacity to present us with new approaches to human life because both genres can change some of the underlying rules of ordinary life. But that can create its own problems: change becomes something brought about by aliens or people who have magical powers. While you can see the aliens as teachers—not unlike O Sensei, really—and the magic as our own internal powers that we have not fully tapped, the fact remains that we can read those books and assume either outside intervention or powers we don't have.

That's where aikido comes in, because aikido taps into our own, very human, resources.

To put this on a personal level: I recently observed to a fellow aikido student that I had become less aggressive. And she said, "Yes, I noticed." (That's one of the troubles with aikido; the people you train with often know more about you than you know yourself.) Granted, it took a lot of years of study—I've been doing aikido since 1986—but slowly the art is making me a different person, one less interested in getting in someone else's face.

I'm sure aikido isn't the only way to make this change in our human nature, and I'm also sure that, as we change, we will bring change about in those who come after us, both culturally and—I suspect eventually—genetically. But to get to that point, we have to survive the present and to start taking steps to make those changes in our own lives. Coming up with a sane approach to the violence and general volatility in the world today and looking clearly at the missteps that led to the major economic crash of 2008 with an eye to really understanding the root of the problem are just two areas where we can apply the ideas of O Sensei, Duchamp, and Marks.

Maybe it isn't an impossible job. Let's begin at once.

Endnotes

1 *Catechism of the Roman Catholic Church*, Section 418, http://www.vatican.va/archive/catechism/p1s2c1p7.htm.

2 George, Rose, Excerpts from *The Big Necessity: The Unmentionable World of Human Waste and Why It Matters*, published on Slate.com in October 2008 at http://www.slate.com/id/2201466/entry/2201467/.

3 Duchamp, L. Timmel, *Alanya to Alanya* (2005), *Renegade* (2006), *Tsunami* (2007), *Blood in the Fruit* (2007), *Stretto* (2008), all Aqueduct Press, Seattle, WA.

4 Marks, Laurie J., *Fire Logic* (2002), *Earth Logic* (2004), both Tor, New York, and *Water Logic*, Small Beer Press, Northhampton, MA, 2007. The fourth volume, *Air Logic*, is forthcoming from Small Beer.

5 Budo is a Japanese word usually translated as warriorship. According to my Aikido teacher, Mitsugi Saotome, "bu," usually translated as war, literally means to stop the spear, while "do" means way or path. So budo means the way of stopping the spear – a much broader concept than the way of war. Saotome, Mitsugi, *The Principles of Aikido*, Shambala, 1989, pp. 191-192.

6 Ueshiba, Morihei (O Sensei), as quoted at http://www.aikidoonline.com/archives/2003/feb/feat_0203_osensei_words2.html.

7 Saotome, *The Principles of Aikido*, op. cit., p. 216.

8 Ibid, p. 27.

9 Ibid, p. 30.

10 Said by Martha Greenglass in *Tsunami* p. 481.

11 The 1951 movie, directed by Robert Wise. I have never been able to find a copy of the short story by Harry Bates, "Farewell to the Master," which was the source material for the movie.

12 For a detailed discussion of the complex interrelationship between government and private enterprise in the world today, I recommend Naomi Klein's *The Shock Doctrine*, Picador, New York, 2007.

13 Suskind, Ron, *The One Percent Doctrine*, Simon & Schuster, New York, 2007.

14 *Tsunami*, op. cit. pp. 477-481.

15 Said by Medric in the Prologue to *Water Logic*, op. cit. p. 1.

16 *Fire Logic*, op. cit. p. 261.

17 Some tantalizing hints about *Air Logic* can be found at http://lauriejmarks.com/books/air-logic.html

18 Ueshiba, Morihei (O Sensei), as quoted at http://www.aikidoonline.com/archives/2003/feb/feat_0203_osensei_words2.html. The full quote is, "Aiki is not a technique to fight with or defeat the enemy. It is the way to reconcile the world and make human beings one family."

Nancy Jane Moore is part of the online writers' consortium, Book View Café— http://www.bookviewcafe.com/. Her collection, *Conscientious Inconsistencies*, is available from PS Publishing, and her novella, *Changeling*, is published by Aqueduct Press. She holds a fourth degree black belt in Aikido and has studied martial arts since 1979. She blogs on self defense matters at http://takingcareofourselves.blogspot.com, and on fiction at http://blog.bookviewcafe.com/ and http://aqueductpress.blogspot.com.

Fanfic and Slash 201

Panel Description: Are you a fan of fanfic or slash? Want to have some serious discussions about pairings/genres/etc? This is *not* a panel for people who have no idea what fanfic or slash is. Serious discussion of fanfic and slash communities and the stories themselves will be discussed here.

Panelists: JJ Pionke (moderator), Beth F., Joanna, Cat Meier, Cecilia Tan

(The audience of 50+ people is all women.)

Introductions

JJ: I'm an adjunct professor of English Composition. I sometimes infect students with fanfic. I give extra credit if they do something interesting. I write het and slash.

Cat: Ferriscat on LJ. I've written a tiny bit, but I read a whole lot.

Audience: She's edited a whole lot.

Cat: And I write a lot about it. I do stuff for meta_fandom. Nine years? Six years?

Ctan: This is not the math panel.

JJ: Oh, and I'm deepforestowl.

Audience: Ohhhhh!!!!

Beth: I'm carbonel.

Joanna: I've been reading fanfic since 1993, starting with Highlanders slash fandom. Never been to any slash cons. LJ funkyreunion. Reader but not a writer.

Ctan: I run Circlet Press; am author of much erotic sf. Harry Potter fanfic, nc 17 slash almost exclusively. For me, if there's not sex in it, what's the point?

Audience: Pairing?

Ctan: My one true threesome is Harry Draco Snape together.

Audience: I think you can say ot3. We will all understand.

Ctan: Snape/Draco. This is the first time I am coming out at a convention to talk as my fanfic persona. It is not a secret I write fanfic. Many of you know many professional writers write fanfic or used to and gave it up. I'm already a maven of erotic science fiction hello!!! So i'm not really worried about losing my rep. But there are no links from my fic journal to my LJ. It can't in any way look like a marketing tool for me to gain readers for my paying work. The whole thing is, it's not a job, it's fun, it's for my own enjoyment.

JJ: What are we dying to get off our chests?

Ctan: Do any of you read warnings as advertisements?

Everyone: YES!!!!!

Ctan: All these people are like, "Warning!!" and I'm like, Oh! This is what I want!

Beth: I put warnings in my zines upside down at the end so they could find them if they want.

Joanna: Really apologetic warning sign is a sign not to read it in the first place.

Audience: GROAN

byplay is too fast for notes!

JJ: Right now my fandom is BSG. My ship is gonna sail, I know it in my bones.

laughter

Charlie Jane: What ship?

Beth: I like Snape/Harry but I hate the term snarry.

Audience: YES.

JJ: Pet peeve, a really new young author, in A/R, I assume a she, very long, they're poorly constructed, they're not beta-ed.

Ctan: And yet people are addicted.

JJ: YES and why? Why? Why?

Audience: There are things that I will read. Terrible stories but it can be as simple as good pacing. In first throes of Harry Potter fandom I read them all anyway.

Sigrid: Marvel comics on LJ is like 35 people. And 35 people who maybe write 1 fic a year and it would SUCK to be in a fandom with like 4.

[This is the most responsive audience ever!]

Ctan: You don't see a lot of the really horrible science fiction published any more, because there are like, contests to make fun of it. And there were really horrible books, and people loved them. I mean there are people who loved the John Norman Gor books. And obviously Norman was getting something out of writing them, and I don't think it was the paycheck, and this is a guy who was a college professor and he had a fetish—he had a kink and he pushed that button again and again. What about when you are addicted to a fic that is bad, you know it's bad, but you read it anyway, and you almost want to offer to beta it, except then it would have your name on it.

Cat: And you would be embarrassed to admit you were reading it.

Ctan: Like that guy who couldn't keep it up, petered out three-fourths of the way through, still waiting. Then you have to write fanfic of the fanfic.

JJ: What are some things you wish would happen or wouldn't happen? What is problematic?

Ctan: More plot. I like sex but I like plots.

Cat: Longer is good, but…

JJ: Too many people write in short little bursts.

Ctan: I just participated in the Harry/Draco world cup, in like 14 teams on LJ; every piece in it is 10K to 30K words, all novellas, a huge fest. They gave us 3 months; other people are like killing themselves to read it all. Knock yourselves out, if you're unemployed, maybe you should get a job or a boyfriend or something.

Audience: Waking up early Christmas morning for Yuletide.

Audience: Ahahaha!!!

Audience: Mom... I have to check my email

Laughter!

Cat: Bandom. Rpf, bands, disco, big bang challenge, fan art, fan mix, all edited and done and in, all goes out together. I was going, oh this is great, except there's been no good fic in fandom because everyone's been doing this. Then like 50 things come out at once.

Ctan: For the world cup it was sort of paced. But...

JJ: Is there anyone who isn't familiar with Yuletide?

dead silence audience motionless

JJ: Wow. Next time we will have a graduate level class.

Audience: Will there be qualifying exams?

Sigrid: We were talking about doing the writers workshop. How to write from that place. But, ficathons, do they improve the quality of the work?

JJ: Depends on the fandom and the purpose of the ficathon. In BSG, used to keep interest high. Especially because frickn' scifi, let's have a one-year hiatus between seasons! And with the A/R ficathon, well, I've run *every* A/R ficathon. My other secret love in the BSGiverse is the Doc Cottle ficathon. **laughter** And that thing never fills.

Panel: Who does Yuletide?

(Many people's hands. Some shouts of "I read it.")

Cat: Underwritten het pairing, Rodney/Taylor. We had twice as many stories after the ficathon, posted after it, as the main archive had had before. So ficathons can be really good for galvanizing interest. People who wanted that fic but didn't think anyone else did.

Ctan: It inspires me as a writer, to know people want it. I run the Harry Potter tarot fest; it's not a smutathon, it's just pairings. It gets a lot of rare pairs — of course you have a lot of Harry/Draco on my friends list. Harry/Padma, and a sequel, etc. So she has a series going. She wouldn't have any other readers at all if she just put it in her own journal. You get to find new writers; it's good. I like having deadlines, it's motivating. Complaints, there's too many. But, how can there be too many? If you're tired of reading...

laughter

Ctan: You pull cards at home or sites online, to make your prompt.

JJ: People can get really creative. You have to insert these five items in your story; a framework you have to work with. Question: are there place we won't go?

Audience: Ha!!!

mass laughter

JJ: Well if you want to read tentacle sex with Harry Potter,

Ctan: It's out there. Come on! There's a squid and a lake.

Audience: The Whomping Willow!

Audience: Dobby/Sorting Hat.

hysterical laughter

Panel: Mostly it's "Your kink is not my kink, but that's okay."

JJ: Let's be honest, what's there not to love about Snape getting pregnant.

Ctan: I draw the line at Lucius/Draco.

Audience: Oh I won't rpf, oh I won't read incest, oh...but then I will read it.

Audience: But not only that, you will drag people like ME into it.

Audience: Curiosity factor.

Ctan: When you notice it enough to say no to it...

Beth: I once read a story that worked despite the, well, bdsm care bears.

MASS ROFL

Ctan: How do I make the transition? You're learning some really amazing skills! But, they lack rewriting skills! Especially, the women who are writing these works in progress; they post, as soon as they finish their chapter, it goes through their beta, you're reading the first draft of someone's novel! Sometimes they need the kick. You have a community you get all this interest from. But you don't get the chance to be like, oh I took a wrong turn in chapter 13. Deadlines, characterization, pacing, training your family not to bother you while you write, all are skills!

Beth: I disagree. You use someone else's voice, you don't make a new character.

Audience: I think worldbuilding suffers too. You don't have to explain what Hogwarts is.

Joanna: Other universes, it can be put into very different contexts...

JJ: Herminone/Snape body swap,

Aud, everyone on panel: "Fire in the Rose."

Liz: WOW!

JJ: Yes, it was a completed piece on their hard drive, and they just sort of dribbled it out to us every Friday. I didn't go out on a Friday, for...

Audience: Ahhahahaah!

JJ: I was in graduate school and I was like, please I need you to save me, save my soul!

Ctan: You need to be able to go back and weave things in, build up a few chapters first before you start to post!

JJ: It is instant gratification, by the end of the night, I will have at least five comments. I don't wrie anything longer than 1 or 2K words.

Beth: Paper zines…

Ctan: Quimby's bookstore after Terminus, HP convention there, people who would want to sell their zines.

Audience: There are not really any Harry Potter zines. They get so many C&Ds (Cease and Desists).

Ctan: There are some comics.

Audience: Serialization thing. I'm a serials serializer. I've been listening to Count of Monte Cristo audio, and it's very slashy! And somewhere around 40,000 words there was a bit that said, "We have forgotten to…"

(I missed this, but I think the point was that it felt like a fic-writing mistake Dumas had to try and fix but couldn't go back and edit.)

Audience: Amplificathon.

JJ: Record it and send it to Alison and multifandom archive.

Audience: We're entering the last of 10 weeks; I'm pretty much having a nervous breakdown.

JJ: Audio, an archive — can download to your ipod.

Panel: It's on LJ, google it.

Ctan: Have you guys heard the recordings of "A Year Like No Other."

Beth: What is it?

Ctan: Most popular Harry Potter gen fic of all time: Snape adopts Draco and Harry story.

Audience: awwww

JJ: Everybody — **gestures**

Audience: AWWWWWWWWWWWWWWWW

Sigrid: My fandom is 1930s and '40s black and white movies with marvel comics! Only seven people but still fun. AUs (Alternate Universes).

Cat: Biggest thing of doing an AU. Choose where you're diverging from fic and where you're not.

Sigrid: Make the choice for a reason.

Cat: If you're going to change the situation a lot, different jobs, etc., keep the character relationships intact, best friends, enemies, making them higher up in hierarchy. On other hand, change things about the characters. Or, keep setting, but change characters. But don't change both.

Sigrid: Melissa Scott, "Creating the Heavens," had a maxim, keep the weird (...). If they have a weird gender thing, put them in a city the reader can understand.

Beth: In Professionals, Bodie and Doyle and god knows the number of stories I've read where Doyle is the prostitute!

Ctan: Whole subset of no magic. They're just at a boarding school. Or not in school at all. Snape is in a rock band, and Harry is a roadie. Sounds like crack fic but can be done very sensitively and well. I am supposed to be writing a non-magical gift fic right now... Still them but they've been transported to a parallel universe. I couldn't just transport them to Arizona.

Audience: I've tried that one!

Cat: What is the one where Remus and Snape adopt...

Panel & Audience:"Stealing Harry."

Cat: It's by sam_storyteller.

Audience: Ohhhhhh!!! (knowingly)

Audience: He is the one straight male slasher foretold by prophecy.

Audience: Slash goggles. I find them very academically useful. Subtext is the best thing to look for! Politically! Once you see one subtext you see the others. How can I subvert this and read it differently...?

Cat: It's made me more critical and more picky when I'm reading things that aren't fanfic.

Audience: Writing fanfic makes me look at movies that way.

Cat: If I'm paying money for it now I need it to be at least consistent quality with the stuff I'm getting for free. I can get the stuff that hits my narrative kinks but isn't well written, for free.

Sigrid: I think watching, oh come on! Two lines 15 minutes ago would have set that up correctly.

Ctan: Often it was, but it got cut.

Audience: Ahhh, yes.

Audience: Otherwise excellent books, I find myself putting it down and going Hmmm.

[Missed a bit while thinking]

Audience: Stuff where Batman is very terse. Batman speaks for real, you can tell who said what anyway. It is tough to go back to writers where the sentence structure is all alike no matter who is speaking.

Cat: Penknife. She had a post on basically what you are asking. New media, new show, when she approaches it, whether or not she is interested in telling stories about, that is part of how she enjoys it. So part of the fannish enjoyment of something comes from the reading and the writing. I don't put as much attention and emotion into it, if it doesn't hit that thing I'm looking for.

Audience: It's not necessarily everything you really like. I have never had the least inclination to write any BSG. But yes, I love it. Yet for some reason I'm beating my brains out writing hornblower slash. I could use commercial lube instead...LOLLLLZZZ

Audience: Are you in age of sails?

Audience: Yeah!

Audience: BLD. Yes.

Audience: AHHH.

Ctan: There is so much sexual content in Harry Potter, trying to get out—you can feel her tamping it down (hand motions) desperately.

Beth: The very best shows don't get as much fan fiction. Buffy didn't get it for such a long time.

Ctan: You had Buffy. You didn't need it. Long waits between books! You couldn't just read them AGAIN.

Beth: Star Trek—there's so many holes to be filled, it just calls out,

hysterical laughter that goes on and on

JJ: And yet when the canon fulfills our desire, we don't need the fanfic. Once they're mainstream on tv in a hot tub, who needs the fan fic.

Audience: Enjoying the heck out of House/Wilson subtext until they started making it so overt, till I was like DUDE. That's… DUDE. Leave it to the professionals. Don't have them making slashy jokes!

Beth: But I trust Doris Egan. She's not a slasher.

Audience: Gail Simone's another one. All the girls in Birds of Prey. I mean, jeez.

Audience: Friends who don't fic or vid, but I feel a theological divide, when I'm talking to them and when I'm talking to other people who do. There is a difference in wanting to participate, a really participatory feeling, not so much love, but you want to be in it, you want to make it.

Beth: Fanfic is a gift economy.

Cat: Active engagement with the text.

Ctan: I started writing meta essays about it, the theme of flying—god, I'm such a Ravenclaw. Publishing them on the Internet; my mother leaves a comment, very good daughter—all these years of great books, this is what I'm getting out of it. And then I was like, this wasn't enough. I'm a canon nut. I wanted to get in there and wrestle with it. Those first two months are so fucked up, learning it! A whole new style of editing…

Ctan: You know what's funny? My spellchecker in Microsoft Word already knew the word Dumbledore.

Audience: Question for all panelists, What is your most non-obvious paring that kind a works?

Someone: Once I read one with Angel turned into a puppet, somehow getting it on with Miss Piggy.

Laughter

Beth: Jane Carnell, writes fanfic. Wrote whole bunch of pairs that you don't want to see, 100 of them; okay if I pick one will you do it, and it was, Cowley/Chewbacca. And it sounds awful, and she makes it work! Cowley is a Jedi knight who's old and tired, but he runs into this young strapping hero who... Well, it's cute.

Audience: Didn't someone slash fanlib and LiveJournal?

Audience: And Netscape/IE and Yahoo/Google.

Audience: Yep, that's going on amplification.

Cat: I'm on the OTW (Organization for Transformative Works) Finance committee.

mass applause

We weren't sure where our chair was, so a committee member wrote several paragraphs about the tension and something was going to have to give. It was completely meta.

JJ: I tend to specialize in them. Weird ones: Doc Cottle, Adama, and Roslyn, BSG.

Ctan: I'm picturing some sort of weird fertility treatment.

JJ: Cecilia don't be hateful.

laughter

Ctan: Filch /Mrs. Norris.

Audience: Nearly Giving Head Nick?

LOLZ

Audience: Shadowfax/Bill the Pony.

> [This is a rough transcription from notes taken by Liz Henry during the panel; it is not transcribed from a recording and may not be precisely what was said.]

Panel Review: Fanfiction & Slash 201

JJ Pionke

For the last several years at WisCon, there has been a fanfiction/ slash panel whereupon newbies and veterans alike would come from far and wide to talk about what they love about fan written stories. The panel always got bogged down in discussing and defining terms for the newbies, and the veterans were always left with a feeling that there could have been so much more, but there wasn't because of newbies.

For WisCon32, I suggested a fanfic and slash 101 panel and a separate fanfic and slash 201 panel. The idea being that 101 would answer the newbie questions and 201 would delve more deeply into the serious discussion of fanfic and slash. To my delight, it worked beautifully. A lot of 101ers did come to the 201 panel, but were mostly quiet as the 201 panel ranged all over the place with plenty of audience participation. That said, a lot of 201ers were in the 101 panel and were mostly curious as to what the 101 panel was going to say about fanfiction and slash. 101 was styled more as a question and answer type of panel rather than a panel discussion, and as such, the panel did very well with many people's questions being answered in what I hope was a satisfactory way.

201, on the other hand, was a boisterous good time with a lot of laughter, but we discussed many really good topics like what wouldn't we write in fanfiction and why, as well as how, warnings on fanfic are like advertisements. We also talked about quality of writing, specific fandoms (mostly Harry Potter), why we write, and how fanfic writing is often like a gift economy. An interesting topic that was bandied about was how we expect real world books, that we spend money on, to be as good as, if not better than, the really fantastic fanfic and slash that we are reading on the Internet for free. This was something of a key argument in the panel: that writing fanfic and slash is a great time and so is reading it, but because we are reading so much well-written fanfic and slash, we expect better from the publishing world. There was also some discussion regarding the changing nature of fanfic and slash, in this case Amplificathon, which is an archive of fanfic and slash that has been recorded and uploaded as audio files that people can listen to.

Overall, it was a great panel that encompassed a lot of the hard questions that many of us had been dying to talk about with other hardcore fanfic readers and writers but hadn't been able to because of the constraints on having to define terms for newbies in years past. Plus, in years past, scaring away the newbies with discussions of twincest (incest between twins), darkfic (very unhappy, often brutal psychologically), and mpreg (male pregnancy) wouldn't have been such a great idea. I made a passing remark in the panel that we would have to have a graduate level course at WisCon 33 and that might not actually be a bad idea. There were a lot of things that we wanted to talk about but ran out of time to discuss, some of them being specific writers in specific fandoms, meta, fanfic and academia, and many other topics. Here's hoping that the discussions of FFS 201 will continue at WisCon 33 and beyond!

JJ Pionke is an adjunct professor of English in the Chicagoland area. She has a teaching interest in SFF, nuclear culture, pirates, and graphic novels. When she is not teaching, she can be found working on various conference papers, stalking her mother's cat, riding her motorcycle, or thinking about her next tattoo.

Last Time, on Battlestar Galactica… Panel Review

JJ Pionke

When I proposed the Battlestar Galactica (BSG) panel, I knew the series wouldn't be over but that we would more than likely be at a mid-season cliffhanger and that fans would need to squee and speculate. Much to my delight, the panel made the final cut for the program. Much to my horror, it was put in the 11:30PM-12:45AM time slot. My only thoughts were that I was going to be the only one in the room with my fellow panelists and one or two diehards that may or may not be drunk.

Surprisingly, the panel turned out to be a hell of a lot better than I had expected, in part because half the audience and the other two people on the panel, Ben Burgis and Maddie Greene, were a bit tipsy. The booze effect, appropriate for BSG, led to some rather hilarious discussion about who the final cylon is, whether or not we should trust Ron Moore (the show's creator), and will Adama and Roslin get it on by the end of the series? You know, we discussed the important questions like that. I also learned that in order to distinguish the elder Adama from the younger Adama, I should call him Papadama. It was rather enlightening in so many ways. Of course we took a vote on who the final cylon would be. Dee won with Roslin a close second. I pushed for Doc Cottle, because what's there not to love in the good doctor, and hello, been around since practically the first episode with access to basically everyone because he's a doctor? So what if he is a tertiary character!

I somehow managed to hijack the panel from the moderator, Ben, I think in part because I felt like the BSG panel was my baby and I was sober, but he didn't seem to mind and professed that he had wanted to be on the panel to know more about BSG anyway. Apparently, the audience rather enjoyed my sense of humor because there was a lot of laughter in the panel as well as some really great discussions of fanfiction with the BSG fandom. Considering that a good chunk of the audience had come from Fanfic and Slash 201 earlier in the evening, it worked out pretty well. Since there were many fanfiction readers and writers in the audience, we progressed to the inevitable discussion of where to get our fix.

Other discussions involved the fact that everything seemed to have come from IKEA because there was lots of shiny new stuff floating around like Starbuck's viper and baby stuff. Papadama's shaving mirror actually is from IKEA and is called Frack. Considering that humanity was running away from their devastated homeworlds and all of their resources, where is all of this new stuff coming from? IKEA of course. It's the obvious answer. **snicker** Silliness aside, there were great discussions of disability, prophecy, technology, and feminism. Overall, it was a hilarious panel, made just a little bit better by libations and the late hour, much to my very pleasant surprise.

Panel Report
Publishing, Profit, Agendas, and Ideals: The *Eclipse One* Cover Debate

Micole Sudberg

> **Panel Description:** Last year when Night Shade Books released the cover for their anthology *Eclipse One* a debate broke out over the names represented on the front. In an anthology that had 50/50 male and female authors, only male names appeared on the cover. The ensuing argument centered around two main points—the publishers felt that, of the authors in the anthology, the names they'd put on the cover were likely to attract the attention of more casual buyers. And because they were in the business of making money, they could not afford to put an "agenda" ahead of anything else. Readers felt that, because no women were given a slot on the cover, the publishers were reinforcing patriarchal assumptions about who sells books, and who doesn't. Some expressed the opinion that the lack of women on the cover was actually likely to deter them from buying the book. In this panel [...], let's explore both sides in depth.[...]
>
> **Panelists:** K. Tempest Bradford (moderator), Robyn Fleming, Eileen Gunn, Jeremy Lassen, Micole Sudberg

That is one long panel description, and I even left out some of it. I'll leave documenting the panel to someone in the audience and focus on the points I wanted to make during the panel and my reflections during and after the discussion.

My take is that there was a lot of sexism and male privilege displayed in the cover design, the name selection, and the ensuing conversation, including but not limited to people representing Night Shade Books. There are many different ways to dissect this, and these are some of the approaches I took.

1. Marketing

I work for a website optimization company. We break Web pages down into different aspects or areas called "variables" and test different values for each variable to see which variables affect user decisions and which combination of variables will be most effective in getting the user decisions a business wants. What my company does is called "multivariable testing," and it lets you test for interaction effects. An "interaction effect" is when two or more variables interact to create an effect neither of them would have alone. For example, you might get a great response rate when you use black text and a great response rate when you use a black background, but if you use black text on a black background, your response rate will drop to zero. Jeremy/Night Shade chose the five authors listed on the cover based on their sales records, reasoning that this would enable the book to reach an audience = (some fraction) * (the audience for Author A + the audience for Author B + the audience for Author C...). The problem is, though, that there is an interaction effect created when all the authors listed are male: the audience drops by the number of women who perceive the book as being intended for an audience that excludes them. In this case, the effect is exacerbated by what Eileen Gunn, during the panel, called "the semiotics of the cover image," which compounds the impression that the anthology is meant for a male audience.

This is complicated, as Jeremy and Eileen both pointed out, by the issue of gatekeepers. Jeremy's initial audience for the cover is not, in fact, the consumer end-user but the "gatekeepers": the buyers for the large bookstore chains who will determine the book's availability to consumers. This is a very small number of people (two?), both of whom are in fact male. However, I don't think this eliminates any of the issues addressed above: If your cover gets your book past the gatekeepers but doesn't appeal to the consumers, you're still not making a profit.

On this level, sexism/male privilege is operating by making the gender of the authors "irrelevant" to the decision-making process. Jeremy said, during the panel, that he made a choice based on sales metrics, but the fact is, in a very real sense, he didn't make a choice because he didn't see that there was a choice to be made. It is clear from his responses online and during the panel that he simply didn't notice that he'd picked five male names.

2. Customer Service

Sexism/male privilege also operated in Night Shade's reactions to the complaints made. Tempest in her panel description and on the panel itself described the sides as "readers" vs. "publishing professionals," but to me the division looked more like "women" vs. "men." (Both descriptions are, of course, simplifications: there were women and men on both sides, and readers and publishing professionals likewise. But both Tempest and I did perceive general trends, even if we identified those trends differently.) As I said during the panel, my only involvement in the online debate was to observe in my LiveJournal that there had been four or five instances of men telling women what was or wasn't sexist. The initial debate took place in coalescent's LJ, and indeed I was quite certain that Jeremy, Jason (the other Night Shade representative who was posting), and many of the publishing professionals posting were aware that coalescent is Niall Harrison, i.e., male, not to mention the Reviews Editor for *Strange Horizons* and the Features Editor of *Vector*. But most of the fans/readers commenting were women, which I knew from previous LJ acquaintance and also because many of them identified themselves as women when discussing why they found the all-male list of names off-putting. The publishing professionals dismissing their concerns were male—and it was noticeable that when someone with a male username repeated the same arguments the women had been making, he got a more respectful reception, not to mention praise for his "calm tone."

The sexism/male privilege here lies in the disrespect automatically accorded to the consideration of sexism in publishing practices—even the question is seen as too offensive to entertain seriously, and many of the typical deflections about personal character and institutional history are pulled out. And, as usual, men making observations about sexism are seen as automatically more worthy of attention than women making the same observations. This is, again, a place where sexism is negatively affecting the business's reputation and therefore its profits. To put it bluntly, it's standard business practice to suck up to customers. The business has the institutional power, but the power depends on sales to customers. Whether or not a business is going to listen to customers, it makes business sense to look like it's listening to customers. There were ways to respond or not respond to customer complaints that wouldn't have blown up nearly as badly as the tack Night Shade took.

3. The Economics of Reputation

I'd like to step back and re-consider the "five best-selling authors in the anthology" and what names on the cover do. Jeremy repeatedly cited the sales records of the authors listed as if this were a politically neutral factor. But reputations aren't natural; they're produced by social interactions, social expectations, the type and quality of work, and the way that the work is marketed. An author's name on an anthology uses the author's name to market the anthology and the anthology's name to market the author. The author gains exposure in a way that may produce future sales and that influences readers and reviewers to consider that author's story a "significant" one: the author benefits in increased sales and increased reputation. Obviously, the name on the cover isn't the only factor that affects this. But by putting only male names on the cover of an anthology, Night Shade perpetuates the sexism of a publishing, academic, and cultural system that continues to value art produced by men over art produced by women.

4. The Assumption of Capitalism

I didn't manage to raise this point during the panel, but Alaya Dawn Johnson brought it up from the audience: Much of the discussion operated under the assumption that sexism was okay—or at least a necessary evil—if it resulted in increased sales. The argument largely focused on whether or not Night Shade was unwittingly harming sales by failing to account for or appeal to a female, or at least a feminist, audience. But why should we accept this assumption? Don't the people involved in Night Shade have social responsibilities beyond the success of their business? Many of us have been pointing out that it's not okay to put white people on the covers of books starring people of color, even if the publishing industry is convinced that the "audience" (i.e., the white audience) is too racist to buy them; profit isn't the only factor to take into consideration.

Conclusions, Inconclusiveness, Afterthoughts

> The book's sales history: Jeremy said it "sold to expectation," that he's already contracted for Volumes 2 and 3, and that based on the authors already accepted for Volume 2, there will be multiple women on the cover.

This was a pretty frustrating panel for me. I came out of it feeling like I hadn't made the points I'd wanted to make and, worse, that I'd failed to support the points made by women online (as Eileen pointed out, everything we were saying had already been said online) and that I'd failed to represent the women in the audience adequately. A lot of my frustrations revolved around the granting of cookies. In the debate in person, I was willing to and in fact did give out cookies—that is, explicitly reassuring Jeremy and the audience that I didn't think he was a bad person, that the problem was cultural and institutional rather than personal, and that I was willing to engage in debate because I had a previous knowledge of Night Shade's work publishing feminist writers. And all the things I stated were true, but in most online debates I will not state them, because it is a strain on the emotional and psychological resources of the debaters to have to provide them; it shifts debate from the issues to the personal interactions. I did not want to be the Good Female Critic, as opposed to Those Crazy Women Online. I did not and do not think those women were crazy. I did not and do not think they were obligated to re-phrase their objections in a more acceptable tone. I chose voluntarily to take a more conciliatory approach in person because I did appreciate the difficulty in being the one person on the panel everyone else disagreed with, and because of my personal response to Night Shade's history, but I do not believe that a more conciliatory approach should have been required, or that the approach taken by the initial critics was rude or over-the-top. I very much stand with the women who made the complaints last year. And I'm not sure that this came across, either to Jeremy or the audience.

Micole Sudberg lives in New York City.

Notes on the *Eclipse One* Cover Debate

Notes by Janice Dawley

> **Panel Description:** Last year when Night Shade Books released the cover for their anthology, *Eclipse One*, a debate broke out over the names represented on the front. Namely, in an anthology that had 50/50 male and female authors, only male names appeared on the cover. The ensuing argument centered around two main points—the publishers felt that, of the authors in the anthology, the names they'd put on the cover were likely to attract the attention of more casual buyers. And because they were in the business of making money, they could not afford to put an "agenda" ahead of anything else. Readers felt that, because no women were given a slot on the cover, the publishers were reinforcing patriarchal assumptions about who sells books, and who doesn't. Some expressed the opinion that the lack of women on the cover was actually likely to deter them from buying the book. In this panel, which will be a debate, let's explore both sides in depth. Does indulging agendas and ideals hinder profit? Or can adhering to an ideal lead to different and/or better ways of creating more profit?
>
> **Panelists:** K. Tempest Bradford (moderator), Eileen Gunn, Robyn Fleming, Jeremy Lassen, Micole Sudberg

Tempest gives some history of the controversy (which she says took place the Internet equivalent of five years ago—in other words, last August). She and Jeremy decided this would be a good jumping off point for a WisCon discussion about the world of publishing and why certain decisions are made.

Eileen Gunn says she used to be the Director of Advertising at Microsoft, back in the '80s, "when it was small and cute." Cool! (Then she adds, "It was never cute.")

Lassen says that the decision of which names to print on the cover was based simply on sales metrics and categorization (people known as sf authors, since the book was going to be displayed in the sf section). His description of the name selection process actually sounds pretty vague. Garth Nix is sold in the sf section? Really?

Eileen makes a distinction between marketing to the chain buyers vs. marketing to the actual readers. Jeremy says he was trying to appeal to both. Eileen also points out that the cover is less important than the spine after the initial display period.

Her first reaction on seeing the collection in a bookstore: "This book is for guys." She had just rejected another collection as being almost entirely stories by men, and was irritated when she saw *Eclipse One* and assumed, from the cover, that it was full of sci-fi adventure stories aimed at men as well. But then, she said, it dawned on her: "*I'm* in this book!" She considers the art and the list of names on the cover of *Eclipse One* to be a misrepresentation of the contents; it's kind of a miss in terms of advertising.

Micole talks about her reaction to the book. But first, her work in web response testing. She says this testing isn't practical for books, given the technology and the size of the audience. She clarifies that people aren't saying Jeremy is a sexist asshole, just that the results in this case perpetuate sexism. The names printed on the cover act as publicity for the authors, in addition to reflecting their current popularity. Reinforcement. Male privilege was also displayed in the online conversation in which some male publishing professionals (Jeremy and Jason) were outraged at the criticism. Conflation of personal opinion with corporate opinion when people post as "nightshade books." "You want to suck up to your customers"—these guys didn't. Instead, they said people just didn't understand marketing, didn't get what they were trying to do, etc. She says that Tempest saw the conversation divided along publisher/reader lines, but Micole saw it as male/female. Examples of women being ignored and men being listened to when they said the same things.

Robyn looks at the cover: "There IS a woman on there! I thought that was something else" (i.e., a penis). Laughter. She says the cover was completely unappealing to her; her eyes slid right over it.

Tempest asks if there is a way for anthology covers to appeal to buyers without having names on the cover at all. Jeremy says no, and Sharyn November in the audience says loudly, "Yes!" She says she took herself off this panel because she knew she'd be growling the whole time.

Jeremy admits that he got heated in the online debate because he was so invested in the project. He says some people maintained that he "shouldn't have bothered" putting out the collection. He says the cover is by Michael Whelan, cost a lot less than it normally would, and codes just the way he wanted it to. Eileen points out that it doesn't even look like Michael Whelan art. "OK," says Jeremy. He admits that the entire production process was rushed and could have been better thought out. "Those are excuses," says someone, and he agrees.

Eileen says the cover reminds her of literary fiction of the '70s, which means it seems completely out of date.

Jeremy says there is a "zero sum game" in marketing. Once you position yourself for one market, you are closing yourself off from another one. He was trying to trick readers of sf adventure fiction into reading his anthology, even though it is full of literary sf.

Eileen: "If you were at Microsoft, I would tell you that you should never try to trick your customers! That's a very bad approach to marketing. You should try to APPEAL to your customers."

Robyn says that she might have wanted to pick up the anthology if either the art or the cover copy were different, but the combination really doesn't work.

Micole says it really does look like a "boys' own adventure" book. She says the process of marketing doesn't really matter to her; it's the results that matter. Regardless of the "ungendered" nature of the marketing/production process, the fact that the book will actually turn off potential women readers is a gendered failure.

Eileen challenges the "zero sum" theory a bit by saying that when you market a book, you have to keep in mind your various audiences and give "tidbits" to all of them. This book didn't do that. She also says that this panel has brought up a whole lot of things that were already mentioned online, and now, as then, she thinks that Jeremy's reaction ought to be "Wow, I made a mistake; I apologize." The response should absolutely NOT be, "I DIDN'T make a mistake. You just don't understand."

Jeff A. Smith in audience asks if Night Shade will market test covers more online after this experience. Jeremy says he would love to "if [he] had [his] shit together," but he doesn't. As for what's up with *Eclipse Two*, he says he will be using the same metric method as before, and in this case at least two (maybe three) of the four names will be women. Also the choice of cover art will consciously not be "boys' own."

Sharyn November says she is not going to ask questions, she's just going to make points.

- This conversation wouldn't have happened with a major publisher.
- She would have advised Jeremy to not respond to the criticisms online because it makes more trouble than it's worth.
- She likes the cover, actually. Would she have bought it? She doesn't know, she got it for free.
- She produces anthologies and never puts names on the front; they're always on the back. She said "what about this idea?" online, and there was NO reaction. It really pissed her off because it made the conversation almost entirely negative.

She also asks "how did the book sell?" Jeremy says it sold exactly to expectations, and they have a commitment to at least three volumes.

Alaya Dawn Johnson asks how far you can excuse marketing decisions in pursuit of sales. What about cover art that portrays black characters as white? Is that OK? Jeremy says he has published a lot of women and marginalized people, but he feels more able to "fight those battles" with novels and single author collections. The audience member says that his plan to use the same rationale for picking the names on the cover for volume 2 is not OK just because it HAP-

PENS to result in some female names this time. Does he really think this is a good idea? He says, "If it means we can have another discussion like this next year, yes." Oooh, sarcasm.

Pat Murphy in audience says the point about the "gatekeepers" of publishing is really important and could be its own panel at a future WisCon. She also says she almost never browses in bookstores and questions how many other people do. Almost all her reading choices are made because of online recommendations.

Robyn said that as a reader, she DOES browse in bookstores, especially when it comes to anthologies. So the cover, presentation, etc. are very important to her.

An audience member asks, "how important are the names below the first two?" Can't you put some potentially less saleable names below? Jeremy says he could if he had a real Hugo-winning bestseller in the collection, but in this case the influence of the names was more dispersed and he was taking a chance that any one of the names would be recognizable to the readers.

Ysabeau Wilce in audience says that as an author in the collection she supports whatever needs to be done to sell the book, even if it means a bunch of men's names on the cover.

Janice Dawley is a computer geek and contributor to the Feminist SFFU wiki and blog. She lives in Burlington, VT.

Elves and Dwarves: The Racism Inherent in Fantasy

Panel Description: Elves are slim, tall, light-skinned forest-lovers. Dwarves are stout, working-class, good craftsmen. Asians are good with math. Jews have a natural gift with money. Issues of racial stereotyping in fantasy are generally passed over pretty lightly. If a race of lizards are portrayed as slow-moving and lazy, well, that's to be expected, they're cold-blooded, right? They're biologically different from the rest of us. Is it OK to casually make generalizations and judgments about cultures and races in SF/F, whether real or imaginary, or is this dangerous racism? Do responsible authors owe it to their readers to avoid using simple biological imperatives instead of carefully developing alternate cultures? And what of the characters that rebel against the norm? Are they brave iconoclasts, or merely the exception that proves the rule?

Panelists: Vito Excalibur (moderator), Alma Alexander, Carol Hightshoe, Elise Matthesen, Janine Young

Alma: It's not Tolkien's fault, he just started something, and everyone else just followed doing the same thing!

Carol: So, he created it, it became a stereotype, we have to follow it?

Alma: Yes.

Carol: My elves have black hair!

Vito: Any of them blonde?

Carol: Some, but we don't care about them.

Alma: They live in a gated community?

Audience: "Elvenhome!"

laughter

Elise: Gated community—they can arrest you...variations in class panels. "Dwarves are stout working-class repairmen."

In my manuscript, when you've got your people investing, dwarves know a lot about working with iron and stone and they have a lot of money! So the dwarves in the 1800s come in with their money! The railroads own a lot of the judges. In my story the dwarves have more money.

My second point, that Tolkien is entirely at fault. **laughter** I will point out that Gimli as soon as he sees Galadriel falls in love with her and puts her on a pedestal. The poor guy can't even fall in love with his own kind. My point is, it's actually pretty scary that Tolkien started this; it's a marvelous book, he's a great writer. But everyone copied him, and they have created this status quo in fantasy where it is very hard to say, my elves are black. R.A. Salvatore, the black elves are bad, and there's the one black elf who is good. Are we not seeing the inherent racism in this! The one good black elf who is mistaken all the time for one of the Drow.

Vito: These black elves live underground and Drizzt has purple eyes and has inborn goodness. They have a matriarchal society with a spider goddess and he fights the evil black elf female-ruled society. **groans from Audience** He's a super special snowflake.

Connie (from audience): I was so happy to see a black character. I don't care if they're good, or evil, or what, I loved Drizzt anyway **laughter**

Vito: What happens to a story with...

Alma: We're geared to judge. My father, he's not American...he found this party...he went to the NAACP party and was the only white person there. My father probably would not have noticed this. He doesn't really cotton on to the fact that there's other people who don't necessarily look like him.

Vito: I want to move on. We can recognize that there are people who see race and people who don't.

Alma: But is it racist to see race...

Vito: It isn't.

Carol: Having the character who stands out if he's well written, it helps to exemplify where the stereotypes are in writing and gives us something to think about, beyond the story. Like the young lady who was just glad to see Drizzt, so something good came out of it. And it's those types of stories that got readers to think. And that's the most important thing to come out of writing. How many children did Harry Potter reach?

Elise: About the special snowflake. There's the inherently good one and then the comic sidekick character; the story says to that character, you got lucky, you were picked up by the grace of the wonderful protagonists who will let you eat at the big feast and you'll get some of the jokes and you'll pine hopelessly for the girl you'll never get. So what they are saying to the good dwarf—you are there by the grace of us, the story is not for you.

scattered audience applause

Audience: We can't pick on R. A. Salvatore, we have to go to Ed Greenwood for that because he is the one. It's D & D based; it's in the setting that certain races are certain ways. Dwarves get bonuses; elves, hobbits get bonuses to dexterity. Humans...it's enforcing what we're talking about.

Janine: We do not live in a world that is fair in regards to our physiology. There are special people. I am not going to the Olympics. They are beautifully built, and they've got whatever bodies they've got to do the extraordinary thing they can do. So it is not in my opinion racism to say that say elves have a genetic trait that make them good at shooting arrows. What does start to make it racism is that the only people with this incredible dexterity and good noble traits and aristocratic manner, belong to people who are fair haired or blue eyed or light skinned. That's when things begin to get a bit iffy. Well sure your physiology may make you super strong...you are the dwarf who is super strong and muscular. But if he has the mentality of always greedy for gold, well now we get to wonder about that.

Vito: The laws of D & D were not handed down from on high. Gary Gygax; he chose not to subvert that steretotype. Look at Otto the vampire from Pratchett.

Audience: Fantasy highlights things about humanity through metaphor. If so then what does it say to have different races in fantasy?

Vito: Excellent question! What is the function of different races in fantasy?

Carol: To have fun. Also, readers expect it.

Elise: It's fun to write in code. It's fun to mess with your head.

Audience: If it's code, then what's it code for?

Alma: It's far more fun when you turn it on its head. I've made dwarves in this world be the bards. There's two kinds of elves, the Tolkienesque tall pretty people who buy everything they can get their mitts on and then a Shakespearian elvish peaseblossom race… I've just HAD FUN. I've just created all these races to have fun with them.

Janine: Okay. **deep breath** I'll make a political comment. We'll talk about elves and elves, or fairies, instead of talking about Israelis and Palestinians, but it'll be in another world, but they've got magic powers instead of guns. So I feel sometimes like—Oh, come on, just talk about them if you want to talk about them.

Alma: It's a way of deflecting fire.

Janine: It's a way to talk about something you can't talk about or work out, let's magically work it out. Another thing of course is fantasy is wish fulfillment, well, human beings can't walk on snow, I wish I was an elf. They quantify it, which makes things really easy. Fantasy is so popular because it's really easy to create characters that way, take one quality and turn it into a race.

Vito: One of my favorite books is *Blindsight,* where Peter takes an alien race and makes it NOTHING like humans.

Alan Bostick (in audience): We are talking about race, but it is species. Post-renaissance construction… **scattered woots from audience**…

the elves/dwarves/men thing comes out of Nordic and Teutonic mythology.

Vito: There you go, it's the fucking Vikings.

Elise: Thank you for saying the thing about conflating species and races, because that has a tang of eugenics.

Vito: That said, if they can interbreed they're the same species.

Elise: It's not even about that; it's about culture, cultures bumping. I was visiting Jo Walton and talking about racism in Britain and in the US, and how you categorize someone. In Minnesota, you categorize them based on what they look like, before they open their mouth. Jo was saying no, here we categorize them based on how they speak.

Audience: We are sticking to the humanoids, different flavors, dwarf, elf, here are the blond, or short. What about *A Companion to Wolves*, or other races...

Vito: Let's talk about the Horta.

Janine: Bilateral symmetry; it is a fantasy novel (Vito tries to interrupt as moderator), if there's a half elf or half dwarf they're not a different species... When we get to *Companion*...no breeding.

Alma: We are humans who are reading...responding as humans to the story. From our point of view.

Elise: How to subvert and mess with it.

Janine: Animal companions, the lion is in charge in Narnia, one of the few.

Audience: In Tolkien, it's not just elves or dwarves. In Narnia, there's the Calormen, Turkish, dark people = evil. In Tolkien, the Southrons are dark.

Vito: Here's a question, why are we still writing and reading about blatantly racist fantasy worlds?

Liz (from audience): "It's FUN!"

Janine: (There's not many) books where the hero is not white, and the world he's in not very white. Readers still love the Tolkienesque world, which is actually England and it's white. It's really hard to get away from that and integrate this world.

Alma: Seeing vs. hearing, I spent my growing up in mid-Africa, Southern Africa; a lot of people grew up (...). To my ear, if I heard a black person talking with a certain accent, it was African to my ear, and then I'd be in England and I'd hear two people talking in a strong cockney accent and I'd turn around and they'd be black, and I couldn't wrap my head around that — my brain exploded.

Elise: I have a story about meeting John, a Star Trek fan, and when we finally met it was a deep shock to me for a minute that he was white and we all had a good laugh, and I thought about it and tried to figure out why, and we talked about it. (She had assumed he was black as she had built a mental model of "male Star Trek fan with pagan leanings and certain sense of humor.")

Audience: (muttering about red shirts on star trek)

Audience: (something on trolls)

Kirsten (from audience): It's fun to write in code.

Connie: Well, when white people write fantasy, here's one thing, what about when black people write fantasy...

Liz: (Said something about the assumptions of some of the panelists, especially that the reader is white like them.)

Someone on panel: Yes we play with race and replicate it, because it's fun.

Alma: There's a danger of people writing and misunderstanding, because they don't know about that culture and the people might think it is wrong and something is off.

Liz: You mean you're talking about white people trying to write in other cultures, and it is sort of cultural appropriation and that's difficult?

Alma: I'm not talking about white people, I'm talking about everyone.

Liz: No, I think you're talking about white people!

Audience: What about throwing out the elf/dwarf thing and making new stuff up.

Vito: Oh good, let's talk about Steven Brust!

laughter

Audience: (An example.)

Vito: Fun, but not actually true in real life. Breeding humans with other animals, that was something Brust decided to write about and make up.

Audience: What about Greek mythology...

Vito: Also not true.

Vito: Except for the Tekla.

Alma: But there's this instinctive jerk of, they're not *Us*. They're different.

Elise: If you've read his books you remember the way the word Human is used. Humans = Draegarans or Easterners. Or, the humans are the Easterners. The word for themselves is "the people."

Audience: Everyone's middle class...

Audience: Let's not go there on Steven right now.

Carol: The People. When we're talking about race, isn't it just perpetuating things to say black people, white people.

Liz: Who is "we"! And, omg!

Vito: NO. Just NO.

Alma: This is how wars start.

Liz: So when we talk about racism, wars start?

Vito: The answer to problems is not to take away our vocabulary for TALKING ABOUT THEM. Which they did recently in California, making police stop taking data based on race; this means there is no way to prove police racism! So, no, that is not a good way to fix racism.

Gregory Rihn (from audience): It is due to sloppy writing, you can't write an alienpological treatise, unless…like Tolkien was doing creating his whole Middle Earth. Do you need an alien to do this? Do you have to have an elf or a dwarf? Maybe it's a cliché…

(More audience comments)

Gregory: D&D derived from Tolkien, and people take it as a handbook for writing a novel.

Audience: You make an allegory using fantastic races in order to get anyone to actually listen to you.

Vito: We've danced around it, now let's talk about it. What do you gain and lose, when you talk about the Battle of Deeping-Coomb instead of talking about Israelis and Palestinians?

Janine: Entertainment. Rod Serling was not allowed to talk about race on TV. He had to do it with aliens or whatever. But if we can really talk about it, I see no reason to couch it in metaphor, unless people will get to read it.

Elise: Oh come on that's "fantasy race as condom." You do it because you have a story to tell. Who is the kid in *47*? He instantly was identified as character from myth.

Diantha (from audience): Commented on Native Americans and culture, and the history of race in the US and assumptions about who's reading.

Audience: Who is the reader, and who gets published is predominantly white, when white people are less than 20 percent of the world's population.

Audience: Well, what if you're not talking about English? We don't know what's going on in languages other than English.

Diantha: Yes, I do. And other people do. And it is inherently racist, what gets published in fantasy. Many people of color are writing fantasy and we can't get it published in the US If we live in Africa, or Latin America…

Jody: We've come so far. In 1948, it was very different in publishing. This blows my mind. It's better now. On that 20 percent white business? Go read *Guns, Germs, and Steel.*

Audience: Well, do you mean we should all be reading realistic fiction instead?

Diantha: *Guns, Germs, and Steel*? Go read *Bury My Heart at Wounded Knee*, lady.

Carol: As an author, when I write about other races, they're easier for me to play around with, without insulting people.

Liz: "Real" people, that is...

Elise: Even if I'm writing a privileged character, everyone else in history comes through in the story... (a woman) saying she has worked on her garden for 20 years, and you look around, and three men with dark skins are there bent over, weeding the border.

Alma: My advice to authors is that if you're writing a story that matters to you, then the reader will find it matters to them.

> [This is a rough transcription from notes taken by Liz Henry during the panel; it is not transcribed from a recording and may not be precisely what was said.]

A Request, to Authors of Traditional Fantasy Novels, from Sigrid Ellis

I walked out of the "Elves & Dwarves: Racism Inherent in Fantasy" panel in baffled anger. I wrote in my notes — which got messier and less legible as the panel progressed — a remark I repeated aloud as I walked into the hall of the Concourse Hotel. "Just because something's traditional doesn't make it right."

Races other-than-human are used in fantasy worlds to represent aspects of humanity, to represent ourselves at our best and our worst. They are also used to represent The Other, the unknown stranger who shares nothing with us. All of these things are true, sometimes in the same work of fiction. It is therefore difficult to tease out what is a condemnation of the other and what is an indictment of the self.

It is perfectly fine for a fictional race to be an indictment of a specific human trait — rash decision-making, for instance. A child-like emotionality, let us say. When a Race is used to describe the dangers of this, that is acceptable. But when the same child-like, emotional, rash Race is also dark-skinned with jug ears and big lips and lives in huts in the jungle, when the cultural trait is linked to racial and ethnic stereotypes of our own culture, that is unacceptable. It propagates damaging racist assumptions and values. Edgar Rice Burroughs romped through that territory with his fantastical jungle tribes in the Tarzan books. It was the racism of his day, unquestioned and unremarked.

A current Wikipedia definition of racism states that "Racism, by its simplest definition, is the belief that race is the primary determinant of human traits and capacities and that racial differences produce an inherent superiority of a particular race." Burroughs carried the cultural values of his time. So did Tolkien. The dark and swarthy dwarves — crafty but not wise — are, Tolkien says in his letters, his representations of Jews. Elves "really represent men with greater artistic ability, beauty and a longer life span." They also happen to be fair-skinned, fair-haired, and based on northern European ideals of beauty and purity.

This sort of thinking continues in Tolkien's heirs. The Dragonlance books, by Margaret Weis and Tracy Hickman, divide personality traits according to race or species. As do books based on the Dungeons and Dragons role-playing game, such as the Greyhawk and Forgotten Realms series. These books assign virtues and vices according to genetics because they are based on games whose codified rules are based largely on Tolkien. In a sense we can hardly blame the authors for writing the races as they do. But in another sense, we can blame them — for not noticing or thinking about what they have inherited.

We can do better than that. And, in order to avoid being a racist right here, right now, we have to do better than they did. We can no longer replicate the racist assumptions of our culture and defend it by saying we've always done things this way.

Indictment of humanity at its worst is the privilege and responsibility of fiction. Models of humanity at its best are our prize. The writer of fantasy, in choosing to represent aspects of our common nature through the prism of non-human race, gets a toolkit more powerful in magnitude than realistic fiction can afford. Build your race with the tropes — don't be afraid to make your villains vile and your heroes flawed. But carefully examine the racial packages you've constructed. Know why you choose the appearance and traits you do. Don't give an entire race an identical personality as an ethnic characteristic. Know your reasons. Think about what you are doing and why you want to say it in the first place.

Races other-than-human are a powerful tool in fantasy. Make sure you know what you're building.

Reference

The Letters of J. R. R. Tolkien, Humphrey Carpenter ed., Houghton Mifflin, pp 144, 176. 1981

Sigrid Ellis is an air traffic controller. As such, she is, in fact, from the government, and is here to help. She blogs at http://sigridellis.wordpress.com and is one of the four Fantastic Fangirls, discussing comics, here: http://fantasticfangirls.org. She also writes comics. http://slightlyobsessedstudio.com.

Panel Report
Elves and Dwarves: The Racism Inherent in Fantasy

John Kim

The Friday session on "Elves and Dwarves: The Racism Inherent in Fantasy" illustrated a pointed contrast. The panelists were largely authors who wrote about elves and dwarves, while the audience had a number of outspoken members who were interested in the topic of racism in fantasy. At the heart the split was over fictionalized fantasy races, or more specifically Tolkien's. The two sides could agree at least in principle that parallels to real-world races are problematic. Though the example was not used in the panel discussion, such allegory can be seen in races like the "Shemites" and "Kushites" of R.E. Howard's Hyborian age. This sort of real-world parallel is rare in modern fantasy, though, while elves and dwarves still flourish. One case would be Jacqueline Carey's Kushiel series, with races such as the D'Angeline that essentialize certain stereotypes.

Elves and dwarves, though, have no direct real-world parallels, in keeping with Tolkien's stance against simple symbolism. However, he still presents a reality where race is of exaggerated importance compared to our own. In every way, these races stand apart from each other in sharper contrast than any human grouping. Height, features, culture, talents, and personalities are all strongly controlled by race. For example, dwarves have beards, while hobbits and elves do not.

Within the *Lord of the Rings*, race is of primary importance. Characters of different races may cooperate and respect each other, but their racial identity is primary to what they are like. This vision has been imitated by many authors since. Exaggerating the influence of race in this way can be an allegory used to tell a good story. However, one should question what the allegory is saying—and especially question using this allegory by default. In much the same way, there is nothing inherently wrong with a story that has only male characters in it, or only white characters. However, if this becomes the assumed default, then the result is problematic.

There are roots of this idea in some mythological sources — but there are also many myths and earlier fantasy stories that do not have exaggerated races. Many stories instead have magical individuals, enchanted places, and/or fantastical cultures. For example, the Amazons were a fantastical culture, but the descendents of an Amazon woman were not a genetically distinct race. Hippolyta's son Hippolytus was not a "half-amazon," say.

An author who writes a story with only white characters is not making a statement that white people are the only ones of import. However, if this becomes the standard within a field, then it has an impact on the readers. Readers — especially young readers who grow up as fans — are influenced if all of their favorite characters are of a particular race.

There are many fantasy works without fantastical races such as elves, dwarves, and orcs. These generally have only more realistic human variation, however. Realism is a limited choice for fantasy, and it would not do to call for more of it. The problem is a lack of fantastical allegories where race exists, but is overshadowed rather than exaggerated.

For example, what if the lands of the world were alive, and the land that you were born and raised in changed you? The people of the forests are tall and slender and sharp-eyed because of their homeland. Rather than "supposedly" genetic races, these stories would tie into allegory about homelands and nationality. What if the stars slowly shifted, and a series of celestial signs that change only once every generation changed in those born under them? The change of generations could be exaggerated. There could similarly be allegory of religion — where baptism in one church might mark your features and bring out your talent of sight, while another might foster your crafting talents.

Humans vary from each other in many ways, with race constructs being only one of them. Why is it that in fantasy, only race is commonly exaggerated?

Response to the Elves and Dwarves Panel

Bridget Collins

Perhaps the most thought provoking panel I attended at WisCon 32 was also the most frustrating. "Elves and Dwarves: The Racism Inherent in Fantasy" promised to be a reflection on the purpose of races in science fiction and fantasy, but I left feeling like the program had been a panelists vs. audience stalemate. The authors on the panel had all used races in their work and defended their use on the grounds that they subverted them or that species were different than races. Many of us in the audience saw this as simple semantics; essentializing a race or essentializing a species is still essentializing, and whether or not you essentialize them to something "good" or "bad" it does not change the fact that they have been othered.

It's not that readers think there should be no races or non-human species in our science fiction and fantasy, but we are often frustrated by the lack of self-reflection a writer may exhibit in the choices they make. We want characters of color in science fiction and fantasy, but the fact that they often appear as the bad guys is troubling (the Drow Elves of the Forgotten Realms universe came up in regards to this issue). Races and species are often used as metaphors for humanity, essentializing one characteristic in order to explore our entire humanity. Must we always ascribe negative traits to characters of color?

Furthermore, implicit in the use of races or species is often the reduction of behavior to biology and this makes me very uncomfortable. Evolutionary psychology has been used in our own culture to defend rape, sexism, and violence ("men can't help it, they have to spread their seed!"); reducing the artistic talent of elves or the greed of dwarves to biology functions in the same way. It is also lazy writing. Rather than take the time to build a world in which cultural traits exist within biological, social, economic, and political networks, the author employs a stereotype that the reader is probably familiar with from countless other science fiction and fantasy books (the role of Tolkien in this could be a panel in itself—"It's all Tolkien's Fault?").

So, where do we go from here? I would love to see a redux of this panel, perhaps with authors, readers, and academics on the panel who had spent some time reflecting on what exactly the role of races and species is in science fiction and fantasy. Perhaps some examples that subvert stereotypes or use race/species to critique racism could be a jumping off point, rather than starting from a defensive position. We use science fiction and fantasy to explore our own humanity and society, so what are we saying when we "other" pejorative traits or naturalize cultural characteristics? Is it just lazy writing? Is Tolkien really to blame? Will the real Drizzt D'urden please stand up?

Bridget Collins is a PhD candidate in the Program in the History of Science, Medicine, and Technology at the University of Wisconsin–Madison, where she focuses on the history of public health, environmental health, and women's health. Her dissertation will detail the history of domestic medicine in twentieth century America.

It's Not About Identity: Transcript with Several Responses

Transcript notes by Josh Lukin
with additions in italics by Liz Henry

> ...At four I returned to the second floor to attend my first-ever Science Fiction Convention Panel, "It's Not About Identity," with L. Timmel Duchamp, Andrea Hairston, Joan Haran, Sylvia Kelso, and Lauren Lacey.
>
> > **Panel Description:** In the wake of the demise of "woman" as a unified category, many second-wave feminists felt undermined, saying that there could be no feminism unless there were some absolute, essential definition of the category woman. Other feminists (both second- and third-wave) have argued, though, that this attitude rests on a misunderstanding of the relation between political theory and the practice of politics. This panel will explore some suggestions for new ways of thinking about feminism and its future.

Timmi spoke of the elision of class and race in the "we" of second-wave feminism and the challenge to that elision leveled by the Combahee River Collective. She was very excited at the time to read of interlocking oppressions, as she had seen her own working-class origins elided in the claims that groups styling themselves "Women's Organizations" made on behalf of "all women."

Joan: We need to be particular and located. My engagement with feminism comes from a different local culture. You bore people to tears by assuming people have the same experience and priorities as you. And if you're *not* located, you run a greater risk of your knowledge being appropriated and used against you.

Andrea: I agree with everything—I'm in the Amen Corner here. I come in as an artist, a director in a field my race and gender aren't associated with. And I've seen, for example, a nineteen-year-old white man sitting beside me mortified when people came up to him and said, "You directed that, huh? It was great!" And he had to say, "Uh, no, she directed it." These assumptions, these categories *are* our social realities and are constantly in our brains.

Lauren: I'm seeing a backlash against postmodernism. My first impulse is "Don't assign me to anything—I want to be free of those." But there's a movement to reclaim those identities, while keeping the knowledge that these *are* constructed categories.

Sylvia: How do we put these insights into practice? As soon as you go outside your circle of shared values, you have to qualify the word "feminist."

Timmi: It's like maintaining double-consciousness.

Joan: Can postmodernists and poststructuralists really claim to be the ones who discovered constructed categories? We need to historically situate feminisms. Within feminism, there's been a lot of polemical misrepresentation by some feminists of other feminists.

Sylvia: In the 1980s US feminism got so fissured-up that there was no sense of collectivity.

Andrea: How can we work out a common language or a consensus? When I work with visual artists and see what visual artists do in my field—'cause having a director in charge of design would be a disaster—I have to learn to compromise with other modes of creativity and to open myself up to what I'm at first uncomprehending of. But we don't want to say, "What don't I know? And what can that other group offer me that might allow me to see more?"

Timmi: That's a great figure for coalition politics. It connects to maintaining awareness of who is included in our "we" and who isn't.

Lauren: "Transnational" is a word that's become fashionable in the academic jargon of late, but academics can do a lot when they take their students abroad to learn about the Other—starting with getting them to wonder, "Who made that sweater?" and showing them.

Joan: Haraway tried hard in the "Cyborg Manifesto" to address coalition politics. But she misrepresents people who ought to be part of the coalition. There are people she doesn't talk about, and she styles Adrienne Rich a poet without acknowledging that Rich is also a great theoretician. But it's true that people need to give up on believing that things are resolvable.

Timmi: We need, to use a favorite verb, to bracket some things.

Andrea: We need to relinquish the sense that the world is absolutely knowable and that we're progressing toward that knowledge. You speak of Adrienne Rich and being categorized as a poet—I had a student who wanted to do a play as a senior project, and I lobbied to have that count instead of, rather than in addition to, a lengthy written thesis; and I kept hearing "Do you really think directing is that much work?" and various questions as to whether the collaborations, the planning, the dramaturgical work, the preparatory research, and so forth weren't just an attempt on the student's part to "get away with" not doing the thesis. Finally I persuaded them to recognize that the student's program notes were "real work." But my friend the Women's Studies chair—any production of knowledge that those of us in the theater would take seriously, she's suspicious of, 'cause it's Just Art!

Nancy Jane Moore, in the audience, says she's convinced art is far superior to theory.

Joan: Judith Butler has written, "I work in the area of feminist theory, which is not distinct from feminism as a social movement. Feminist theory would have no content were there no movement, and the movement, in its various directions and forms, has always been involved in the act of theory. Theory is an activity that does not remain restricted to the academy. It takes place every time a possibility is imagined, a collective self-reflection takes place, or a dispute over values, priorities, and language emerges.

Timmi: The term "sexual harassment" is an Act of Theory—before its existence, it was impossible to articulate that issue as political.

Andrea: Things that we take for granted, even among people that don't self-identify as feminists, are a product of theorists, of narrative, of analysis, of consciousness-raising.

Sylvia spoke of how she responds to "I'm not a feminist."

Timmi: So we've come up with two strategies: bracketing and respect.

Sylvia: We're just gonna have to learn to compromise somewhere.

Timmi: There are different standpoints.

Audience: What's something that's unresolvable?

Lauren: Female Genital Mutilation.

Andrea: Or Female Genital Cutting, to use a less judgmental name.

Lauren: This is one of those Really Hairy Moments where people draw the line—it's a Local Issue.

Audience: What exactly is it and why are there people in favor of it?

Andrea: Take the Mende, for example—and I'll try to be as neutral as I can on a practice that I in fact oppose. There's a whole value system around Initiation, a year-long education process in which the young girl learns to be a woman, that's sanctioned by the narratives of the society and is very performative. For the Mende, being a child is horrible: you have no rights, you can't speak—and if you don't do this, then you aren't agreeing with all the values, the morals, the community, and you're ugly too; but if you do, you can proudly say, "I am Mende!" There are women in that society who do say it's mutilation, but some say it's all we have left of our culture after Western encroachments.

Audience: Could we add Empathy to the list?

Timmi is delighted.

Audience: Could you clarify what you mean by bracketing?

Joan explains what it does; Timmi explains why we do it.

Joan: How to contain a set of ideas that are paradoxical, that can't be resolved, that you're not able to work through, leave something aside to address another issue.

Timmi: I use it often, I read theory and like some of what they say and reject utterly some of it and call that bracketing so I don't have to say I can't stand X, so I can save authors from the dust heap.

Hairston: So it's not all or nothing.

Audience: You're dealing with individual differences. *I'm a descendent of the consciousness raising movement.* In the many years that I worked for the LGBT Speakers' Bureau, we were told that you can't claim to be "speaking for" — it's just you speaking.

Timmi: It's good to have more stories, a plurality of narratives.

Andrea spoke of having done a performance piece among refugees in Germany from lands and cultures that were at odds with and stigmatized one another. They had to figure out how to respect one another and were helping each other tell their stories, even though one participant's story might denounce another participant's people. And the audience, too, when it was performed, would empathize completely with a member of a culture when they'd just heard — and empathized with — the experience of one of its enemies. And a German official said, "Thank you for doing this on our soil." Which Hairston took to mean that it clarifies the audience's life, too.

Andrea: I worked with group of refugees from all over the world. Our common language was German. We were going to create a play. Get everyone to tell her story, we were all women, but must tell it in German, because the Germans thought it would help them assimilate into German society, so they asked me to do it as an expert on multiculturalism, (laughter from all) we had to figure out how to respect one another, what was going on for each individual woman, we had to be on her side. That was our form of listening. You must come from that point of view. You can't argue with her, you are helping her tell her story. That is what we do in theater. When it got to her story, she could contradict in her own. When we performed it the audience was weeping. The stories were so different, saying oh horrible group x; no, not group x, oh horrible group y. At the end we were all together. The Ger-

mans were very happy, the German guy says "We've had a checkered history"

everyone laughs

*"What we need are more instances of this on our soil." He went to English to try and say this. And thank you thank you thank you. I took it as him saying, I didn't know what to do, and the more I see this the more I know what to do about who *I* am. In other words his life was now clearer to him, because he listened to a woman from the Sudan talk about her experiences getting to Germany.*

Joan: That is one of the things that feminist science fiction does for me. That kind of performative walking in other people's shoes doesn't work for me, but reading does. And for me narrative fiction really does work. The more voices in the narrative fiction that you have to imagine yourself into, the better. Sandra Harding talks about feminist standpoint is not something you have, it is something you struggle to achieve, one of my hopes for utopia, is you don't just stick to reading things of a particular type. So I think, yes, as many stories in as many genres as possible.

Timmi: You're both talking about people collaborating to help construct the narrative. When you read you are constructing a narrative, you've given what you need to make the story but the reader has to make the story work. With theater you're making clear each of the stories, activity is more powerful than knowing.

Andrea: Reading a novel is about getting into a voice other than your own, even when you wrote it. You have to give yourself to the story, and be taken where the author and chars are going. If it is really good fiction for me it takes me somewhere I haven't gone. And particularly with feminist sf I find that it does do that.

Beth, from the audience: *I am not in academia, had a bad attitude about it. I live in rural small town Wisconsin. Basic question, narrative fic of sf is part of the answer, but how do we get the feminist narrative out? Back in early '70s, was in consciousness raising, in a lot of those discussions and meetings, with people with different backgrounds than mine, trying to solve some issues, but if you talk to any woman in my small town, the media has told them what feminism is for: either feminism has fixed this for me and I don't have to think about it...and what it is, is it's a way of destroying the conversation. What they think feminism is really isn't relevant to them.*

Timmi: It's not part of the public narrative.

Lauren: *I have students from that town, and I ask them, write about feminism, and they get really uncomfortable, yeah I know it was important and I'm happy about the things it did... At best, many of my students think it did all its necessary work long ago.*

Beth: But they still accept all the inequities of the patriarchal domestic arrangement. Those women are going to have a job, and they are going to do all the housework and organize the childcare, and...

Lauren: When you start talking about the transnational— Well, what about here? The progressive conclusion, I suppose, is that we all need to think about our lives. But women in Middle America already feel overwhelmed and see it as just another demand on their time and energy.

Women are caught up in many different roles, so the idea we want them to fight for something else is a little too much. For me it is the stories that are important. Uhh...as an English professor... We can give them a book.

Andrea: People aren't happy with what they have but feel it's inevitable and immutable: consider *Kindred*. If we believe in change, that you can start out with nothing and figure out strategies—we have to ignite the feeling that change is possible, to get women to figure out what they'd like to do, what they'd like to be...

Things that are not working for us, by us I mean, all of us, the state of our society, people are not happy with what they have because it is inevitable and immutable, and if you feel that then you 're just like what the fuck? Why be an activist?

laughter

Butler, writing Kindred, *consider what did the people in slavery think, how could they get through every day, how do you prepare for the next generation where it isn't going to be this way? If we believe in change, if what Octavia writes in* Parable of the Sower *that god is change, if we convince people of that as a possibility, the character might think there is nothing I can do, but they intervene in small ways, and then bigger, and end up mothering another generation, so we have to ignite, we have to figure out what those changes are going to be. If you're thinking it's possible to change, then, change is going to emerge. I grew up in the '50s and '60s Pittsburgh, their thoughts, got me to college and doing the things I ended up doing. Get those women thinking, "What do I like? What do I want to be in my life, and how do I move toward it?" What does feminism have to offer us in our lives? They are invested in it if it's their day-to-day lives.*

Joan: Feminism ought to be a social justice project, but Humility is probably another word to add to our list.

Coming back to coalition politics. Feminism as a social justice project, coalition doesn't have to be labeled feminism. There are places you can intervene, consonant with feminist social justice but what you're doing isn't necessarily called feminist; humility. You can be feminist, but decenter your feminism.

Karen Joy Fowler, from the audience: *For a coalition*, be really strategic about your project and why you need to come together—what you need to bracket, and what you need to want to change.

Audience: Think hard about how to intervene and where to intervene. Working in rural development in Ireland, I've had to figure out what's relevant to the people there and why.

Lauren: Otherwise you're just perpetuating the problem.

Timmi: Linda Zerilli in *Feminism and the Abyss of Freedom* says, "If there is only the name with which a political collectivity calls itself into existence, then we can never be certain that speaking in that name is correct. Contrary to the claims of feminist standpoint theory, there is no extrapolitical standpoint from which we could determine the correctness of speaking in someone's name. This means that every such speaking will be inescapably political and open to question. And yet the very fact that a political collectivity such as 'woman' must call itself into being from a place where it does not yet exist means that there must be some form of closure. Insofar as second- and third-wave feminist theory has not been wholly blind to this constitutive condition of democratic openness and closure, it has tended to see that condition as installing a crisis at the heart of feminism: posited as a unified category given in advance of politics, 'women' generates exclusions; posited as a site of 'permanent openness and resignifiability,' 'women' precludes the possibility of speaking collectively. Although the tension between openness and closure can be experienced as a crisis for political actors, we have seen that it is also the irreducible condition of feminist and democratic politics." Do you care to respond to that?

audience laughter

*Joan: I don't know that I follow the quote! *laughter from all* I can speak, let's say, adjacent to it…*laughs* Not a Derrida scholar at all, but notion that there's some language we just have to use, because you're not sure that the thing is that thing. So the category of "women," we don't buy that there is a [truth] to that category but we have to use the word.*

Andrea: It's like the electron: all of our language fails us at the borders of things.

It's like the electron. We don't know how fast it is or where it's going, but we have to talk about it. We cannot get to it with our words.

Joan: Sometimes we have to use language "under erasure," saying things like ~~women~~ to show that we know how problematic and inadequate the term is and are using it provisionally.

There are times when acting as and speaking as a woman will be [appropriate] and times where it's not appropriate, and during exclusions, there may be particular moments and painful ones…there is the issue of conflict resolution and being able to speak about what we've done and why. And there may be costs to it. E.P. Thompson, The Making of the British Working Class. *(nods from Timmi) The self consciousness of it and the temporality is what is important. It might be putting language under erasure. Provisional use of a word.*

Joan: There will be times when acting "as women" or speaking "as women" will be what serves…there are structures out there that we're forced to operate in. Just stay conscious of their contingency.

Timmi: Self-consciousness, positionality.

Andrea: Here's why I don't like academia: Zerilli's poetry is not up to her ideas. I read things in which the ideas are wonderful, wow, but the language is frustrating. The problem we're trying to talk about is that of the electron, or of polyrhythm *[Hairston begins drumming three-against-two on the table while talking].* My Yoruba percussion teacher showed me that to be a Yoruba drummer is to be able to listen, to talk, and to play different rhythms with each hand: we have to be able to do polyrhythmic thinking. [Audience applauds when she's done]

Lauren: Zerilli's point is that our democratic society is based on identity politics—unless we want to make a whole social paradigm shift, we have to think in those terms.

Beth in the audience: We have come in our society to think that it's a zero-sum game in which there is no we—how do we get around the paradox Butler identifies in Xenogenesis*? It goes back to Octavia Butler, I'm going to point at my husband, who knows the quote.*

Beth's Husband: "Human beings are both rational, and hierarchical, that's why you blew yourselves up."

Andrea: You're a woman you're not a woman, it's the simulteneity of contradictory things, you have to act as a woman because society...and yet woman isn't real, it's a construct, it's a fiction, it's made up, and you have to hold those things in yourself and not lose your mind!

Lauren: Maybe it's like voting Democratic while keeping in mind how much better things could be.

Audience: I don't know if you noticed it, but the rhythm of Andrea's speech was affected by her drumming: these things have an impact on one another.

Audience: We live with contradictions all the time and are miseducated from a very early age that they're not contradictions, which makes us impatient with those contradictions we encounter later on that are not Officially Sanctioned Contradictions.

*Audience: We already hold contradictory ideas all the time in our society, we vote…in our free individual democratic society, and we don't think of this as a contradiction, because no one came in and says, "You know that doesn't make sense" and it has to make sense because as a child the world does. We so much want to *say,* instead of assist. We're assisting people already in a situation, not trying to make their situation OUR situation. Below, above, we think we're above, and then I'm gonna turn around and say someone else is above me. What people want vs. what they think.*

Timmi: Figuring out how to ask the right questions and listen to the answers.

Timmi reads off a list of concepts we've pulled out from this discussion: respect, bracketing, empathy, plurality of narrative, listening, which involves construction, polyrhythmic-ness, contradictions, self consciousness, compromise.

Sylvia: We think of Foucault's concept of the Regulatory Ideal as negative, something social structures pressure us toward; *the concept you are never going to get to, you can hold it in your head, it can be a bad thing*, but it could be a Good Thing to establish such an ideal and try to get there, you might have one, like feminism, democracy, activism, so long as you remember that you're not going to get there.

Timmi: That's our feminist utopia.

Andrea: And it's FUN trying to get there.

Audience: What are the possibilities for dealing with irrational actors?

Lauren: The ideal is a social structure that wouldn't reward such behavior.

Joan: But be aware that means can become ends.

Guy from audience makes a very long question/statement. How do we do this without compromising ourselves…

Timmi: Great question. (Shakes head, smiling.)

Sylvia: That's what I JUST SAID about the regulatory ideal.

Joan: It is important to hold on and act according to your values. But, one of the principles that I hold very dear from Starhawk's The Fifth Sacred Thing, *is that means become ends, so ends don't justify the means, whatever your regulatory ideal, what you do to approach it, matters. Don't do shit, to get to something good.*

Andrea: If you shit on the road, you have flies on your return.

Timmi: There's no better way to end!

** applause**

> [This is a rough transcription from notes taken during the panel; it is not transcribed from a recording and may not be precisely what was said.]

Josh's Responses

I came away from this panel with a pedagogical, a theoretical, and a collegial insight.

PEDAGOGICAL: Just over a dozen years ago, a teacher of mine at Youngstown State defended their Professional Writing and Editing program against its detractors, saying "I'm very proud that it teaches skills that will enable our students to work in strata of society that would otherwise be closed to them." And that idea became central to my philosophy of teaching freshman comp in grad school; and then, when I came to Temple U, I realized that students tended to want more than that, so I worked on various ways of giving them analytical tools to address the world around them. In particular, I sought to let students know about alternatives to voluntarism: Some students like to argue that "you can achieve anything" and consequently protest against the idea that a fictional protagonist can be constricted by her background and circumstances in her decisions. In such situations, I have had classes confront the question of whether people have complete freedom in defining themselves. Some conclude that one can talk about the limits imposed by social structure without reducing people to passive sufferers or dupes of the machinery of the world; others stick to their original criticisms but are better equipped to argue for their views in a context where they can better articulate what's at stake.

But it gets tricky: one wants to encourage neither despair nor victim-blaming. Randolph Bourne, whom Lauren Lacey's remark about the "transnational" reminded me of, demonstrates the problem in his wondrously self-contradictory essay on "The Handicapped": first he argues that his disability has enabled him always to consider the circumstances of those society would write off as reprobates; then he admonishes his fellow disabled citizens to stop whining and realize what they can do. It's the old "I won't attribute an undue level of agency to Others, but I can't be as flexible with myself and those I identify with — I need for therapeutic reasons to believe in Personal Responsibility as far as my own life is concerned." How does one address that paradox? It seems to me that a good goal would be to teach students to think about cultural options: who has more, who has fewer, what they do with them. And in the process, to expand students' knowledge of their own cultural options as well.

THEORETICAL: At MLA (but probably not at the American Studies Association), a panel with a title like "It's Not About Identity" would advocate the views of Todd Gitlin or of some of Walter Michaels' epigones, the idea that the Good Sixties when we were all united by universal class-oriented goals were succeeded by the Bad Sixties, when "Identity Politics" destroyed the Left, what with those pesky blacks, gays, women, and people with disabilities demanding that their difference be recognized. Why not, I've always wondered, conclude that the strength and resources of the Right are what damaged the Left? Why insist that we were stabbed in the back by our own? Isn't that a creepy mirroring of a right-wing narrative about how we lost Vietnam, or Red China, or atomic secrets? Does the Left need its own Dolchstosslegende? None of that here, in part because nobody wanted to look down on everyone else and make hortatory judgments.

COLLEGIAL: Look at how disagreement, even strong disagreement, worked on this panel. Nancy's opinion didn't elicit expressions of scorn but powerful and sober arguments and historical analysis. And Andrea's response to Beth — saying that "we have to get women to" do this and that — is framed in the kind of imperialist language that Spivak would not like (remember Spivak asking why Nussbaum was so intent on teaching Indian women what they should want?);

but it was contradicted so gently by the four subsequent speakers that one could have learned a lot and still barely noticed that there was a disagreement there. Nothing confrontational.

References

Full text of The Comabhee River Collective Statement http://circuitous.org/scraps/combahee.html.

E. P. Thompson, *The Making of the English Working Class* (New York: Vintage Books, 1963).

Linda M. G. Zerilli, *Feminism and the Abyss of Freedom* (University of Chicago Press, 2005).

Sandra G. Harding, *Feminism and Methodology; The Feminist Standpoint Reader.* New York: Routledge, 2004.

Donna Haraway, "A Cyborg Manifesto: Science, Technology, and Socialist-Feminism in the Late Twentieth Century," in *Simians, Cyborgs and Women: The Reinvention of Nature* (New York; Routledge, 1991), pp.149-181. http://www.stanford.edu/dept/HPS/Haraway/CyborgManifesto.html.

Transcript from Liz: http://badgerbag.livejournal.com/112027.html.

Transcript from Josh: http://aqueductpress.blogspot.com/2008/05/wiscon-32-panel-6-its-not-about.html.

Josh Lukin specializes in literature of the 1950s US and in disability studies. He has published on the work of Walt Whitman, Oscar Wilde, Grant Morrison, Philip Dick, Jim Thompson, Justine Larbalestier, Samuel Delany, and Patricia Highsmith as well as the future of black disability studies, the Black Panther Party and disability, the film *Tshe Men*, and Colson Whitehead's *Apex Hides the Hurt.* His edited collection *Invisible Suburbs: Recovering Protest Fiction in the 1950s United States* was published in 2008 by the University Press of Mississippi. Josh teaches at Temple University.

Response to "It's Not About Identity"

Micole Sudberg

I liked this panel a lot, I agreed with it a lot, I wanted it to dig deeper. Joan Haran had a critical point about conflict management and fear of conflict, and I wanted more examples of conflicts being managed in the panel.

For example, I often felt like Sylvia Kelso was talking about one thing, and the rest of the panel was talking about something else; or else that there were differences in her approach to feminism and identity, and the approach that was more-or-less the consensus among the rest of the panel that resulted in her being fairly silent most of the time. I agree more with the approach I perceived the rest of the panel as advocating, so I was more interested in hearing their takes, but I also feel like this was an example of the kind of differences feminists need to be exploring rather than smoothing over — that there was a lot of talk of conflict management and managing disagreement, but that what was operating was often an all-too-familiar dynamic of "feminine" discomfort with disagreement and patriarchal deliberate obliviousness to difference.

Or I could have been projecting. It's hard to tell.

What I'm more sure of is the discomfort of unacknowledged power difference in other examples brought up in the conversation, notably the use of Female Genital Cutting as an example of bracketing, the practice of Western students visiting India for "feminist observation," Andrea Hairston's account of working with refugee women in Germany, and some of the discussion of the resistance of the "white women in Middle America" to feminism. To borrow the phrasing of one of the audience members, many of these discussions seemed framed in the language of "saving" rather than "assisting."

I will try to break down my discomfort into specifics:

1. I really, really, REALLY wish that the example for bracketing had been a familiar, American issue, rather than the "exotic" example of female genital mutilation. You are just not going to find many Americans of either gender or any ethnicity who

are willing to argue for this practice, and using it as an example of "bracketing" relies on and reinforces the tropes of the West needing to save women of color/women from the rest of the world from their own prejudices. I know it is easier to see examples from outside your own culture, but this particular example is so tightly interwound with the practices of colonialism and neo-colonialism that it runs the risk of perpetuating the assumptions of colonialism while attempting to dismantle the assumptions of patriarchy. Andrea Hairston in particular tried to unpack some of these issues, but I would have liked to have seen them addressed more bluntly, and I would have liked to have seen the panel expand on more familiar, Western examples of conflicts that must be bracketed for coalition work.

2. I can see the potential in Western students visiting India to learn how much they don't know about the lives of Indian women, but again my immediate reaction to the suggestion was a kind of horror, because the practice also seems to have a lot of potential for misunderstanding and abuse: for the Indian women to be treated as objects for observation, or for their activist practices to be misrepresented or appropriated, or for Western students who cannot afford to travel to India to be again and doubly penalized for class status and economic hardships. I don't know that any of these things happened; the actual trips and trip organizers may be cognizant of and careful to avoid all the pitfalls I see. But these pitfalls weren't discussed, and that troubles me.

3. Similarly, Andrea Hairston's story of the German-speaking refugee women theater group had some elisions that troubled me. I don't think it's impossible that the man she spoke to really had an experience of connection and realization—in fact, there are often nonverbal cues that convince us of the reality and trustworthiness of this connection that are hard to convey in words—but this was another example in which people of color, colonized people of color, performed (in this case literally) alienation and connection for white people. And yeah, we can see things more clearly in other cultures

than we can in our own sometimes, but—I want to know how you ensure, or at least try to encourage, the audience to complete the connection, so that they are not just looking at others as others, as objects of pity or disapproval, but as fellow humans, who have their own subjectivities, who are able to look back.

4. The discussion of the failure of (presumptively white?) Midwestern women to identify as or be active as feminists troubled me because it put the feminists in the roles of saviors, of knowing better, of... I don't know! Because I don't live in those communities or live with those particular frustrations, and I do in fact think feminist theory, activism, and practices are tools for change that could be helpful to those women, to all women. And in some cases the women speaking were teachers, academics—they were in positions of power (however tenuous), and they were looked to for explanation and teaching. But I wanted more discussion, more problematization, more investigation of how much work the women at WisCon were doing to understand and work with the priorities of the women who frustrated them, versus how much was despair and frustration at the women in their communities not agreeing to the priorities of the feminists trying to motivate/catalyze them.

And I'm uneasy saying this, because it's the kind of criticism that's easy to make from a distance. Certainly the media-depicted conservatism of small Midwestern towns is one reason why I have never considered living in one—and that means that I am speaking from a position of ignorance myself. Certainly I am aware of, encounter all the time, frustrating misunderstandings of what feminism means (to me) and have to decide in every individual encounter how much education and explanation I am willing to do.

But I do think there were conflicts, potential faultlines, in the conversation at those points, conflicts that we might need to acknowledge before we can build bridges across them.

Reflecting on Josh's and Micole's Notes on the "It's Not about Identity" Panel

L. Timmel Duchamp

After reading both Josh Lukin's and Micole Sudberg's notes on the "It's Not About Identity" panel at WisCon 32, it occurs to me that another item that ought to be added to the list I compiled during the course of the panel is reflection. Reflection, in my view, is de rigueur for feminist process. And so it is, for me, that post-con discussions of WisCon panels that go beyond brief sketches (as Josh's and Micole's sets of notes do) are of interest not only to people who didn't attend the panels but also to the panelists and audience members who did. This, of course, is one of the assumptions underlying Aqueduct's WisCon Chronicles series. And it is the reason I wrote the essay examining last year's Romance of the Revolution panel.

The assumption doesn't make sense, of course, unless one regards panels as instances of public discourse. (I.e., takes panel discourse seriously.) WisCon's status as public space makes it vulnerable, of course, to hostile interference; that's the nature of public space. But it's important for women to occupy public space: this is something feminists have been insisting upon for centuries and is what makes WisCon more than just a fun social event (which it also, of course, is).

But to get back to reflection. Josh's and Micole's notes have helped me reflect on the panel. I can certainly understand Micole's discomfort with the choice of FGM as a make-or-break issue among international feminists working in coalition; the example that came into my own mind was abortion, but another panelist was quicker with this other example, and it's not my way as a moderator to override panelists when they're on-topic. When I mentioned FGM as partly a matter of social hygiene, I was specifically thinking of the still apparently little-known parallel to the fashion of cosmetic clitoral cutting in the US today. A few years back in my annual reading list for Fantastic Metropolis I recommended an article by Simone Weil Davis, "Loose Lips Sink Ships," published in the Spring 2002 issue of Feminist Studies, about “the new elective sex surgeries”—“trimming” the labia and “cleaning up” the vulva—an article that drew some startling parallels between “aesthetic” plastic surgery and FGM. I didn’t get a chance to expand on that but was happy to cede the floor to Andrea, who explained the social issue of adult identity involved for the Mende.

As my memory has it, no one on the panel talking about the two sides of the FGM issue ever suggested there was any question of saving non-Western women from FGM. I assumed we were talking about what sort of issues might have to be bracketed when working in coalition. And so the question in this case would be “Do you work with women who favor FGM [thus bracketing your moral or political opposition to FGM], or do you refuse, no matter how important it might be to work with them on another issue, because you don’t want to be complicit?” That’s what bracketing is about. It seems from Micole’s post that that must not have come across as clearly as I’d assumed.

IIRC, the only patronizing/missionary-attitude expressed was toward the women in Beth’s small town, as Josh pointed out to me not long after the panel, noting the irony. (And I do think he and Micole are right to mention this.)

Perhaps if we’d used abortion or frequent elective plastic surgery as examples of an issue that might require bracketing, the panel might have ventured into the area that I’m guessing (in retrospect) Sylvia may have been interested in talking about. Abortion, I’ve been told by people who teach university-level Women’s Studies courses, has become a taboo subject for many college-age women, too shameful to be mentioned (much less discussed) in public. And as I know from personal experience, sometimes feminists find it necessary to work in coalition with stridently anti-abortion groups.

Micole put her finger on an important problem when she wrote:

> I agree more with the approach I perceived the rest of the panel as advocating, so I was more interested in hearing their takes, but I also feel like this was an example of the kind of differences feminists need to be exploring rather than smoothing over—that there was a lot of talk of conflict management and managing disagreement, but that what was operating was often an all-too-familiar dynamic of “feminine” discomfort

> with disagreement and patriarchial deliberate obliviousness to difference.

On the one hand, if the panel had lacked the fragile bit of consensus that it did have, we probably would not have had such a lively discussion and would have gotten bogged down in matters of definition. On the other hand, if the consensus had broken down at any point, it might have offered some (perhaps painful) illumination into the very issue we were talking about. Part of the problem, I think, is that these discussions aren't ongoing—being one-offs, there's no opportunity to reflect and then re-engage—there's just the moment, and then, sometimes, the possibility of reflecting (with the help of comments like Josh's and Micole's)—and that's it—unless there's a second round at the next WisCon (though usually follow-up panels don't work quite like that).

Thank you, Josh and Micole. The art of conversation, as I'm always saying, is not easy, even though, at its most exciting, it tends to look that way.

Notes on the Narrative and Politics Panel

Victoria Janssen

These are my notes on the narrative panel at WisCon. Mostly, I didn't write down attributions, or try to make a sequence (or narrative!). This is just the bits that struck me, and that I wanted to refer to later. Also, there might be some of my own thoughts and interpretations, but not a lot.

The panelists were L. Timmel Duchamp (moderator) Carolyn Ives Gilman, Eileen Gunn, Pat Murphy, and Susan Palwick.

Received narrative as a force/atmosphere and combating/resisting received narrative; reader reading subversively, and writer leading/seducing reader into the subversive reading. The latter sounds like the hard part.

How do we make new narratives/stories for which the models don't exist? Subverting the conservative force of narrative: this equals story, this does not equal story. Making new story understood as story.

Narrative arc can be independent of structure; for example a single narrative arc, but structured as scenes going forward and backward in time. Structure can reinforce narrative arc, also. Thematic reinforcement ought to work as well.

The game of reading is to see narrative in a collage of events; seems to happen naturally when you have three random events; even two will do.

If reader is faced with a puzzle, must read interactively to assemble the puzzle/narrative.

Writer can write a story and then distance herself from the story, allowing her to rework it with greater freedom. "That story is done. I am now working on this story." (William Gibson recommended this technique to Eileen Gunn.)

Once a narrative is out in the world, it's no longer yours.

Exploit the holes in the story. [I think this meant, exploit the holes in one story to make a new, more interesting story.]

Carolyn Gilman: narrative is not explanation, it simulates explanation; narrative stresses competition and conflict; narrative tends to stress the personal and private over the public and political. Sequence in narrative implies causation.

Original version at http://oracne.livejournal.com/1037244.html

Victoria Janssen's first novel, *The Duchess, Her Maid, The Groom and Their Lover*, was published by Harlequin Spice. She's a member of SFWA, RWA, and a writing group known as The Nameless.

Comments on the Dissecting Privilege Panel

Janice Mynchenberg and Beth Plutchak

> **Panel Description:** Few words are more likely to provoke a rapid, vehement response than "privilege," whether it's agreement, accusation, or fervent denial. What made this nine-letter word a four-letter word? From its beginnings as a "private law" to the current bugaboo, panelists will discuss what privilege does and doesn't mean, determine how we can get past fighting about the word itself, explore the situations and structures that lie behind it, and reflect on the implications for societal change.
>
> **Panelists:** Laurie Toby Edison (moderator), Steven Schwartz (SS), Alan Bostick (AB), Richard F. Dutcher (RD), Paula Fleming (PF), Naamen Tilahun (NT). At the last minute Laurie was stricken with the wischolera, and moderating duties were assumed by Richard Dutcher.

Janice and I ended up discussing this panel for the remainder of WisCon. There were a number of things that didn't work, and we both wanted to figure out why. After leaving WisCon we continued the conversation through email. Diantha Sprouse and Dan Dexter are our partners and are included by reference in our conversation, although they did not take part in the email correspondence. Bracketed comments are added to fill in background for the reader.

Beth,

I wanted to write because I've been thinking a lot today about the privilege panel. Diantha and I bought the first *WisCon Chronicles* book. Today I was reading the last few articles in it before taking off on my trip. There was an essay by Samuel Delany about gender equality. He told a story about a time when rape-warning posters were all over a campus he was visiting, and the mood was fearful. His life partner was out walking and saw two women. He tried to approach them, but they ran from him, thinking he was intending to rape them. They didn't realize he was a gay man and just wanted to walk with them because it was after dark. Delany went on to comment that male privilege and power are not something men can relinquish at will, because others will continue to see them through that lens. But if others don't use the lens, then a gender power balance may be at least temporarily possible.

That got me thinking about the privilege panel. It struck me that privilege is not a fixed entity. It grows out of a particular social context. It is not something that the privileged person can claim as a right; it is something others agree to yield to him/her for whatever reason.

Now, when the moderator began by listing all the ways he is privileged, he was speaking as if these qualities were always and everywhere advantages. But that's not true. Privilege is much more fluid. The privileged status items the panelists listed may have functioned that way in many other settings. However, in the context of a WisCon event, it is not a privilege to be male; if anything, women have the privileged status for the weekend. Nor is it a privilege to be heterosexual at WisCon; sexual orientation is not considered especially relevant to social ranking. Nor is it a privilege to be literate; everyone is assumed to be literate. And so on.

In the context of that panel, the privilege that mattered most was the difference between being a panel member and being the audience that had to wait upon the acknowledgement of the moderator. And that privilege was neither named nor dealt with.

So the moderator listed a bunch of largely nonrelevant things that he claimed gave him privilege—as if his privilege was an objective reality rather than a social construct. It's not that simple. Any "privileged" status is ours (the assembled people) to grant in the context of WisCon, not his to permanently possess—regardless of context.

Am I making sense?

Janice

Janice,

I've also been trying to get a handle on the privilege panel in relationship to how those topics fail time after time at WisCon, and also to understand why I was so personally upset. [I found the panel very upsetting and ended up having an emotional meltdown by the end of the convention.] I think you are absolutely right about privilege being fluid. It is also something that is "granted," if that's the right way to think about it, without any input on your part. It's not something you claim and can take advantage of or step back from at will.

If you could step back, how would that help anybody anyway? Even if white people "step back" in certain areas, that does not change the relative position of anyone else in society. Without acknowledging that reality, the discussion, as structured, becomes a discussion of the uses of paternalism.

Dan and I have come to the conclusion that one of the things that happens at WisCon is, many of the people who attend WisCon are writers and/or academics, and their hold on privilege (however that's defined) is pretty tenuous. When the debate is framed by first stating what my privilege is, we are already going down a path of solidifying my position, and once that is secure I am willing to help the "underprivileged." After that, the conversation was unavoidably sent down the path it took. I still believe that until people at WisCon take a good hard look at where they really fit and what that really means to their place in society and their relationship with other members of society, no progress can be made. I've also come to the conclusion that this is not necessarily the spot we get "stuck" every year. It is more likely where the battle line is drawn.

Beth

Beth,

I think you and Dan are on to something. Many of the WisCon folks have always had some kind of privileged status and are blind to that fact. I agree that many others have worked hard to gain a little ground and are terrified of how easily they might lose it. So they insist it's solid earth rather than shifting sand under their feet. That's a lot of denial to break through in a panel or two once a year.

From a global perspective, though, every single WisCon attendee is pretty privileged. They are educated, have easy access to books, can afford to take off time from work, have travel funds, know how to find grant or scholarship aid if they need it, etc. What percentage of the world's population can say the same? My eyes were opened to the incredible privileges Americans take for granted years ago, in a school assembly, when the dean of students chastised us: "I'm tired of listening to you complain what a burden it is to have to read Tillich. Do you know how many people on this planet never have a chance to sit back and read Tillich—let alone be able to receive grants and take out loans to put off earning a wage in order to read book after book? You are among the most privileged people in the world, and you are absolutely blind to all the advantages you are enjoying while you're in school."

I guess a lot of my thinking has also been influenced by gaining the privilege of being an ordained minister (after centuries of the church denying the job to women) and then seeing how easily it can be taken away from me by the same processes that granted it to me in the first place. In my own denomination there are some who seriously argue that, for the sake of better relations with the churches who don't ordain women, we should stop doing it. The recent battles over granting ordination to GLBT individuals have (re)created difficulties for many folks who are otherwise perfectly qualified but cannot find a congregation willing to have a GLBT minister in their midst. My ordained status is far from secure, nor is it ultimately in my power to protect it.

Janice

Janice,

It sounds like your experience as a minister likely parallels mine as a banker. After years of building a career, I was one of the early casualties of the current financial crisis (without Chuck Prince's golden parachute, alas).

I've been reading and thinking a lot lately about not only privilege and class, but also about theory. I have had a pretty deep-seated mistrust of theory as I've seen it handled by white feminists and left-leaning social studies professionals, but I am rethinking some of that in light of Timmi's guest of honor speech. Most of my experience with theory has been through academia, partly driven by the fact that it took me so many tries to get my BA. I was in school for what I think is known as the second wave of feminism. At that time my activism had been informed by listening to radio accounts of the freedom riders on practically a daily basis while in high school, and then my involvement in the Vietnam War protests in college. Although I was aware of the feminist movement at that time, it was as an adjunct movement to the other two. Then, I got pregnant at nineteen and dropped out of school. I became someone who was no longer a potential member of the movement, but someone the feminists were trying to help. That experience of being an "other" in terms of what I saw as the theory of second wave feminism meant that even though I have always considered myself a feminist, I have never felt that I belonged to any of the feminist movements.

Beth

Beth,

Diantha and I bought the two *WisCon Chronicles* books, and I've just finished reading them. There's some pretty interesting stuff in there. One of the last pieces in the second book was a bunch of people writing about how they do or do not deal with sexist/racist writing in workshops. Quite a range of responses from people who all claim to be committed to battling these demons.

I just started a book of essays on feminism, faith, and the family. The first essay reminded me about the hidden privileged point of view in a lot of feminist thought—though only briefly, and not directly using that term. But it pointed out the hubris of assuming that one cultural/economic/social context is pretty much like another—and assuming that all women's problems require pretty much the same basic solutions. That's part of why I'd like to write a piece with two voices instead of one.

Janice

Janice,

What I am particularly hoping is that we can add personal experience in our discussion. The weakness of theory, for me, has always been that it never seems to account for my personal experiences. As someone who's lived with gender discrimination and spousal abuse, and is white and well educated, I never exactly fit the narrative. Bringing up my personal stories sometimes works as a vehicle for taking the conversation beyond the common narrative of what it means to be poor and female in this country. This was problematical this year when I was not on many panels. Speaking from the audience, I was able to tell stories, but the interpretation remained with the panel, so that deeper level was lost.

The way a question is framed has so much bearing on how we are able to answer the question. This was a good WisCon in the sense that there were numerous panels on issues of inequality. However, at the basic level of panel descriptions, we were being guided in the direction of an oppressed-and-helper dichotomy. This trips my buttons to begin with, as you know. Bad enough to deal with the issues of being poor and homeless and all the rest of it, without having to spend energy warding off all the well-meaning, ill-advised "helpful advice" you have to pretend to pay attention to.

I think part of the problem is the need to narrow the discussion and define it in such a way that it becomes easier to talk about. However, so much is inevitably lost in that process. At the same time, we do need a way to talk about the relationships of oppressions in a larger context—if we don't we end up effectively promoting the right-wing agenda of making every oppression at best a personal problem, and at worst getting into the battle of the hierarchical "isms," where we take over the work of supporting discrimination in defense of our ism.

That said, I'm going to try to impose some order on my own thought process. First, I want to talk about the "arc" of my WisCon and how that experience showed up some specific weaknesses in the framing of the discussion of inequality. I'll admit I reacted badly to some of the titling and descriptions of panels on what I'll call the political track. In particular I was concerned about the uses of the terms ally (as in white ally or male ally) and privilege as they functioned to create insider/outsider spaces. Now, I obviously have not been involved in a lot of group discussions that are already in existence with a history of using these terms. I also know that the intent of their usage is to set up a space to have a conversation that acknowledges the different divisions of power in society and how "I" may have benefited from that to "your" detriment.

In the "Dissecting Privilege" panel specifically, the panelists were directed to begin by defining the ways in which they were privileged. There are a number of problems with that approach. The subtext is that the panelists are solidifying their claim to whatever privilege they identify. Framing the question that way makes it very difficult to question the structure of privilege itself. So, how are the panelists left to deal with the problem of confronting inequality, oh no, I mean, of helping those less privileged deal with their problems? One of the panelists explained how she thought she could help educate people who were poor, because, after all, poor people didn't make bad choices on purpose, they just didn't know how to make good choices. Dammit, I used to do this all the time with my money when I was a welfare queen. Buy food or pay the rent...buy food or pay the rent... I always ended up making the *bad* choice. Shame on me.

That's the other problem with this framework. The only solutions available to us are solutions based on individual choice. It becomes difficult to analyze the economic, sexist, and racist structural underpinnings of society and how they play off of each other.

Part of my experience of the convention was attending a number of back-to-back panels that seemed stuck on the "us and them," "helper and helped" level of discussion. An advantage I have, which many of those involved apparently don't, is that I've crossed a lot of borders in my life. I moved from poverty to the middle class and on the way saw a side of racism that I wouldn't have if I had always been comfortably middle class. I can't tell you how many times I have been reassured in the following way: someone says something stereotypically demeaning about welfare mothers. I point out that I have been a welfare mother. They are quick to point out that they never meant people like me, they meant black welfare mothers. At this point I'm beyond trying to point out to this person what is wrong with what they've said because my head is spinning too fast with what what what??? You can say you didn't mean me, but I can tell, and what what what?? How is blatant racism supposed to make what you said better?

Forgetting what I could have said if I could think faster in the moment, what about the larger systemic issue? We have a political economy where the oppression of poor women, and in particular poor women of color, is carried out at a grassroots level. Why do we continue to allow that to happen? Let's not be afraid to take the conversation there.

Beth

Beth,

I think one of the issues we need to discuss is what we mean by "privilege." The panel seemed to be unclear about their definition and sometimes seemed to equate privilege and power. I think especially of the claim that sometimes a poor black Christian women has more "privilege" than a white male CEO. Well, she might conceivably have more moral authority in a given scenario—and if she was with a group that outnumbered the CEO and he was unable to access his company security force or the police, she might have been intimidating, etc., etc. All of which changes the power balance—but "privilege"? I'm not so sure how that would be affected.

A person can be privileged but relatively powerless. I think of the aristocracy in Russia or France before their revolutions. Many privileged folks were clueless and chasing pleasure, but not exercising much power. Or the way royal women were bartered by the men in their dynasties and unable to inherit the throne—but were also quite sheltered and pampered. Privilege is a very mixed bag. And it is contextual, not absolute.

It also seems to me that it often has more to do with how people believe they should treat you than with your ability to exercise power. Even people who are not Christian hesitate to use bad language or act disrespectfully if I am dressed as a pastor. That's privilege—and very limited power, as long as all other things are equal. But there are situations in which this protective privilege is limited or ignored. If, for example, someone has just died and the surviving family member is distressed and angry, I—as God's representative in that moment—might (or might not) be treated quite abusively, depending on the person's social conditioning and their stress level and so on.

This is related to your comments about looking at the issue of privilege as us versus them. That line is always changing and permeable. Which is part of the reason that "helpers" are often so patronizing. They are not really superior—just at that moment in a position to do something that the other can't do as effectively or quickly or such. Is that because of privilege? Sometimes, but often that is overlaid with other factors such as wealth or employment or social connections or training that empowers—things that may matter more than the privileges of gender, race, etc. in that moment.

Privilege is only a factor as long as everybody agrees to recognize it as valid. At WisCon, male gender is not "privileged" nor is a heterosexual orientation. The social norm negates it—though there are individuals at the conference who still act as if those qualities deserve preferential treatment. But at WisCon we tend to grant privileged status to, say, the handicapped, who had special spaces marked out for them in every audience, whether they were present or not.

Granting such privileges is not necessarily a bad thing. In the Christian ethic we do a good thing when we honor the outsider, the foreigner, the poor, the sick. They are the privileged in God's table setting—the last being the first, etc. It is a question of whom we honor and why and how that makes "privilege" status problematic. Who does it help or hurt? The goal of granting privilege to some and not to others is to create a more level playing field for everyone—not to perpetuate the status quo of our society.

Am I making sense, or am I just rambling? I think I'll stop here and see what you have to say about whether this note is gibberish or gets us somewhere in our discussion.

Janice

Janice,

Definitely, the concept of power as well as privilege needs to be addressed. I think the relationship of the individual to the societal structure of privilege needs to be addressed as well. I think addressing the panelists' relationship to the audience, as an example of the impact of framework, would be useful.

When SS proposed the panel, he had some specific interest in looking at the word privilege as it pertains to its origins in "private law." He spoke about that in his introduction, but I don't think anyone else on the panel or many people in the audience understood that reference. I know I didn't. According to the panel description the panelists were directed to discuss what privilege does and doesn't mean. I think AB and SS did try a few times to go to what privilege does and doesn't mean, but the strength of the way the original directive to the panelists was framed, "How am I privileged?" was never overcome. When AB gave his example (from something he'd read) about the black woman preacher having more privilege than a white male CEO in a certain environment, he may have been trying to go to what you are talking about with granted privilege and honor. Then NT responded by gently reminding people (is it reminding when people don't know it in the first place?) that black people are taught from an early age a specific way to behave around white people and that the preacher may have been evidencing that training rather than her experience of privilege (except I believe by then privilege was being taken to mean power). I think if that concept had been explored more fully, the panel might have been able to do something useful.

The composition of panel participants also worked to undermine any meaningful discussion of the issue. There were three white men on the panel, including SS who is Jewish and for purposes of the panel discussion included himself as someone who had white male privilege. There was one white woman and one black man. The three white men started by doing some of the traditional male preening and display to establish their position in the hierarchy. AB backed off from the contest pretty quickly. I don't believe SS and RD recognized that that was what they were doing. PF appeared pretty nervous and uncertain as a panelist to begin with and played a typical female role of supporting all of RD's points. NT was particularly gracious in his attempts to broaden the discussion, but when it was pretty clear that he was having no impact, he became somewhat disengaged.

I, unfortunately, attended that panel primed to be misunderstood. I had taken part in the Writer's Workshop for the first time in many years with a story that I had workshopped before and recently rewritten. The main character is a woman in a dead-end job who is obsessed with her disabled son. She does some cool skiffy things with time travel and computers to change things for him. On rereading the earlier version, it was pretty clear that my level of skill was awful at the time, and I was confident the new version was much better.

I workshopped it, hoping to get some feedback on my current level of skill. At the earlier workshop, half the people that read the really weak version of this story loved it, and half felt that the main character was ill-defined and that it was implausible that she could have taught herself enough programming to carry off what she did. I was prepared for, hoping for, criticism at this year's workshop. I was not prepared for getting the same criticism. So, maybe my skill has not improved; fair enough. But, it is often believed plausible in skiffy land that a young white boy can tap the technology in ways unthought-of by the highly trained and highly funded, and save the day. Why is it an implausible idea for a woman who is marginalized to do the same? No one argued that the skiffy things themselves were implausible, but that this character couldn't possibly pull them off. All of which is not to say the story isn't crap. I don't know. It's to say that if you choose to write about people who are marginalized or invisible, it's really hard to get useful feedback.

Then I started attending panels. In the past I've been assigned to a number of panels and had the ability to speak from that vantage. For some reason this year I was only assigned to one panel, which was not a political topic. I knew I would speak from the audience, but I knew I had to be brief because many people would be anxious to speak. So, I spent some time trying to pick succinct-enough examples from my experience to make my points, and at the same time, not sound like I was simply saying white people have problems, too. I raise all of this not to whine about my being misunderstood, but to try to illuminate the way the structure of panel discourse at WisCon works to continue to marginalize certain groups of people.

WisCon panels tend to happen with a number of predictable structures. For instance, the political panels often start at the level of definitions, where the moderator goes up and down the line and asks the panelists to define the main term to be used in the panel discussion, whether it is class or privilege or whatever. The common critique I have heard is that so many of these panels get "stuck" on definitions, or we are constantly "stuck" at the level of 101. This is partially due to the nature of WisCon, where you have so many people with different enough backgrounds and levels of experience with personal/political struggle that there isn't a shared definition or group of definitions to work from. It is the great joy of WisCon for me that that is true, that there is always the possibility of pushing beyond a level of complacency and superiority that tends to happen when we think we understand the problem and know how it can be solved. This level of complacency and superiority always works to continue to marginalize those people who are already marginalized. Science fiction is as good a place as any to start to question those assumptions.

When RD responded to my criticism of the narrative structure of the panel being used to establish privilege by challenging me to come up with a better way to do it, right there, right on the spot, I did feel like I was being personally attacked. I gave an off-the-cuff answer about including more people of color on the panels. RD condescendingly replied that it was unfair to ask POC to have to explain things to white people, and we needed to do that work ourselves.

Instead of acknowledging my criticism (whether he agreed or not) that the way the issue is framed will determine the conclusions that are drawn, he attacked my personal qualifications to understand or talk about issues of race and privilege. The white panelists backed him up, with PF saying she was sure she could do enough reading on her own to figure things out. What was effective in the way RD handled the exchange was that I was thoroughly derailed from my initial point into wondering whether I was now perceived as just another clueless white person.

After that, the panel continued in the vein of who and where to help, with examples from as far away as possible seeming to be the preferred choice.

I like your notion of honor and would also add respect. The reason I burst into tears the next time I saw Diantha, and couldn't stop crying until after the end of the convention, was that according to the narrative of the privilege panel, someone like me—who is now professional, middle class, white, and well respected in my community—should be trying to figure out how to use my privilege to help someone like Diantha—who has been marginalized by race, class, sex, and sexual orientation. As you know, Diantha has been a huge support to me over the years, in encouraging me to acknowledge and hang onto the parts of myself that are mired in a past of poverty and violence.

The panel got it totally backward as to who's helping whom. I think until we can deal with the issue of framing a discussion in a way that honors and respects the experience and insight of the marginalized attendees of WisCon, we will continue to be a place that largely reaffirms the privilege that people bring with them to the convention. So I don't think we're stuck at the level of definition, I just don't think we've made it that far, yet.

Beth

Wow! What a lot to ponder, Beth!

I think we're questioning the very notions of panels as the best way to organize discussions at WisCon.

It seems to me that the nature of panels divides the panelists at the front table from the rest of the participants. The chosen few have the mikes to broadcast their remarks, they have the first and last words, they have the authority to redirect the discussions to suit themselves, they decide when to allow audience members to comment on the ideas they have presented, etc. Every panel is a study in the dynamics of privilege, it seems to me—exercised well or poorly, subtly or blatantly by the panel lead speakers—unless the audience stages an open revolt, which is very rare since we're all conditioned to respect the podium.

You seem to expect to have more ownership and voice in panels than I do. Being an introvert, I've resigned myself to silence most of the time. It takes me a while to absorb ideas and mull them over and then formulate responses, and panel discussions almost always move too quickly for my thoughts to be on topic. Part of the reason I appreciate The WisCon Chronicles series is because it extends the dialogue well past the event—and I have the thinking time I need, as well as more thoughts from others. I feel so much more included this year than in previous years. I have an opportunity for input, if I desire it and do the necessary work to submit my responses to panels, etc.

I've tended to view panels as mini-lectures or rants by more or less well-informed and intelligent people, events that give me ideas to ponder and play with on my own and debrief with Diantha—or, if I'm very lucky, with someone else who's interested and available despite a very hectic weekend schedule.

I believe that the notion of panel discussions was supposed to be more like your vision than mine. So why don't they work that way? Some of it is due to the physical setup, some is ego, some is competing agendas and limited time to cover a broad enough (or deep enough) range of information and insight, some is the number of people involved and their varying levels of expertise/interest/etc.

Perhaps we need a panel to discuss alternatives to panels.

Janice

A native of Ohio, Janice Mynchenberg has lived in several states and now resides in Chattanooga, TN. She was living in southern Wisconsin when she began attending WisCon in the 1990s. After receiving an MA in comparative literature from the University of Oregon in Eugene, Janice enrolled in Trinity Lutheran Seminary. She has been an ordained pastor for 20 years. Her partner is Diantha Sprouse.

Beth Plutchak is a long-time fan of feminist science fiction, and a long-time participant in WisCon. You can find out more about her at http://bplutchak.livejournal.com.

Utopia, Fiction, and Fandom: Conflict, Community, and "Queer Female Space"

Alexis Lothian

1. Utopia and Worldbuilding

Feminist science fiction has long been associated with the category of the utopian. It has also long been known that a straightforward utopia is far less interesting than an ambiguous one. When gender intersects with other forms of difference in the complicated landscape of mundane or fantasized realities, thinking about the utopian becomes very complicated indeed. And complicated utopianisms don't only appear in fiction; they are present in many real-world political and social contexts.

Utopia, conflict, and the politics of community play out in complex ways with relation to radical-left political theory and activism, and to the intersections of feminism, critical race studies, and queer theory. In this paper, I move across some of these complications by exploring intersections between science fiction, fan communities, and the influence of social-justice politics. How do worlds get built and utopias imagined when feminist science fiction and its discontents move away from the page? My main case study here is the sometimes-uncomfortable intersection of queer and critical race discourse in media fandom, specifically around the TV show *Stargate Atlantis*, but the issues I raise apply beyond that example.

"Worldbuilding" refers to something different in the two critical discourses in which I'm most immersed, science fiction and queer studies. In science fiction, of course, worldbuilding is the creation of fictional universes, the making believable of elsewheres and futures that function to provide what Samuel Delany called a "tool to help you think about the present" for purposes of political critique, pleasurable narration, and every point in between ("Necessity of Tomorrows" 34). In queer studies, "worldmaking" is often used in a sense that comes from performance studies. Social practices in space and time make worlds; having a discussion at WisCon involves making a world and so might carrying on those discussions in print and online afterward.

Queer worldmaking is invoked as a utopian practice of dissent against heteronormative dominant worlds by José Muñoz, among others. Muñoz writes that in performance art, "through the transformative powers of queer sex and sexuality, a queerworld is made" (23). Lauren Berlant and Michael Warner have described queer cultural and sexual practices as worldmaking; in *Utopia in Performance*, Jill Dolan writes about "worlds" made in momentary, affective utopias that can be created by the collective sensation of affective perfection, which theatergoers sometimes experience in the presence of a sublime performance. She links these epiphanies to radical politics, writing that they have the capacity to "persuade us that beyond this 'now' of material oppression and unequal power relations lives a future that might be different, one whose potential we can feel as we're seared by the promise of a present that gestures toward a better later" (7).

I'm interested in the continuities and discontinuities between the discourse and practice of worldmaking and utopianism in writing, in reading, and in social life. I wonder about the connections between the politicized worldbuilding that takes place in the writing of feminist, radical, queer, antiracist, and anticolonial science fiction writers and the politics of affective worlds that get performed in and around them. I'm especially interested in the points at which utopian discourses get complicated, where the worlds that get made and built can't be understood to be unmitigatedly positive things. The utopianisms that interest me are not fully utopian in the sense of perfect, but they work with conceptions of perfectibility to make worlds.

2. Political Science Fictions

Imagining a better world and showing how it becomes a worse one is a classic dystopian move, but as Dunja Mohr shows in her book *Worlds Apart*, feminist science fiction rarely produces dystopias with no utopian kernel. In much feminist science fiction, utopia and dystopia, resistance and oppression, get tangled up in complex intersectional worldbuilding.

One of the urtexts of radical science fiction, Ursula K. Le Guin's *The Dispossessed*, gives a classic example of this. In the novel, Le Guin builds an anarchist world that understands itself to be a utopian dream of pure agency. Among Odonian anarchists there is to be no coercive obligation, no power structures, either overt or covert, no inequality—only free action among individuals equal in status and respected in difference, accepting their birthright of solidarity and mutual aid. The existence of the "society without government, without police, without economic exploitation" (256) is a vitalizing force for those who would challenge government, police, and exploitation where they do exist; but by making the utopian society a real one, rather than only a dream, Le Guin complicates her model of agency and freedom. It turns out that it is not, after all, simply the case that people would always act freely and well if they were not prevented from doing so by the machinations of internal or external power. Power, as Michel Foucault's work tells us, is active and intrapersonal as well as externally imposed. By making law of anarchism, Le Guin suggests, the citizens of utopia who believe themselves totally free may have less mental agency than resistant subjects under state and capital power, who are analytical and conscious of the structures they oppose. And they may lack that agency precisely because they trust in their own agency and so cannot examine the ways power continues to operate despite the surface egalitarianism of their society.

The idea that belief in preexisting perfect agency is the greatest danger to utopian realization, presented abstractly in *The Dispossessed*, is suggestive of failures in white feminist movements called out by radical women of color (the 1983 Combahee River Collective Statement is an especially famous example of this, but the dynamics it exposes are present in many contemporary feminist contexts). It is unsurprising that the fictional works that take this danger into account most acutely are those that have a powerful consciousness of race as well as gender and sexuality. Delany, for example, in James Sallis's words, "creates entire societies in order to depict those at the society's margin" (xiii). Or to take a different author from the somewhat restricted canon of widely read intersectional science fiction, the utopian narrative of Earthseed in Octavia Butler's *Parable of the Sower*, which is about the possibility of building a livable future from within a dystopian one. This narrative is not about building a utopian world, but rather about finding means of survival when subjugated by the worlds others have built. A pure utopia, where every citizen would be happy and centrally located within dominant cultural discourses, is neither possible nor desirable. Other works highlight the extent to which one person's utopia can be another's oppression: Delany's *Trouble on Triton* is an obvious intertext to *The Dispossessed*, and the complex and intricate issues of autonomy, privilege, and power raised by L. Timmel Duchamp's Marq'ssan Cycle are relevant here too.

I cite these examples to insist that a utopianism that doesn't claim perfection is perhaps the most useful kind. The moments and the intersections where utopia cracks to reveal continuing oppression must be exposed over and over again as part of any useful process of radical worldmaking. Antiprison activist and geographer Ruth Wilson Gilmore closes her book *Golden Gulag* by suggesting that utopia can best be found by insisting, with eyes open, that collective oppositional action has its effects despite the power of the forces arrayed against it and that the most important utopianism remains the one that can mobilize: a utopia you don't require a spaceship to get to, but that can be found, as Gilmore writes, in "something as modest as people getting on a bus" to go somewhere and change something (240).

3. Community and Conflict

On the theme of getting somewhere and changing something, I move out of fiction and into communities. The most obvious place to look for change would be among activist communities and groups, where people are involved in trying to remake the world in concrete and far-reaching ways. In not choosing that path, I don't want to detract from the importance of that work in any way. But I also want to highlight the work of complicated worldmaking, of utopian discourse and its discontents, of worldmaking critiques of race and gender and sexuality, in more quotidian and less obviously political locations. How, if at all, does this happen in the communities that form around less than radical science fiction media texts, and what role do gender, race, sexuality, and the conflicts around them play?

Stargate Atlantis embodies some of science fiction TV's most common and problematic racial and sexual politics. It focuses on its white male protagonists and keeps the women, strong as they may be, in the background. It insists that there are no queers in space, holding back from more than the slightest subtextual suggestion of nonheterosexual identity or desire. It maps a colonizing discourse of US militarism onto an othered galaxy populated by backward humans properly grateful for rescue from life-sucking aliens. And in terms of race, it falls victim to a combination of TV stereotyping and sci-fi cliché, killing off or writing out almost all Earthling characters of color and carefully marking the alienness of the Pegasus Galaxy natives who just happen to be the only major characters played by actors of color. But *Stargate Atlantis* also has a hugely active online fan community that engages in making art with and from the material the show provides. A significant proportion of fans regularly voice criticisms like mine. Such opinions lead to impassioned blog debates in fan communities, which have initiated many into queer critiques and antiracist ideologies.

When questions not only of taste but also of racism, sexism, and homophobia get involved, the textual and discursive spheres active fans build around and from their objects become very complex. I propose such spheres as modes of worldmaking that can participate in utopian discourses in oppressive ways and also activate the critical intersectional utopianism I've been discussing. Internet drama and Internet pleasure are worldmaking practices of the sort that theorists of performance like Jill Dolan and José Muñoz have described. But what kinds of worlds do they make, what happens when worlds collide, and how, if at all, do they attempt to change wider political worlds?

Media fans' worldmaking practices often invoke certain claims to the utopian. Science fiction fans, mostly women, have been sharing homoerotic, sexually explicit stories about media characters since the 1970s. In Stargate fandom, the two male leads elicit huge quantities of fiction and art. Slash fans' practices build queered worlds on and from shows in which same-sex desire is banished or permitted to very limited degrees. Love, sex, and lust are drawn over and mapped onto characters, and circulate between discursive and physical bodies in front of TV and computer screens. Some slash fans articulate their erotic sociability as a "queer female space" where shared sexual fantasies create a communal imaginary sphere. Kristina Busse, Robin Reid, and I have written about this, tracing the ways slash fans' virtual erotic play in and with a heteronormative text can destabilize it and open intersubjective zones where sexualized fantasy exchanges trouble norms of gender and desire.

Writing about queer counterpublics, Berlant and Warner describe the work of "elaborat[ing] new worlds of culture and social relations in which gender and sexuality can be lived, including forms of intimate association, vocabularies of affect, styles of embodiment, erotic practices, and relations of care and pedagogy." In reframing what counts as sex and blurring these erotic practices with intimate sociabilities, slash fan culture (at its most utopian) is capable of doing all these things.

Based on shared fantasy expressed through the exchange of words and images, these online worlds are framed by relations of cathexis to specific cultural objects and bounded by those objects' accessibility and appeal. In these ways of thinking about practices of fan fantasy, transformation of TV develops into a worldmaking force that seems to have little to do with the representational politics of the show whose subtext provides its jumping-off point. Fans often purposefully transform what they perceive to be their show's crucial lacks. In Stargate fandom, fictions explore the effect of the military's "Don't Ask, Don't Tell" regulations on the possibility of queerness on the US military colony of Atlantis and speculate about the deeper alterities of the show's sketched-out "alien" cultures. In some ways, we might read these rewritings as worldmaking practices in the model of the art queer theorist José Muñoz analyzes. He finds in minoritarian subjects' politicized appropriations of majority culture a way to "disassemble that sphere of publicity and use its parts to build an alternative reality" (196). But is it meaningful to think of fandom as in any sense "minoritarian"? And what violence might such thinking do to the perspectives of those who are minoritized within fan cultures, to those who are excluded from its utopias?

The transformation of TV worlds that have no access to queerness into online worlds that are soaking in it has no necessary relation to the privileges and oppressions that are the conditions of possibility for mainstream TV's lacks. Online queer participation may or may not extend into the offline world, and even there it can mean many different things. This relationship and its politics are cyclically debated in the fannish blogosphere, with the worlds of radical queer politics, liberal gay politics, and various iterations of academic queer theory in contention with one another.

Joanna Russ famously wrote that the "what if" of slash fanfiction was "what if I were free": if women were free to transform worlds according to their own desire. Conflicts over the meaning of slash fiction and the worlds it builds are vital reminders that "freedom" of desire, interpretation, and interaction doesn't mean the same thing for everyone. Fannish participation relies on certain material and social requirements, and for some (though not for all) these include a willingness, more easily accessed by those with greater privilege, to bracket problematic "real-life" concerns. While some fans emphasize "queer female space" as a utopian zone of shared subversive pleasure, those who draw attention to dynamics of misogyny, racism, or anti-Semitism in fiction, discussion, or the source texts around which they revolve may be seen as raining on everyone's parade.

When pleasure is privileged to this extent, any critique that is perceived as endangering that pleasure can be squashed all too easily. The utopian network can end up exclusionary, revolutionizing the lives of only a chosen few, whose belief in the power of their own resistant acts might blind them to their participation in others' marginalization or oppression. Making the white protagonists fuck might subvert the show's homophobic narratives and yet rewrite or exacerbate other dangerous norms. In the case of Stargate, that may mean slashed characters' bodies, and by extension the politics of their writers, can be more easily folded into the US nationalist, pro-military slant of the show. We can imagine other analogies very easily: feminist utopianisms and political organizations that reinforce white privilege, activist groups who claim to be working for equality for all and yet make excuses for sexism and homophobia, and so on. That's not to say that this is what all slash does or what all Stargate fans do; many other readings are of course possible. But a theory of the love- and lust-saturated queer worldmaking of slash fandom shouldn't erase the failures of that transformation, or the extent to which it can participate in building a self-theorized "queer female" world from which some bodies (those not white, not pretty, not normative enough) are erased.

The uncomfortable relationalities that have circulated around race in Stargate fandom on LiveJournal offer some alternative, less easily celebrated worldmaking practices. In March 2007, several Stargate fans angrily complained about another fan fiction writer's problematic representation of Ronon Dex, the dreadlocked Pegasus Galaxy inhabitant played by biracial Hawaiian actor Jason Momoa, as subservient to the white main characters of a story. In response, posts and debates detailing concerns about the interrelationship of privilege, TV stereotyping, and fannish pleasure spiraled across Stargate's interconnected fan networks. These were far from new concerns, having led fans of color to create several online communities dedicated to challenging the racial politics of TV and fandom. On this occasion the discussions had a particularly broad reach, variously emerging as flamewars, intense discussions of race and class privilege, and challenges to fans' desires to see their televisual transformations and queer female spaces as exempting them from potentially offending. The racially problematic dynamics underlying the show's presentation of a happy multicultural team were discussed by several commenters along with the significance of fannish transformation, of the queerness and femaleness of the spaces fans create around their shows, and of the challenges of acknowledging and combating racism within them.

One commenter described fandom as the "least fucked up, racist, sexist thing in this patriarchy," especially in comparison to the show itself (Jessant). For this commenter, perhaps by virtue of its queer female spaces, fandom as creativity is always already outside the patriarchal, racist paradigms of mainstream TV—and yet watching mainstream TV automatically embeds one in supporting said paradigms. Yet for others, the transformation of TV politics is not only possible but ethically imperative for fan writers. This interpretation rests on the worldmaking potential of fandom that is so powerfully expressed by proponents of fandom as queer female space, but brings it into an intersectional sphere where the utopian tendencies of fandom's self-description require serious autocritique if they can be taken seriously. Arguments made by many fans insist that being pro-gay, porn-positive, and situated amid queer interactive worlds built by desire is meaningless if the "fandom buzz" is eliminated for white fans by the recognition of dominant paradigms that privilege them (Telesilla; Moxie Brown). Links to the relevant discussions can be found in my blog entry "Televisual Transformation and Its Discontents."

The "queer female space" utopia is very far from perfectly utopian, then. But in the wake of these race discussions it is not entirely without the capacity for getting something done. One implication of these conversations about race seems to be that more intense demands are made of fannish metadiscourse: that it live up to its self-image by making something more of its source material than the source makes of itself. In the wake of this discussion and others like it, Peggy McIntosh's famous white-privilege checklist and antiracist blogs have become required reading for significant sections of media fan subculture. Such conversations are not as sexy as sharing porn, but they do perform their own kind of worldbuilding, challenging the positivity and political irrelevance of the affects most would associate with being a fan and tempering the focus on pleasure. So should this be understood as progress? Is Internet drama changing the world?

4. Worldchanging Argument

Critiques of racial privilege in queer worlds, fannish and otherwise, disorient expected relationships to objects and communities, marking the self-consciously subversive as embedded in dominant oppressive structures. In this case, they call attention to the politics of fannish love and encourage the coexistence of critical ambivalence. In fannish idiom, they engage in the harshing of squee as a necessary political intervention. I think this is a similar process to the autocritiques of utopianism in the science fiction texts I briefly discussed above.

But I want to maintain some caution about this creation of a new quasi-utopian narrative from the dystopianizing of another. We should not forget who is called upon to do the work of this valuable disorientation and the dangers of framing its progress as an educative and enlightening project. Fans of color may become the voices whose self-evident oppression does the work of a discomfort made political that may, in the end, be expected only to teach white fans to be better liberal multicultural subjects, who can talk the talk of avoiding offence but don't actually participate in the work of unmaking the worlds that overprivilege us. Muñoz writes about the "burden of liveness" that gets imposed on minority subjects who are expected to "perform for the amusement of a dominant power bloc" (187). For fans who find themselves in the racial, sexual, cultural, gender, or ability minority, that burden of liveness may become a burden of critique, where majority fans on the road to enlightenment feel entitled to be led by the hand through their mistakes. In decentering the utopian modes of worldmaking pleasure for privileged subjects, the comforts of fannish pleasure should not be denied to others.

One of my colleagues likes to complain about the structural tendencies of radical scholarship, which shows in detail how we are all enmeshed in oppressive ideology and then ends in upbeat fashion by finding a small glimmer of hope. My work tends to follow the opposite trajectory, beginning with hopeful possibilities and then dashing them. So why do I cling to utopia as a concept and a politics if it's so problematic and its deconstruction so crucial? Why not throw it away? My answer is that I believe, with Delany, that to think through bad alternatives is as important to changing the world as envisaging good ones. In "The Necessity of Tomorrows" he says:

> Without an image of tomorrow, one is trapped by blind history, economics, and politics beyond our control. One is tied up in a web, in a net, with no way to struggle free. Only by having clear and vital images of the many alternatives, good and bad, of where one can go, will we have any control over the way we may actually get there in a reality tomorrow will bring all too quickly.

Thinking through utopianisms and dystopianisms in fiction and practice, the building of worlds that challenge the ones we receive in multiple ways whether through writing or sex or performance or even getting into arguments, puts these many alternatives into practice. And by embracing this polymorphousness and contradiction, we could find ways to combine multiple realities, multiple pasts, with multiple hopes for better and warnings against worse futures. This would link modes of utopia, dystopia, and even heterotopia as escape, exit, exodus, elsewhere; dissent, fight, struggle; dream, plot, fantasy, theory. We could explore how these modes are all and always connected; discover connections and alliances even with -topias that might not participate in the specific politics of the counterhegemonic modes we prefer; and in thinking between and among different alternatives we might increase our awareness of how power structures define us, reexamine models of agency, and figure out how we can aspire to transformation in fiction, in politics, and in everyday life.

Works Cited

Berlant, Lauren and Michael Warner. "Sex in Public," *Critical Inquiry* 24.2 (1998): 547–66.

Butler, Octavia. *Parable of the Sower*. New York: Aspect, 1993.

Combahee River Collective. "Combahee River Collective Statement." *This Bridge Called My Back: Writings By Radical Women of Color*. Second ed. New York: Kitchen Table: Women of Color Press, 1983. 210–18.

Delany, Samuel R. "The Necessity of Tomorrows." *Starboard Wine*. Pleasantville, NY: Dragon Press, 1984. 23–36.

——. *Trouble on Triton: An Ambiguous Heterotopia*. Hanover, NH: Wesleyan University Press, 1996.

Dolan, Jill. *Utopia in Performance: Finding Hope at the Theater*. Ann Arbor: University of Michigan Press, 2005.

Duchamp, L. Timmel. *Alanya to Alanya*. Seattle: Aqueduct Press, 2005.

Gilmore, Ruth Wilson. *Golden Gulag: Prisons, Surplus, Crisis, and Opposition in Globalizing California*. Berkeley: University of California Press, 2007.

Le Guin, Ursula. *The Dispossessed*. London: Gollancz, 1974.

Lothian, Alexis. "Televisual Transformation and Its Discontents: Online Slash Fandom, 'Queer Female Space' and Race." 2008. May 8 2008. <http://queergeektheory.wordpress.com/2008/04/27/paper-from-console-ing-passions/>.

Lothian, Alexis, Kristina Busse, and Robin Reid. "Yearning Void and Infinite Potential: Online Slash Fandom as Queer Female Space," *English Language Notes* 45.2 (2007): 103–12.

McIntosh, Peggy. "Unpacking the Knapsack of White Privilege: A Personal Account of Coming to See Correspondences Through Work in Women's Studies." *Independent School* 10 May 2008 <http://seas.stanford.edu/diso/articles/knapsack.html>.

Mohr, Dunja. *Worlds Apart: Dualism and Transgression in Contemporary Female Dystopias*. Jefferson, NC: McFarland and Company, 2005.

Muñoz, José. *Disidentifications: Queers of Color and the Performance of Politics*. Minneapolis: University of Minnesota Press, 1999.

Russ, Joanna. "Pornography By Women, for Women, With Love." *Magic Mommas, Trembling Sisters, Puritans & Perverts*. Trumansburg, NY: The Crossing Press, 1985. 79–100.

Sallis, James. "Introduction." *Ash of Stars: On the Writing of Samuel R. Delany*. Ed. James Sallis. Jackson, MI: University Press of Mississippi, 1996.

Alexis Lothian is a PhD student in English and Gender Studies at the University of Southern California. She is writing her dissertation on queer theories of temporality and their imbrication with science-fictional representations of the future, and dreams of one day writing a book about the ways radical political movements and theories play out in online fan culture. She blogs irregularly and academically at queergeektheory.wordpress.com, but spends a lot more time on livejournal reading fanfic, obsessively following online arguments, and watching and making fan videos.

My mother, that old xenophobe,
always said:
Don't lie down with aliens unless you want to get up covered in ooze —
or suckers — or something gross —or possibly
carrying some kind of freaky alien baby in your forehead.

It's unnatural. Stick to your own kind.

But my love for you, dearest
ASofiilkadhnot'tgohewL ; erl
overrules all objections

Even those
of my friends, who've pointed out
on more than one occasion that your genitalia —
at least, what we assume is your genitalia —
is confusingly located, and difficult to classify.

How are you gonna, you know,
do it? Christine asked me,
only last week.

And aren't you worried about those
rumors we've heard, that the Fjalhrfians
eat their mates?

ASofiilkadhnot'tgohewL ; erl, I couldn't
care less. My heart is yours
so you may as well devour the rest of me, as
far as I'm concerned.

I ask only
this one

small

thing:

Tell me that you love me too, as you engulf
me in the manly vagina of your hungry arms.

Robyn Fleming

Section III. Internet Drama

Response to Internet Drama Panel: Four Things I Get from Internet Drama

Micole Sudberg

There are four things I get from Internet drama that I don't get from real-life interactions about political issues:

1. It's very immediate. It convinced me that oppressions that didn't affect me personally were still going on, were critical, were urgent. Textbooks didn't work because they were dated: *The Bridge Called My Back* convinced me that feminism in the '80s had problems, but surely everything had been fixed by the time I was reading it. (I know, I know.) Newspapers I could explain away as isolated incidents, extreme examples. (I know, I know.) But—people I knew and respected were pulling the same shit people had pulled twenty or thirty years ago. People I knew and respected and whose daily lives I followed, even if I wasn't involved in them, were having to deal with the shit of oppressions and discrimination the same way they had to deal with the kinds of troubles we shared. It wasn't something that happened a long time ago anymore; it wasn't just something that happened to strangers anymore.

2. The Internet—and especially LJ—provided backup. In a work situation, in school, on the street, in my family, I was often alone; I didn't know I could ask for help; if I asked for help it was refused; if I asked for help, it was later, after much suffering. Knowing that I have a network of people that will answer the call if I put it out, or take up the work when I can't continue, makes the struggle against oppressions seem much more manageable.

3. Like I said in another post, the time delay in Internet dramas gives me time to strip out the concessions, conciliations, soft-pedaling, defusing other people's anger, disclaiming my own, and the other placatory gestures that are such an ingrained response to power that they often signal female identity even

in text-based conversations. It gives me time to figure out how justified my anger is, how much of it I want to express, how powerful I want that expression to be. This is so much easier to do with an asynchronous medium than in real time.

4. The medium that benefits me. Face to face I'm a short, fat woman with a high, soft, and young-sounding voice; these are all things that work against me, because they cause people to discount me and to discount my anger. I have to convince people that these are personal traits, not invalidating arguments. Online, my voice is text, which is something I have the inclination, training, and expertise to use.

I wanted to add, re: anger and Alexis' point about white people getting listened to more, that the perception of anger is also racialized: I was really surprised when I started reading The Angry Black Woman because Tempest so seldom sounds angry! My friends of color get way more flack for anger in their criticisms of racist actions than I do, even though I think most of them sound far more even-tempered than I do.

Can Internet Drama Change the World?

Panel Description: Impassioned blog debates have initiated many into feminist praxis, queer critique, and antiracist ideology. But they also generate frustration, disillusionment, and flamewars. Participants in online political discussions are frequently derided for wasting energy that would be better expended in "real" political work than in online drama, but many can also attest to the importance of online participation to developing understandings of power and privilege. This roundtable will raise questions of the validity and importance of online micro-political interventions, and their relationship to social justice activism on a larger scale.

Panelists: Alexis Lothian (moderator), K. Tempest Bradford, Woodrow Hill, Julia Starkey, K. Joyce Tsai. Other named participants: Cyn, Lesley Hall, Julian, Ladyjax, Liz, Tisha, Magenta

Alexis: Is there drama as we speak?

Woodrow: Is anyone twittering it?

laughter

Tempest: Did anyone go to the Tiptree auction last night? I could cause some Internet drama right now. There was an invasion of the Tiptree with strange performance art.
(http://www.tiptree.org/)

Cyn: The robots?
(http://sf0.org/lonestar/taskDetail/?id=2137)

Audience: Those were the Think Galactic people.
(http://www.thinkgalactic.org/)

Tempest: Perhaps they think they were clever. I dunno, I wasn't there. But hey, I'm going to blog about it.

laughter

Tempest: There's enjoying yourself and then there's grandstanding and creating a spectacle. That's just my opinion. DRAMA.

Audience: Are there going to be jazz hands every time there's drama?

Tempest: YES.

Woodrow: I need that, Tempest with the jazz hands, DRAMA!! for my email sig. PHEAR ME!!!!!!

Audience: Dun dun DUNNNNN.

Alexis: I suggested this panel because Internet drama changed my world, and sf and the Internet changed my politics. I'd like to talk about whether online political stuff is just drama or what kind of activism it can be. As I was thinking about that, the Le Tigre song "Get off the Internet" was playing in my head, the relevance of the Internet, life, and blogging offline.

Let's talk about drama. Let's not actually HAVE drama. No getting really bogged down in the rights and wrongs of the Open Source Boob Project, or what people have been saying on their blogs or on panels and going, "You're wrong!" I'll say things if we need to get things rolling. Panelists, please introduce yourselves.

Tempest: I'm Tempest, I blog as Angry Black Woman, so you know, already drama. **laughter** Yes, I've been the perpetrator of and participant in much Internet drama in the three years since I started doing Internet stuff. I admit I'm kind of addicted to fighting with people on the Internet. I really really love it. I am the XCD comic, someone's WRONG on the Internet, it's five in the morning! Can't have that! Where I come down on this side of the equation is that: yes, Internet drama CAN change the world and my experience has shown me what ways it can and what ways it cannot. (Links: http://xkcd.com/386/; http://theangryblackwoman.com/)

Alexis: Tell me about times you've been inspired vs. discouraged because of Internet drama, with examples.

Tempest: I get discouraged whenever it's conversation about race. Obviously I have those conversations about race. I always feel discouraged in those arguments because they're the same arguments every time, and it never seems to go anywhere, just having to do it over and over. When I started Angry Black Woman, it was to put up a post about privilege, so that when white people tell me racism is over, I don't have to explain it again, just point people to it and go, "Just look at this post."

But I've been encouraged, because despite all the times I'm in the midst of horrible drama, where the people against you say your tone is wrong, why can't you be nice—bullshit bullshit? There are people who tell me, this post you made helped me understand a thing better, changed my mind. I say to people reading my posts, if you ever feel you are called out on racism/sexism, go find somebody who is of that (type), go find a female friend who will tell you the truth, ask their opinion. A lot of the time, you don't know, you need someone else to check you. I said this to a reader, and he and his friend had a conversation and his mind was changed.

Joyce: I'm oyceter on LJ and inadvertently caused a lot of drama, when I didn't mean to! This is my first WisCon without my head exploding!

I started my blog to talk about depression and Buffy, not drama, unless talking about season six, which, hahaha. **audience laughter** I was lurking on Micole's LJ, watching people talking about Buffy and feminism, and I didn't understand a lot of the arguments a lot of the time. Like when people would ask, "Why are all the men bringing up rape over and over in this conversation?" and I thought, "I don't understand, isn't that a valid point?" And then I started seeing it over and over and I thought, "You know, there's a pattern there!" A lot of my thinking about feminism was shaped by Internet drama.

Two years ago at WisCon 30, at the Cultural Appropriation panel, one of my friends was on it, Yoon, and everyone was talking about appropriation of white culture, culture is free, art changes, and I remember going back to hotel room and talking with my friend and not being able to articulate why it was so frustrating. Not being able to say why. And I went home and Yoon posted on the Cultural Appropriation drama, and I posted, and I said all the talk was about white people. At the time I didn't even know the term POC.

(http://oyceter.livejournal.com/441959.html)
(http://yhlee.livejournal.com/602114.html)

And I had comment after comment after comment of people saying I was not understanding the full intricacy of white culture, and I was like wow. I was really surprised. I had personal interactions with people; I liked you! And I was like, HUH. I was like WOW. Ok*AY*. And then…after a while, after seeing the same arguments over and over and over on racism 101, some of my friends and I decided to do International Blog Against Racism Week, now in its third year this August, one of my positive experiences of Internet drama, it's made me go ahead and do more things. I've done IBARW, not world shaking but it's something. I've found more people in my local community, more to talk about things, sometimes I have to retire from Internet for a while while my head explodes, stop being stupid!!! but it's in how I formulate things and how I look for things. It's make me look for more POC authors and events and things.
(http://community.livejournal.com/ibarw/)

Woodrow: I'm Asim, I'm a male belly dancer and in the SCA, my Internet drama is so old and ancient, the Google does not have it. Usenet. Telnet. More to the point, I've done Internet drama. I like to tell myself I'm done with it, but it's never quite true. I talk in the real world about the same things, pro-choice issues, feminist issues Christian issues, evolution vs. creationism issues. It's an intersecting balance. All of which is still in a stack of papers in a corner of my house. I got re-involved in things in the feminist blogosphere, also reading comics, started taking that up, started converting one of the spaces I was blogging into a safe space (for) egotistical, frustrating, arrogant, I don't understand, can you please explain it to me, people, people who say things like "affirmative action is horrible, you just need to suck it up" and I don't go, "You just don't understand." I have to actually try to explain. People don't understand why other people are angry. Anger is a real emotion.

Julia: I blog as Sparkymonster. I too in the day of Usenet was a little drama llama sometimes. My point was the lack of information about women and sex online. There are a lot of posts about me talking about sex. Like a LOT. For two and a half years. When I first got into LJ, my blog was just fannish, and then local people in my area started adding each other. People I know in my life who aren't fan friends, who don't get what I'm talking about, and then the fans who are like, "Why are you talking about bacon again, omg shut up." So I must give backstory. What is this thing you speak of? Positive, rage coma, this is so wrong.

For example, Supernatural drama. There's a black man touching the lead! And in some cases, guy just kind of brushed against him, people were saying "omg it's so hot brushing against him" and I just lost my mind all over the place. It was kind of great. This one woman, she was black, and she just thought that that basic level of racism was okay, because no one had challenged that woman, and so people were just going, "Oh well I guess you can just be gross and racist like that and it's okay." But, I lost my mind on the Internet and it did have some positive outcomes!
(http://sparkymonster.livejournal.com/182863.html)

The frustrating thing is when I have friends kind of toss me under the bus. Wait what just happened, this was just a horrible racist sexist thing, WHAT? Like the post on Harry Potter fandom was going crazy over "miscegenation." That was fun times. There was a series of slashfic prompts; fetish prompts were like "spanking," "exhibitionism," and one of them was "miscegenation." They were like, "What's the problem? It's listed in a book!" *[Asim headdesks.]* Someone rolled in with bestiality. WHAT? I don't know what your problem is! I went into it. My parents are a mixed couple and I am mixed race and you're coming to me and going, "Hey, you're a fetish object." Thanks. I posted a photo of my parents being snuggly and cute, and my friends said, ohhh I just want to just look at this cute photo of your parents and I want to be happy. Such privilege, not to notice. Well, I too would like to just be happy, but I can't, which is why I'm talking about it. Or people who say "I don't understand why you need to be so obsessed with the racism, I just think of you as white."

(http://zvi-likes-tv.livejournal.com/407901.html; http://oyceter.livejournal.com/629173.html)

Internet drama gives you the comforting sense of back up. People are backing you up. They're not in your living room, but they're there.

Tempest: To what Julia said, you get involved in Internet drama and you find out some of your friends are crazy people. How people act before and after they knew I was Angry Black Woman. Now I have an icon that says "OH SHIT you just found out I was the Angry Black Woman!" There's people who consider me a "safe" black woman. I enjoy the things they enjoy, they consider me one of those black people who're not really black. So many people say some really questionable racist stuff on other people's posts or their posts. The sad thing is, it makes me stop trusting people I don't know that well. I thought you were a friend of mine. And the way they backpedal when they find out. "We're not talking about you, it's those others." Then having to deal with that stuff in real life too. I was at a Thanksgiving dinner with a bunch of friends, in NY, jobs, no family around, and someone talking about Deep Space Nine, something incredibly racist, about this episode Avery Brooks wrote or directed…

Several members of the audience: "Far Beyond the Stars." (http://en.wikipedia.org/wiki/Far_Beyond_the_Stars)

Tempest: Yes! "Oh, I just want to get back to the space station and it doesn't matter anyway because he's black." And everyone laughed, and she went "No, no, that was racist of me" and someone went "No, no, you're right" and she went hee hee hee hee, and I got up and left. And later they went, "Why didn't you say something then? Why go off and post on the Internet about it?" And I'm like, "You laughed at racism and I'm childish?" People don't want you to speak up when stuff like that happens, and then get offended when you DO.

Joyce: In the Cultural Appropriation Debate of Doom, suddenly I was this angry Asian girl! People come into my blog to comment and are SCARED of me. Before, I was like, oh some people are reading me, I was like friendly and happy and nice, I'm not going to bite your head off, and suddenly people thought my voice was scary! It was interesting to see how when anger came up, on race or sex, people would start to back off. It was very interesting to see the polarization of my friends list after that.

Julia: There's a lot of pressure to be polite and friendly. I admit, there are times when I'm like, "Oh I'm sure you didn't mean that," and sort of softball it, but, when people say, "Why do you have to be so angry about that?" I'm like, "I DUNNO, why do you have to be so horrible and offensive!?" Homophobia, racism, sexism, transphobia, no matter what, if you bring it up, you are mean and scary, and it's because people don't want to examine their own stuff! One time this guy I know was like, "Well I'm not racist, so I didn't get involved in that discussion." and I was like "Oh hai, if I can admit to having some racist thoughts, feelings in me, why can't you, Mr. white heterosexual guy," but he was like, "But I'm not racist!"

Ladyjax: And I get that attitude, (of people telling me) you're not like those angry black women, and I'm like, "Yeah I was a debutante, but I can unleash it!" I go into hoohas about (...) and suddenly you reveal yourself and they go oh I didn't know. And I'm like, "Oh, did you MISS the Angela Davis icon that says fight the power???" *laugh* And there is a sense of betrayal, the kumbayah approach, I thought we're all fans together. I make this decision, right now, YOU are the person who's going to get it.

Woodrow: When I started posting on those issues, I have an Angry Young Black man blog, and another blog, and what happens is that it creates that kind of tension and people say I didn't realize, I read your post on that; that's really angry! And I say yes, well that's because I'm really good at packaging my anger into nice discrete elements. Like Malcolm X put it, "Everyone here can easily understand what's pissing me off." *[Ladyjax joins in and recites the Malcolm X quote in unison with Woodrow]*.

Julia: There's people who say stuff like "I don't really think of you as Latina, I think of you as white." My friend had a whole series of things to say, but...she just burst into tears because it was so intense. And actually that made him realize what a horrible thing he had said. I'm not recommending tears as a strategy. But sometimes it is helpful.

Tempest: Sometimes being reasonable just makes Internet drama worse.

general audience agreement

Magenta: Fandom is totally not kumbayah. But it has come a long way in the last 20 years.

Woodrow: I've been in the SCA for (mumble mumble) years. I go to our biggest event, and I can count the people of color on my hands. Maybe a couple of toes. And I go back on my blog and talk about it. There's maybe five black male belly dancers in the world. Now, when I reverse that, I start to see why it's important to understand the issues of women, they're dealing with the thing I'm dealing with, in the real world. People read that and go OHhhhhh.

Joyce: Well, I'm heterosexual, I'm able bodied, I make money and stuff, and I should remember this, and remember how it felt to have people not back me up. And I have to remember how to be a better ally for other people.

Tempest: Yes. Internet drama has made me a better ally. It's made me better at understanding oppressions that aren't my oppressions, and when I fuck up, what to do. I'm black, I can't fuck up! **laughter** I was in a writing group, and wrote an alternate history, where ancient Egypt was the dominant power, and I had these suicide bombers and they were Jewish, and in my mind they were so neat, and I had it all worked out in my head in an 1800-word story. One of the people in my writing group said, you know if I had read this without knowing you, I would be so pissed right now at you, and knowing that you didn't intend to be offensive, I could talk with you. I could feel myself going in my head, "No, that's not what I *meant*," but I shut myself up and sat there listening for 20 minutes and I felt whatever Veronica had to say was more important than what I thought I was doing. After that session I was like, "You know, I'll probably change it."

The next day, Lisa M.'s story went up on *Fantasy Magazine*. She had a story that started off, "Today was a good day to sell a child to the peddlers." The story was about a little girl whose mother sells her to the traveling peddlers and yay we can make her work, but she's so horrible they leave her by the side of the road. But, a guy who is Romany said, dude, this is a selling children to the gypsies story, what the hell is wrong with you. The comments were full of people going "Well, I didn't see the stereotype, so you should stop being offended." So, because of drama, I could just stop and listen, and change my mind. I learned something. In fact, I think I deserve a cookie. **laughter** (http://www.darkfantasy.org/fantasy/?p=544)

Audience: We're working on this, all of us, at WisCon. But on the other hand I've gone to at least one panel where some people were NOT working on it. How do we take that stuff, the drama, and put it in a place we can refer newbies to? It would be so much faster.

Liz: I don't think you can necessarily make it faster. Going through the process is important.

Woodrow: (points at Liz) You have the backup sticker? You have the proprietary boob sticker. The map, it happens that way. The faq is good, but it's not going to go anywhere because the conversation doesn't get seeded properly.

Joyce: That's why I find the Internet valuable, well, I'm like a happy happy Internet touchy person. When I got into Carl Brandon Society, they said we've had this same conversation with the same people, over and over. But I found people coming from all over, of course it's limited to people who have computers, access, it expanded who I know about, or can talk with, besides emailing or meeting.

Julia: I use delicious for my bookmark tagging. "I see you're having that conversation on that issue: LINKDUMP. One of the best ones the Amptoons post, "How to not be an Insane-o White Person."

(http://delicious.com/starkeymonster/forcluelesswhitepeople; http://www.amptoons.com/blog/archives/2005/12/02/how-not-to-be-insane-when-accused-of-racism)

Audience: YES. Mmm-hmm!

Julia: If I just gave them the right article, tragically that is false, some people aren't interested in working on their own issues.

Joyce: Actually, could we compile a list of links?

Julia: I don't understand about feminists and women of color, it's like "Wow, here's a LIBRARY."

Cyn: Kate Harding, Fat is Unhealthy, that's another one.

Lesley: I'm a historian. I work on issues of gender and sexuality and history. These things just have to keep going on and on and on. There is always someone coming in for the first time who has not encountered these ideas. They're not in a position where knowing the history will speak to them. They have to have that conversation real time. I'm not being a nihilist historian, but I'd like to perhaps quote you a woman called Stella Brown, who was a British feminist socialist sex activist of the early twentieth century, at the age of 75, seriously crippled and going blind, she wrote to her friend about the seriously unsatisfactory progress of abortion reform, "You did not expect to win at the first battle, surely?" On birth control, we get there in the end, long hard struggle, doesn't happen because we have the brilliant idea things could be better, it takes a long process of dissemination. Things do change, for example the campaign to abolish slavery started with handful of people everyone thought were raving mad. It's funny when people write novels that are completely ahistorical and the characters think, "oh, slavery, terribly bad."

laughter

Alexis: There's the feeling people have that we are moving on, but then suddenly, you link into the conservative blogosphere and it's hard. They're having their own drama, and they think they're changing the world in the opposite direction.

Woodrow: I have a couple of friends who are very conservative. Part of what I've taken on is to talk to them about the issues that are important to me, and to find that middle ground. Understand the enemy by talking to them. There may not be a way to live in harmony with them. And it's gonna be on the good guys. Because I think we all know the bad guys aren't going to make the effort.

Ladyjax: Being the special colored friend. I know a black person. Then you get the black person who shows up and says, "All you crazy negros, I'm not like you." And I'm like, "Okay, sooner or later something's gonna happen to you, and you're gonna need some backup."

And it's a way in which people are totally wrong, and do you value that friendship so much more than this shit that's going down right now, and this is bad but, trying to be patient and hold someone's hand and then making the decision, you know, I don't care—we're telling you get off the Internet and go to the library and better yet, go talk to someone my age, and ask them. My lack of patience has increased on certain issues. I'm sorry this is hurtful, I'm sorry you're crying, guess what, this is 24/7 for me. Put on your big girl panties and deal.

Joyce: It's important to take things offline as well. I was like, "OMG my friends in real life don't know my politics, and my family, I'm not out to them." The time, the energy, the bravery, to go to work and having people go "I don't think the Muslim terrorists in *Iron Man* were that bad," and I'm like, "Okay, I cannot lambaste you because you pay my paycheck." Weighing the consequences: is this the time to make a stand, is this something I should lose my job over? Making these choices, not like, "This is at work and I can't say anything," but more, how can I let people know this is not okay in front of me. In my presence, please don't do this. It's not funny to me, it is a real issue. And I've been that Asian friend who goes hahaha and then thinks later, "OMG what was I thinking?" When you're here, I don't want to hear this stuff.

Julian: How do you address it in different situations? Making it about yourself. The other point, about making a point over and over? The original people burn out, but someone else takes up the mantle.

Tempest: I have tried hard recently not to treat people who wander by my blog like the last 10 people who did it. Sometimes it is brave of them to come to a blog called Angry Black Woman and go, "But I don't understand! Aren't we all human?" There is a learning curve. I have been trying really hard. Sometimes I have to kind of retrain my regular commenters not to attack. Sometimes there's an overreaction. I have stages. One: here's some resources, go educate yourself. Stage two, no really, go educate yourself. Stage three, get the fuck off my blog.

Julia: It's so important for allies not to always punt that up to people of color all the time. Go do it yourself, don't kick it to me. It's exhausting!

Woodrow: I opened it up for the political debacle, as a safe space for you to be essentially racist. And people, well, they did it. People stepped into this debacle. It was a teaching moment. I wanted them to teach themselves, and me, where they are coming from.

Joyce: Just rant! Not having to worry about being polite and stuff, the separation of education vs. MY need.

Ladyjax: I'm done with talking about white people, let's POC talk with each other.

Joyce: It's very important to have that space, to have other people doing that educating, doing that stuff, and today I can relax. Or can be like, "OMG!" and have other people there, having your back.

Alexis: It's so uncomfortable, I'm often the white person saying exactly the same thing people of color have just said, like twelve of them. I say it and everyone goes OHHHH. How horrible!

laughter

Tisha: I teach a women's studies 101 class, I bring issues from Internet drama back to the classroom for teaching purposes.

Liz: People use "Internet drama" as a put down or to trivialize a discussion. But it's activism and political work.

Audience: Personal drama, too, might be important.

Woodrow: I lost a girlfriend that way. If it's personal, I take it off the net.

Sarah: Anger keeps coming up, and drama as a synonym for anger. Anger is expected, conflict, drama, on the Internet. People are less freaked out on the Internet than in real life. That's why it's great ally training. So many of us are trained to run away from conflict.

Joyce: I learned how to be angry on my blog. As a small Asian girl I'm not expected to be angry in real life. I express myself better in writing, I have time to think about things. I learned how to process my anger and be okay with it on my blog.

Julia: Personal drama on the Internet can be good way of personally processing, but it's a crap way to settle an argument. It can't fix it.

Tempest: Personal drama actually relates to the larger issues of racism and sexism, things are going south, a person said something crazy on the Internet about race, or about me, but it intersects in the larger context. It's really hard to deal with in the larger context. It's not just between me and you, it's about larger things, and you make it not about me and you when you put in on the Internet.

Alexis: Anyone have one sentence more?

Audience: Thank all you guys for doing this. Last year, all these people were running around, my eyes were bugging out of my head. I didn't realize, can Internet drama save the world? It can transform it; it certainly transformed mine. I went from Jewish woman who happened to be Hispanic to a Latina who happens to be Jewish, and last year when I was like BLACK PEOPLE omg, and I started reading all these LJ things, and it has transformed other people's lives. You have had an influence.

> [This is a rough transcription from notes taken by Liz Henry during the panel; it is not transcribed from a recording and may not be precisely what was said.]

Not All Trolls Lurk Under Bridges

Cynthia Gonsalves

§§§ where I was then §§§

Many of you out there have heard about the systematic trollage of one of my favorite science fiction and fantasy conventions, WisCon, over this past weekend. A young woman managed in one fell and pestilent swoop to hit all the spaces for a blanket win of Asshole Bingo. The troll thread she started on SomethingAwful.com was full of attacks on fat people, transpeople, people with disabilities, women, etc. You get the picture, don't you?

I was moderating a panel on self-care strategies for activists, which got caught up in the trollage; one of my co-panelists was singled out for abuse as a transperson, and the other co-panelist had her chronic disease [fibromyalgia] labeled "imaginary." Me, I was just another fat woman offending the troll's sensibilities by being Openly Fat in Public. The substance of our panel seems to have been too twee for her tastes; she was more offended by who the people in the front of the room were. And of course, if any of you had the misfortune to read the original posts (which have now been taken down), the troll got me and the other woman panelist confused. Sloppy, sloppy troll.

When I found out about all this crap last Sunday night, my initial desire was to smash her like a bug with my fat self; however, I got over that quickly. Losing my temper wasn't going to be effective, and I needed my friends around me not to lose their tempers either. My wrath got hot again when I heard that children of some of my friends and acquaintances had gotten targeted, but seeing effective group action beginning to take place helped me cool off again.

When I found out that this person had been identified by tracking the slime trail she'd left on the Internet, I knew the Threefold Rule [whatever you put out in the universe will come back to you three times as strong] was kicking in. The technopagan part of me was nodding. I have no problem with people having brought the troll's behavior to the attention of the Dean of Students at her university, but I firmly disapprove of making physical threats against her.

I found out later that she is a troubled person struggling with an eating disorder, and that elicits some compassion for her in me, but not enough to give her a free pass on this one. Actions have consequences. What makes me particularly sad is that as I've begun on a size acceptance path, I've found some tremendous writing about struggling with and recovering from eating disorders out in the fat blogosphere that the original poster rejects so violently. She's managed to piss off and alienate people who could have been strong supporters in her path to healing.

Part of me is somewhat surprised that the WisCon community hasn't had to deal with this kind of attack sooner, because we collectively give the finger to the sexist, racist, homophobic, transphobic trolls' sense of what is right and proper in the universe. I'm hoping that we can work on protection strategies against the inevitable attacks; we can't lock things down hard without killing the vitality of the community. There are always going to be People Being Wrong on the Internet, and directing their wrongheaded nastiness at us.

§§§ where I'm at now §§§

Now, looking back almost six months, the most important thing to work on is our community response. This really is part of the Women (and their allies) Back Each Other Up concept. We have to make it clear that no matter what nastiness comes our way, we aren't going to be silenced by the attacks. The trolls want us to shut up and go away so that they can remain comfortable and righteous in their worldview. Our response needs to combine protection from attacks without making it hard to talk about what happens at WisCon among ourselves and the outside world.

I continue to be saddened by the knowledge that some of the people who were singled out in the troll attack may not feel comfortable coming back to future WisCons, and our community will be lessened by their absence.

As for the original troll, a tiny part of me hopes she eventually figures out where she screwed up so badly. It's a useful lesson to figure out who your real allies are, and the troll communities don't seem to be where they'll live, because they'll turn on you if you're no longer amusing.

Cynthia is a fourth generation native of the SF Bay Area and earned a BS in chemistry from Santa Clara University. Her career in the Silicon Valley has combined various uses of analytical and surface chemistry techniques with electron microscopy and focused ion beam milling. This enables her to keep her indulgent feline overlady supplied with cat food and kitty litter and maintain her love of reading, knitting, jewelry making, and San Jose Sharks hockey. WisCon has been a treasured part of her calendar since 1998.

An Open Letter to Zathlazip and the Rest of WisCon 32

Hederahelix

There is a lot of confusion about what happened at WisCon. This was my first trip to WisCon, and my trip began with a red-eye flight; so I started the con with a pretty substantial sleep defecit. However, I do have a lot of rather strong feelings about the incidents of harassment, so I'm going to write up what I know. Plenty of other people have written about this, but I wanted there to be an article in which we all get to see the actual consequences on some people of the actions of the person in question. I have tried very hard not to cue as fact anything here that I could not personally verify.

Here's what I know. At some point toward the end of the con (please don't ask me exactly when, the whole con is a blur), I was sitting around having some drinks with some friends, both old and new. We were engaging in a very casual post-mortem of the con: what went well, which panels didn't, what we'd like to talk about next year—you know, like you do. Then someone in that group mentioned having heard that one con participant had been spouting fatophobic and transphobic stuff. Even then, there were rumors that it had been significant enough an expression of those forms of hate that the person was escorted out of the con, but I cannot confirm that rumor.

At some unspecified point in time later on Monday night after the Dead Cow party, I found myself in a hotel room with about five other people. Being geeks, we all had our laptops. We were, you know, cruising around, reading fic, generally having a good time, like you do.

Then someone found the link to the reposting at SASS. I am clear on that for two reasons. First, it was only after I got home to California (a day delayed because of weather in Dallas that canceled my flight) that I saw the second half of the post in the Google cache linked to by Angry Black Woman (ABW). I mention this because I was in the room with three people who appeared in the photos that were being mocked in the SASS thread, but after I got home, several more people in that room got mentioned in the second half of the post. In fact, I think by the time all was said and done, between the full original post and the SASS thread, everyone in the room but me was mentioned. So, it is fair to say that I've actually seen plenty about the way that both the initial post in its Google cache form and the SASS thread affected people, because I got to watch a lot of it play out in real time as the people whom it happened to saw it, which is frankly an experience I could have lived without. Because I saw how hurt people were in private. That is just not okay. Period.

Now, look. I know that everybody in the United States has a legal right to free speech. I have the legal right to say most things I want to, with a few notable exceptions. But there are legal rights, and then there is common courtesy, and the people at SASS are made of fail on that front. I have read or skimmed every page of that thread. I am perfectly aware that the posters at SASS could give a rat's ass about common courtesy. I don't expect it from them.

I do, however, expect better from people who attend WisCon. When I write up my con report, about all the good things that happened and the other less good things, I'm not going to leave out the things that I thought were problematic. But even the people who totally steamed me under the collar at panels (and lo, there were many) were people who were implicitly committed to working toward common courtesy. We might disagree about how to get there; we might be at very different places in the process. But everyone I met at WisCon, including the ones who said really problematic things, were trying. Everyone except for one person: Zathlazip.

One of the things about the WisCon program book that impressed me was how clearly it laid out that common courtesy was a good thing and that sometimes the needs of one group came into conflict with another. Let me quote from the "Navigating the Crowded Con" section of the pocket program: "Smoke and scents travel quickly, and air won't move if you ask it to. The hotel uses scented cleaning products, the Gathering features perfume and spices; the Dealers' room includes incense and old books. Some members need fragrance to manage pain and mood, and some medications have strong scents. For some members, smoke or fragrance triggers asthma, migraine, or illness; these effects are cumulative. We ask that you limit your use of scented products when possible. Washing your hands after smoking makes a difference."

Now, see, *that* is common courtesy in a situation in which peoples' definitions of courtesy come into conflict. Some people with issues with scents want to be in a completely scent free zone because scents set off very real health issues. Other people use scents to manage their own health issues. How do you negotiate that conflict? You talk about it openly and try to limit the impact of your issues on other people as best you can. And you warn people who have issues in advance where those issues are most likely to be triggered. You do that regardless of how trivial you think the issue is or how much you dislike the people or group in question because that's what it means to live in groups. Our conflicting needs and different opinions crash into each other and create conflicts. There isn't an issue to argue about there; conflict is inevitable. The question is how you deal with that conflict.

The organizers of WisCon thought about the consequences of the actions of the con members and made an effort to foresee reasonable outcomes of various events. This is what grown-ups do.

And here's where we get to reason number two that I remember perfectly clearly where I was when I saw the thread: I saw the emotional fallout as people who were in the SASS post saw what was being done to them on SASS. I watched as smart, funny, beautiful people were deeply hurt by a bunch of small-minded people without lives or human emotions mocking them for sport. Trust me, as for the targets of that hatred, these are folks whom I'm sure get this all the time, as a number of them have rightly said on LiveJournal and in other places. The mocking on SASS isn't really what people are hurt and angered by, especially since the information has come out that it's possible that the poster at SASS who appeared to be the troll in question might not have been her but a hacked account. (Again, nobody's yet sure who did what at SASS. Yet. The Google-fu is strong in this group, and that may also be revealed later.) For now, I am willing to err on the side of giving the initial troll the benefit of the doubt, but that does not reduce her culpability in this in any way. Even if I write this post as if the poster on SASS using the icon of the photo of the WisCon troll was a fake account, Zathlazip does not get a pass on anything.

What people are hurt and angered most by is that someone paid $45 in membership and came into the con with what appears to be the express intent to mock the congoers. And that she saw nothing wrong with posting that mockage to a hateful website.

How do I know that she's not sorry? I've been closely following what she has said in public. She has continued to say in her "apologies" (which read more like her being unhappy than she has been caught and called out on this than anything resembling remorse for her actions) that she thought her original post was funny and that she was not sorry for most of what she wrote. In posts well after the initial Something Awful post was taken down, she has continued to refer to all the con attendees as lesbians, which you know, would totally work for me, since there were plenty of attractive women there, and I'd love to think that they were all part of my community, but it's clear from her use of the word that she thinks that the word *lesbian* is an insult. I do not put up with it when people at work use that language around me or when family members do that, even if the people in question are teenagers who think they know everything. I would have hoped a 25-year-old graduate student was more mature than that, and most of the ones I know are, but clearly this one isn't.

I could do nothing but watch as people were wounded not because they were mocked for their size, race, gender, disability, and/or sexuality, but because it happened to them at one of the places where they worked hard to try to create space where they did not have to deal with as much of that shit as they do on a regular basis. I watched them wince as they braced themselves knowing what the kind of people at SASS did for sport and knew that it was only going to get worse. I felt the rage swell as we all realized the level of betrayal of community norms that the person in question had perpetrated.

That is not okay. Nobody should go into a con and photograph people for the express purpose of mocking them. And you sure as hell don't post that stuff to a place like SomethingAwful and not expect this to happen. And then! And then, you really, really do not continue to use the same kinds of insults in your posts after the fact.

Look, Zathlazip and your ilk, if you don't like women, fine. You don't have to. Engage in all the self-hate you want. If you aren't interested in talking about gender, race, sexuality, ability, etc. in a meaningful way, find another con to go to. Go to Comic Con. That is totally boy space with lots of boy gamers. (Incidentally, there were plenty of gamers at WisCon. You were sitting next to one in one of your panels because you were, I realized belatedly, sitting next to me.) We weren't there for a gaming convention; we were there for a feminist science fiction convention. We were there because having been to gaming and comic conventions where the fanboys run the show, having been to academic conferences in which the papers of fangrrls are not attended by the fanboys, we wanted a place to express both of those parts of ourselves and not have to defend or justify our right to be both. Perhaps it is unfortunate for you that the con that happens in your geographical neck of the woods isn't focused the way you wanted it to be focused, but if that's the case, go to your local comic convention and mock women's bodies there. Lord knows that too many comic books and games, much as I enjoy them, excel at that. Go. Be with your people.

But do not come into my space and wreck it for us. Because even before this happened, there were plenty of problems with that space. The difference is most of us there who had those problems were strategizing about effective ways to change that. You seemed to have no investment in doing so, which as far as I'm concerned means that you don't belong there.

As I mentioned before, this was my first WisCon. I attended with several people who had been before, and when we got there on Thursday, one of them immediately made plans to go help with packet stuffing. (For people who haven't been, at registration everybody gets a packet with your badge, your pocket program, and a few other forms. Those packets are assembled partly by official Concom members, but also by regular attendees who help out at the beginning of the con.)

In retrospect, this was the best thing I could have done as a newbie. Because when my roommates went to volunteer, I tagged along and volunteered too. What that meant was that even before registration happened, I felt a sense of partial ownership of the con. (I also helped with breakdown after the Gathering. I didn't volunteer for the rest of the con, but I'm glad I did at least that much.)

At opening ceremonies, the Concom members asked all the volunteers to stand up. I felt like a total dweeb standing up since I had barely volunteered, but I was glad I had when the Concom members then told the assembly that the people who were sitting down needed to look around and realize that if they weren't standing up, they should know that without the people who were, the con wouldn't happen, so they should get themselves involved.

It seems like a small thing, but sometimes small things are symbolically important out of proportion with their perceived size. It might have been my first con, but I was a part of it. I owned it. I had an obligation to work to make it better.

Clearly, the WisCon Troll never felt a part of WisCon. (Perhaps it is therefore inaccurate to call her the WisCon Troll.) I don't expect people who use hateful mockage for sport at SASS to feel that way. But I do expect the people who pony up the money and go to the con to feel that way, even if they only feel it some of the time.

Were there moments that I didn't feel a part of it? Sure. Were there people who said things that pissed me off? Sure. Did I mock some people when they said things that I thought were stupid? Sure. I'm only human.

But—and it's an important but—I mocked things that I thought violated the spirit of the community. I mocked the behavior of people who seemed to still be lacking a clue when it came to say, racism, not the people themselves. And I got involved in ways that would help change the con for the better. Most importantly, I had the good sense not to post that mocking in places where it would spiral out of control.

What I never got from the troll was any sense of how her very public mocking was designed to make the con better or what community values she thought the people in question violated. This is particularly fascinating since she conflated one person with another fairly often, gave inaccurate physical descriptions of several others, and demonstrated a pretty impressive level of misreading of the political opinions of people in the panel on politics—to say nothing of the utter lack of subtlety in how she read the unspoken dynamics of that panel.

True, if it turns out that the poster at SASS using her photo in the icon is not her, she did not post the photos that revealed the identities of the people in the photos. But there is no way in hell that that kind of outing was not a foreseeable consequence of her actions, so she bears some culpability that it happened even if she did not do it herself. The people at SASS were going to escalate to doing things that even the WisCon Troll didn't want them to do. Any idiot who's been online for more than 3 minutes could have foreseen that, so either she didn't care or she didn't think, neither of which is excusable in this case. Whatever personal issues she has with body image do not mitigate that fact.

Moreover, if you are kicked out of a con (or if the collective membership is crying that you should have been when the membership is 1000 people at that con who don't agree on much else yet are collectively begging for your banning), this is a sign that you have done something wrong. Fannish communities do their best to incorporate as many people as possible; in order to have violated norms so completely that you are exiled and/or shunned, you must have done something of a pretty significant order of magnitude to end up in that position. That should be a sign to stop and think and spend some serious energy reevaluating what precisely got you there. I have seen no proof that such energy is being expended. Moreover, I have seen plenty of proof that the contrary is true.

Based on that, I have no problem in the world with the circulation of Zathlazip's various names to feminist communities, academic networks, and fandom far and wide because her behavior is not acceptable in any of those circles. Zathlazip is not a person who should be welcome in fannish, feminist, or academic communities, because she clearly has no respect for the norms of those societies. It is, perhaps, poetic justice that since she violated those norms, other trolls have stooped to that level in their response to her instead of providing whatever kind of approval and validation she sought by mocking us among them; this is why women ought to stick together and support each other instead of allowing other people to play on our differences and divide us.

I am perfectly okay with fandom/academia/feminist communities circulating her various names, and here's why: she went into feminist fannish space and took photographs of people there and posted them in a public place with the specific intent to mock them in ways that completely activated fatophobia, transphobia, racism, misogyny, ableism, and homophobia, to say nothing of the shameless dismissal of whole categories of medical issues. In no way and at no time has she demonstrated any remorse about her actions, even after (if the rumors are true) the convention asked her to leave as a result of her actions.

Based on posts that I am reasonably sure she herself committed, I am convinced that she represents a threat to our safety in fannish/feminist space. I have seen nothing that will convince me that she will not go right out and do this again. Her own issues, whatever they may be, may in fact call for compassion from us, and I am trying very hard to keep that in mind, but compassion asks that we understand where she is coming from, not that we do not speak out about the wrongness or her actions and how those actions hurt others, nor does it dictate that we must welcome her back into our communities until she has made progress on controlling the behaviors that led to that pain, regardless of the source of her acting out.

Let me give you a hypothetical. I still think, like LiveJournal blogger cereta, that if the WisCon Troll Zathlazip were in my workplace, and I were asked to write a letter of recommendation, I would want to know about this, because if I endorsed her without knowing about this and then she did this again, it would be my professional reputation on the line. Plenty of people at WisCon are academics, so that's less of a hypothetical situation than it might first seem.

In addition, I think the move to circulate her name is as much about making sure she is not allowed to pass freely into safe fannish and feminist spaces in order to do this again as it is vengeance. I would not feel safe with her at any convention I attend, and I think everyone in fandom/feminist circles has the right to know who she is so we can protect ourselves from this behavior.

There's been a lot of discussion about the idea that women need to have the backs of other women, especially in fannish spaces. I was thrilled to get to WisCon and get my little "Proprietary Boobs" and "Backup" ribbons to wear on my badge as a physical way of marking my frustration with the insane debacle known as the Open Source Boob Project. However, I am sad that we so quickly had an opportunity to put those promises to support other women who were being hurt into practice. I am proud of how so many people whom I had not met before WisCon, whom I now consider friends, responded swiftly and smartly to this assault on our space. I am deeply disappointed that that assault was instigated not by a man but by another woman who should have been standing shoulder to shoulder with us and our allies, regardless of their sex or complicated expression of gender, instead of attacking us. I hope that Zathlazip and other people who think like she did will learn from this; but I also plan to work to change structures so that it'll be harder for her or anyone else to do this or something like this in the future. No, we can't stop it entirely; that's not the point. The point is for us to do what people at WisCon have done for decades before I got there: speak out when something is not okay, support each other when someone else hurts us, and continue to celebrate ourselves when too much of the rest of the world will not. That's my obligation as a new member of the community, and I hope everyone who was there will take that away from WisCon 32.

Hederahelix is the alterego of an acafan with an interest in science fiction, feminism, and the queerest corners of the places where they intersect. She lives on the left coast and envies Madison's supply of macaroni and cheese pizza.

Trolling for a (Not So Good) Time

JJ Pionke, December 2008

The short version of the Troll Incident: A woman, Zathlazip, lashed out against science fiction convention attendees. The Concom of the convention kicked Zathlazip out and warned its membership in a post on LiveJournal to leave her alone and not threaten her. The Concom told various people who were concerned that there would be a statement forthcoming. Six months went by; no statement came. WisCon's membership was left wondering what happened. Many of the membership started to question whether or not they wanted to go back to WisCon. I have to wonder, what the hell were they thinking?

The long version: At one point over the course of the fabulousness that is WisCon weekend, a woman who has a history of eating disorders, took pictures of "non-normative" people in general, altered the pictures with unhappy faces crudely drawn over people's real faces, and then posted the pictures to a website so that all and sundry could then make fun of, and post hurtful comments about, said people. I choose to believe that she was bored rather than that she was being malicious, or evil incarnate. While Zathlazip blocked out people's faces, she made no move to obscure their name tags, which are clearly readable in some of the pictures. She also crossed a line and especially angered con members by making fun of a child in her post.

As WisCon wound down, and the news about this attack on congoers spread like the WisCholera that was going around, blogs lit up and people posted all about how they felt about these attacks. Zathlazip never posted a public apology for her actions, rather she posted an apology buried in comments somewhere in her blog and tried to make herself out to be the victim by saying that she had lost friends over her own stupidity. On the other side of the table, some people who had been affected by her indiscretion posted threats and were told by a WisCon Concom member to "Cut it the fuck out." Though I do not know the nature of these threats or even why they were made, the fact that Zathlazip made fun of minors in her ill-thought post might have something to do with it.

In a very short time, Zathlazip realized that she had stepped onto a hornet's nest and managed to get her original post taken off the site that she posted it to. By then, it was too late, of course. Those that had been making malicious comments on the original post started a new thread on a different forum, one set up to make fun of the original forum; and then started raiding public photo pools for pictures tagged "WisCon." My picture showed up in the reposts.

It was a picture from WisCon 31 and is of me wearing my *Battlestar Galactica* uniform. I found out about the reposted picture at WisCon in a roomful of people, all of us on laptops. The picture and the comments associated with it were pointed out to me in that room and my face burned with shame. My feelings of shame stemmed from the fact that my *Battlestar Galactica* uniform was a kick-ass costume that was the hit of the party at WisCon 31, and the comments made about me were incredibly hurtful and hateful on the repost thread. In short, a really cool experience with a really cool costume was tainted by a bunch of jerks looking to get their jollies by making fun of my love of an awesome show, my size, and my being a butch woman. Zathlazip is responsible for those attacks on not just me, but the countless others who were targeted because, more than likely, no one on that website would have ever known about WisCon if Zathlazip had not brought us to their attention.

I personally finally decided to send a letter to Zathlazip's Dean and her PhD Advisor, as her behavior was completely inappropriate at an academic conference. From one academic to another, her behavior caused harm to a number of people, including myself, and was reprehensible in a setting where the exchange of knowledge is on an academic and fan level. I have absolutely no idea if any action was ever taken against her or not because of my letter, nor do I know if she was punished in any way for her actions other than "losing friends."

More than anything, however, what hurts the most is that the Concom of WisCon has done nothing as of December 2008. There has NEVER been a post on the WisCon website about this incident, nor has there been any word from the Concom other than to "Cut it the fuck out." In short, it's been months since this incident and I, and many others, are still waiting for the Concom to say something to those of us who were attacked. They have said nothing and their silence is perhaps the most telling. Though there may be discussion going on in Concom circles, it's not something that they want to discuss with the outside world, and further emails to the Concom about this issue have largely gone unanswered. It makes me wonder if there will be any kind of policy changes at the next WisCon or if this will all just be swept quietly under the proverbial rug.

During the drafting process of this article, a discussion was created when various friends, who were and were not at WisCon, proofread this piece and realized that I was indeed correct in stating that the Concom had not publicly responded to this situation other than to tell us not to threaten Zathlazip. Over the course of the discussion, that was on a friends-locked journal post and then went into an email discussion, a Concom member strongly disputed my statements that the Concom had done nothing public. Shortly after, a message appeared on the WisCon LiveJournal community that read in part, "...we are now in the process of finalizing our response to this incident. We will have decided our course of action by the end of November, and information will be included in the eCube mailed out at that time." It is now the week of Christmas and the year a breath from over, and still, nothing has been done.

Responses to the WisCon Troll Incident have varied from anger to aggression to forgiveness to hurt. This single event will forever change the face of WisCon. Undoubtedly, at next WisCon, people will be nervous about being photographed and there will be discussions, moderated and not, about the Incident, WisCholera, personal space, and photography. In the end, Zathlazip has not been held accountable for her actions, and the Concom has done nothing public to date to support those that were attacked in Zathlazip's original post or the reposts that happened afterwards. The carefree nature of WisCon has been irrevocably changed, many would argue not for the better.

When Zathlazip first surfaced and my picture appeared, I thought to myself that maybe I should take a break from WisCon. I love WisCon and have been going for years, but can I continue to go to a convention that apparently isn't interested in my mental health and safety? When I look back on this incident, I don't remember my shame at being singled out or even the turmoil I went through composing the letter from one academic to another. I remember the silence from the Concom. I'll be at WisCon next year, but if something happens, I know not to get my hopes up in regards to support from the Concom. The fact that the Concom has failed to act publicly, even after so much time has lapsed, is an indication that the Concom has perhaps forgotten that it is not them, nor the programming, nor anything else that makes WisCon. WisCon is made by its membership. The people who pay to go to the event, have a good time, and contribute to a larger discussion on a variety of science fiction feminist issues. The fact that the Concom seems to have forgotten this is perhaps the largest tragedy of all out of this incident.

Links:

http://community.livejournal.com/wiscon/173722.html
http://community.livejournal.com/wiscon/156955.html
http://community.livejournal.com/wiscon/152457.html

Safe Space vs. LOLspace in the WisCon Trolling

Liz Henry and Debbie Notkin

> *Trolling is a game about identity deception, albeit one that is played without the consent of most of the players. The troll attempts to pass as a legitimate participant, sharing the group's common interests and concerns; the newsgroups members, if they are cognizant of trolls and other identity deceptions, attempt to both distinguish real from trolling postings, and upon judging a poster a troll, make the offending poster leave the group. Their success at the former depends on how well they— and the troll—understand identity cues; their success at the latter depends on whether the troll's enjoyment is sufficiently diminished or outweighed by the costs imposed by the group.*
>
> —Judith Donath, Identity and Deception in the Virtual Community, 1999: http://smg.media.mit.edu/people/Judith/Identity/IdentityDeception.html

The WisCon community is still actively reacting to last year's trolling of WisCon. Many people are angry and upset, still concerned with the issues brought up by the chain of events that followed the original incident. The person who posted the WisCon photos and detailed mockery, Zathlazip, is also still being affected. I (Liz) would like to bring up several issues to complicate how WisCon folks are thinking about the incident. I formulated this article in conversation with Debbie Notkin, so some of this is "I" or "me" writing, but when it is "we" or "us,"it's me and Debbie thinking together.

As is true for many people at WisCon, I was upset at being trolled and having my image and my family's offensively photoshopped, and at seeing my friends and my community mocked in ways that hurt them and made them feel unsafe. Humor that uses racism, misogyny, homophobia, fatphobia, and transphobia is hurtful and contributes to silencing of entire communities. It reinforces the ways that disempowered individuals are discouraged from simply being visible, let alone from making personal and political connections. However, I don't believe that making fun of people on the Internet is a horrible crime and the people who do it deserve ousting from the realm of humanity. I also think it can't be, and shouldn't be, forbidden.

WisCon has particular community norms developed partly from feminist consciousness raising and the notion of "safe space." These are progressive concepts that emphasize consent. They may also include respect for the expression of particular emotions with an expectation of extremely limited consequence. What is safe space, to the WisCon community? How is it perceived and how is it really? Who is it safe for? For example, WisCon is a space that is likely safest for white middle-class women, but can feel unsafe for men and for women of color. As with the Internet-based culture I describe below, these norms are often unspoken and/or taken for granted at WisCon.

We believe there is no safe space—only safer space, just as there is no safe sex—only safer sex.

The forum members at Something Awful and at SASS as described in the introduction to this volume are operating from a different set of assumptions than the WisCon norms. They are part of an Internet culture of machismo, which values freedom of expression, sharp-edged humor, and being tough, but which does not lack rules. Even the trolls of the trolls have community norms, the transgression of which is frowned upon. They see their own community boards as their space, liminal space in which the rules of being polite do not apply. It is more like a flyting from Norse saga, or some other duel of verbal insults, but done non-consensually. Part of the goal is to freak the mundanes, épater la bourgeoisie, not just to get attention or lulz, but, often, to point out hypocrisy or put the targets of their mockery through what they perceive as a needed learning experience. This can become a competitive game of who can be the most inappropriate. (Of course, they are also just in it for the lulz.)

We believe it is productive to examine the ways in which, in safer space such as the semi-private venue of WisCon, members put increased weight on our own feelings. In the everyday world, people are perhaps more or less used to having to suck up hurtful comments.

In feminist safe space, some feelings are privileged over others: being hurt, lonely, outgroup, or alienated, for example, brings responses of energy, respect, compassion, and attention. This is a strength of the community, though it is an incomplete strength. White women's feelings are regularly privileged in the community over those of people of color and middle- or upper-class women's feelings over those of people from poverty or working-class backgrounds, revealing the racist and classist flaws in the safety paradigm. Nonetheless, in general, foregrounding feelings is seen as difficult and useful work that people need to do as part of political consciousness-raising and personal development, and this framework is also used to deepen anti-racist discourse at WisCon and elsewhere. Unlike sadness or exclusion, anger, including feminist rage, is generally not an acknowledged emotion at WisCon, and certainly not a privileged one.

In contrast, at Something Awful and in performative Internet culture, foregrounding emotions such as hurt and loneliness is precisely the behavior that gets a person reviled. Being "butthurt," or demonstrating too much sensitivity in the face of emotional suffering that is a part of the human condition, is a weakness that must be strengthened by attack. In the LOLspace view, the spectacle of Internet drama results in the shattering of false perceptions and in another form of individual improvement and consciousness raising. Crying in response to something cruel or unfair in a game, for example, would be seen as bad sportsmanship. Theater and games have this in common with the LOLspace view of the Internet; they exist in a realm outside of the rules of day-to-day interaction. Being upset in the context of this game, and showing it, demonstrates that a person needs to be critiqued, mocked, or defeated more intensely in order to be taught how to take it with the community's or the game-players' concept of grace and humor. In our media culture it is commonly and legally accepted that famous people can be parodied in any way. In the Something Awful style of Internet culture everyone is a public figure, a potentially famous person, and is fair game for that game, which is assumed to be played on a level playing field. However, that playing field is not level at all.

SA members pointed out in their forums that several WisCon bloggers wrote that it was as if Zathlazip had raped them. In their view, Zathlazip made fun of some people on the Internet by calling them fat. From the SA point of view, words on the net are not something that can be equated with rape; doing so has also been described as bad feminist practice because it trivializes physical violence. It might not be fruitful or wise to compare and rank the emotional damage that stems from differing sources. But we still feel that talking in public space is a different animal altogether than physical violence; in fact, it is part of our goals to encourage public discourse and difficult conversations in the belief that it encourages the examination of diverse ideas, and that it might actually defuse impulses to violence. In other words, we think that as a global culture, the more we talk in public, the less we're shooting each other in the head.

I would like to describe a part of my own participation in the incident and how it affected me. I found that the posts that mocked me and others stuck in my head—the hateful words were hard to shake, or would come up unbidden in my mind. They are far from my self-concept, and I am lucky enough to be surrounded in most of my life by a feeling of safety, friendship, love, and appreciation. Yet I am still aware that, unpredictably, others are hostile towards me, and may be looking at me while thinking that I'm an "ugly, wheeled, dykey man-thing" who should be harmed physically. Awareness of this is certainly key to my survival, as I have to keep in mind who might and might not view me in this way. Yet bringing that awareness to the fore in a context where I expect to put my constant armor aside—this causes painful cognitive dissonance. The images were even more powerful than the words, so for example calls for queer and disabled people like me to be raped or gassed to death were combined with images of my head photoshopped onto the naked body of a woman in a wheelchair whose arms and legs were twisted by muscle spasms. My home address was posted and re-posted; however, I did not see this as a direct physical threat; more likely to result in the delivery of a hundred pizzas than actual stalking. And in fact, it was meant not even for that, but in order to provoke a response of anger and hurt—in order to provoke me to flip out in public for further amusement and spectacle value. My assessment based on a lifetime of participation in Internet culture was that the real life threat was quite low. Many others at WisCon judged the level of threat by different standards.

In this context, I was tracking the identities of some of the participants. Zathlazip was particularly easy to track, as her various screen names linked to each other. I found some posts she had made on bulletin boards, and linked to them on my blog, repeating her real name and details of her life, as well. In doing this, I was partly motivated by hope that some of the people she had mocked would understand her possible mindset—would have some empathy for her, and direct their anger at the other, much worse hatemongers in the situation. Yet I think I and others who outed Zathlazip were also motivated by an element of cruelty and self-righteousness; awareness of her vulnerability and the way she could be tarred with the same brush she laid on us; hope that she would become a target of trolls in her turn, and desire for her to feel the uncertainty and fear that shook many of us as a result of her actions. This may still seem well deserved to many WisCon members, but I am less certain now that it was a good response, and I have personally apologized to Zathlazip for participating in the outing of her various identities. As I faced the possibility of calling the high school principal of another person from SASS, I considered whether I wanted to unleash the machinery of the school and possibly the law on this child's life, when as a deeper value than protecting myself from hate speech, I value his free speech and right to make as much of an ass of himself as he likes in public. A call or letter from me seemed likely to set off a chain of events and consequences that I would find completely repugnant and inappropriate. In short: I don't know his situation, and he gets to call me a fat dyke man-thing without being expelled from high school and losing his job and maybe the support of his parents. When I was in high school, I published an underground newspaper that held a mixture of serious critique and sophomoric mockery; what consequences should I have suffered? Perhaps this high school boy, in turn, though he possessed enough detail of my life to call down the law on me, decided not to escalate things, concluding that though he finds my queerness to be unacceptable, he would never call for Child Protective Services to deny my rights as a parent. In any case, I did not make that call. If the boy had threatened direct physical harm to another person, I would have called down the law as best I could. We all, including Zathlazip who found her office broken into, had to wonder if the people angry at us were crazy enough to be dangerous.

In the aftermath of the trolling, we have been shocked to see our own feminist community deal with the trolling by declaring particular people to be non-humans and thus valid targets for real world harm. Many WisCon people refer to the incident as "The WisCon Troll." This demonstrates at least two major problems. The first is that it conflates all the events and posts and the harm all of them may have caused, with Zathlazip's original offensive mockery. The other problem is this: a person who is obnoxious on the Internet is still a person, not a Troll. In particular I am thinking of a fellow WisCon member declaring "I want them (the SASS trolls, Zathlazip, and SA members alike) to lose their jobs, their homes, their families; they aren't even human beings. I want them hurt." Others continue to make similar statements. The level of damage to Zathlazip that some people call for is not in keeping with the level of damage that was caused by the whole constellation of events, let alone the level of damage that she herself caused. The WisCon community was damaged by a complicated culture clash resulting from the initial actions of Zathlazip, but we don't believe that participating in the practice of dehumanizing others will do the community any good. Much of the language around The Troll is perturbing. As feminists we profess to care for all women and all people. When we exclude Zathlazip from the category of person, we are doing something wrong.

I would like to bring up a few counterexamples to compare to the WisCon trolling and our reactions to it. Consider if I were to infiltrate a men's rights organization, a conservative religious meeting, a Scientology gathering, and post my reporting of their event complete with clumsily anonymized photos, mockery of plastic hair and tacky outfits and what I perceive as wrongness, insincerity, hypocrisy. (Something which I am certainly capable of doing.) I believe that quite a few WisCon folks would find it not only amusing but would praise me for righteous action. Would I be a troll, a nonhuman? And would they see me as one? It shouldn't matter that I think I'm "right" and the targets of my mockery and curiosity are "wrong"; I'm still violating their community norms. Consider the increasing participation and the intersection of WisCon folks with people who hang out on forums like fandom_wank. Have you laughed at fandom_wank? Do you think the targets of the mockery there may be as hurt as WisCon members were by the trolling? We are not especially hypocritical. But we are also not always internally consistent in our values.

In my own blog reading habits, I am extremely fond of reading the pottersues LiveJournal community, but I stay aware that it consists mostly of teenage fanfic writers ruthlessly and cruelly mocking the writing of girls slightly younger than themselves who post their fiction online. While I find that and my amusement at it somewhat problematic, the intense critique the younger girls experience is now a part of Internet culture.

Here are some examples of outing and public/private boundary violations from my personal life. In 1990, a university employee was a member of a campus conservative group at the University of Texas. That person looked up the records of gay/lesbian organization spokespeople and gave their permanent addresses to the campus conservative group. Homophobic material, threats, and newspaper clippings outing those students were sent to their parents. I was one of those students. I and several of my fellow activists were then cut off by our families both personally and financially. The campus conservatives, perhaps, sincerely thought that as public advocates of non-heterosexuality, we were harmful to society and that we had to face the consequences of our actions. Was this part of the logic underlying Zathlazip's actions, as well as my own logic when I participated in outing her real name and information? When my college roommate took five people's money and instead of paying the phone bills with it all semester, spent it on pizza and beer—which we realized after he moved out and our phone was cut off—I called everyone named Mayoff in Dallas until I found his parents. They sent us a check. Same tactic; very effective, often problematic. Call attention to what is already public but what might not be obvious; out someone's identity or behavior to their family, their job, to the law. These are escalations of public discourse that we shouldn't take lightly.

We'd like to end with a few related ideas, a bit of a laundry list of complicated points to consider.

In JJ Pionke's essay on the trolling, she critiques the WisCon central committee for its response to the trolling. We think that the committee should have made a sharp, strong, immediate response; however, we are also aware that it did make such a response and use up its energy dealing very effectively and professionally to the

Norovirus outbreak. This was necessary, but it also might have been easier to cope with scientific and medical questions than to address emotionally and socially difficult issues.

My own personal damage from the event was partly caused by having to deal with the anger of my male friends. I experience men's anger as an emergency. I had to put aside my own feelings and that of my WisCon sisters, in order to field the sometimes quite extreme reactions of the men who are my allies.

I would also like to bring up a possible perspective of Zathlazip. She may hold the belief that the fat positive movement is not scientifically based and actively harms people by encouraging them to be fat, or not mind being fat, which will harm their health. To someone like Zathlazip, size acceptance may be the analogue of a movement to empower alcoholics, or to encourage anorexic teens to follow their own desires not to eat. However wrong we consider those beliefs, we should at least be able to imagine that Zathlazip could hold some feminist beliefs and still make the choices she made.

Debbie notes that in analysis of the trolling, she is coming from the perspective of a different age. Her concern was information flow, how it got out there, who found it. She wanted to know how it got passed around within WisCon, and continues to be fascinated with how it got responded to in the moment, long term, and now, as well as the immediate emotional reactions. The intersection of the trolling and the norovirus outbreak created an emotional impact, as if WisCon were under attack. Meanwhile, out of the 1000 people at WisCon she only knew a few people who would understand Internet culture and what was about to happen in all its dimensions, where it could go, and how big it could get, and what it meant to hit the front page of Digg and stay there for days. WisCon, as a community, was out of its depth.

Many conflicts arose around the idea of "Don't feed the trolls." This is likely good advice in some ways, and yet it is only effective in a community if everyone follows it. Speaking up gives fuel for more mockery and makes the speaker and those close to them into easy targets. Not feeding the trolls can also play into the silencing of women and of the various other identities and communities under attack. It also can be seen as in conflict with the concept of backing each other, which we had promoted through Project Backup, described in articles at the end of this book and in its introduction. And for women to expose conflict at all is a violation of many norms of dominant culture in the United States. So "not feeding the trolls" is hard and yet it's socially reinforced. Asking people not to process their thoughts in public damages our participation in public discourse and our own history; for example, I watched people lock their public journals temporarily or forever, deleting posts and blogs, removing their names from websites. We saw the WisCon committee take down the year's program item descriptions and the feminist sf wiki group decide to block the wiki from public view, at least temporarily. We respect these decisions and are aware that being out and public is a function of privilege. There are many shades of identity and outing, so that many of us have screen names, pen names, or other pseudonyms, either loosely associated with our real names or carefully kept separate.

In the end, my (Liz's) decision personally and as an editor was to speak up in public, in my own space, and to my own community. Many other WisCon members and allies spoke up against the hateful ideas expressed during the trolling; we are proud to stand with them. It is our goal to complicate people's thinking about the trolling. Please comment online if you would like to discuss what we've written and we will answer.

By day, Debbie Notkin works for a major publishing company, acting as a watchdog to make sure that publishers' rights are unfailingly protected. By night, she engages in a wide variety of nonprofit and social change activities, including helping authors make sure that their rights are also protected, working with photographer Laurie Toby Edison on issues of body image and stereotyping (visit her blog at www.laurietobyedison.com/discuss), being on the motherboard of the James Tiptree Award, and being very active on the WisCon committee. She is one of the three co-chairs of WisCon 33.

Come on Sugar

Julia Starkey

You know what makes me angry, other than people thinking it is revolutionary to be able to ask to touch women's bodies? People who think no reasonable woman would consent to being touched by strangers. Both attitudes are sex negative.

The first one because it presumes that women who are properly liberated, evolved, who "get it," will never be offended by being propositioned. The second attitude is negative because it presumes women must be offended by being propositioned.

I think that joyful, liberated women who are in touch with their sexual selves are going to make a wide variety of choices about their bodies. Some may choose to run around half naked, others may choose to cover themselves fully, while others may cover their hair and uncover their legs. Some women will decide they want sex frequently, while others want sex infrequently, and some not at all. All of those choices are liberating choices if they are what the women freely choose.

I think one of the most important tools towards liberation, self confidence, love, and joy is the ability to say "no." Physical and emotional boundaries and body autonomy require an individual to be able to say "I do not want that." How sincere is a yes if you can only say no under the most dire of circumstances?

I've been at "those kind of parties" where being propositioned for some kind of touch, sexual or otherwise, is typical. And for me one of the most freeing and joyful experiences is someone saying to me "I would like to kiss you. Is that ok?" and having them react to "no thank you" the same way they would react to me refusing a glass of water. I also appreciate the reiteration of "No I don't want to do that. Thank you for asking." The message behind "thank you for asking" (in my opinion) is to reinforce the idea that, in the event's context, propositioning some sexually is allowable. And also a reminder that "no" means "I do not want to engage in that activity with you" not "you are a horrible person."

People are right to say “if only people accepted no that way.” It doesn’t happen enough. Part of the problem with proponents of the project was that they didn’t grasp that it is difficult for women to say “no” due to a variety of issues like social pressure and safety. Well, and that making general propositions outside of specific contexts (like a sex party) actually is not OK.

Also: “I [theferrett] can’t decry the process of ‘asking repeatedly,’ mainly because it’s the only stimuli a lot of women respond to. Frankly, I think any woman who has to be begged fifteen times before she eventually accepts should be drug into the back alleyways and beaten, because her rampant need for a string of pleadings trains the wrong sort of men that no doesn’t mean no. And then we should go beat up the men for good measure.” That attitude there, is not sex positive. What is the value of that yes, when “no” was ignored until it disappeared?

Oh hi, I have a lot to say about this. *Exhibitionism for the Shy* by Carol Queen is an amazing book not really for exhibitionists, but to help people figure out what kinds of words, fantasies, and actions they like sexually. Ladyjax suggests we take a day to touch our own damn selves, which I whole heartedly support, especially when combined with reading Fat Acceptance blogs. Also, you know what else is awesome? Getting a professional massage. In addition to feeling good and fixing body problems, it can be a healing way to receive touch non-sexually.

Julia is a geeky, mixed race, fat, queer woman who lives in the Boston area. Julia brings her love of intersectionality to the various groups she is involved with. She is passionate about many kinds of activism including fat acceptance, LGBT issues, disability rights, racism, sexism, and of course sci-fi. She earned a degree in Folklore and Mythology from Harvard University, and is in the process of becoming a professional librarian. When not overthinking things, Julia plots new and exciting ways to eat bacon.

A Modest Proposal

Hanne Blank

As we all know, many women long to give a swift kick in the balls to some male person or other. Yet all too often women are prohibited from doing so.

Sometimes this is due to our culture's repressive attitudes toward female violence or because of societal pressure for women to behave in "ladylike" and feminine ways. At times women must censor themselves from administering a good solid boot to the greater masculine crotch due to historically justified fear of reprisal. At yet other times it is nothing more or less than men's self-serving, self-glorifying attitudes toward their precious little patriarchal testicles that lead them to cravenly avoid supporting women's emotional and political expression.

All in all, we live in a culture that routinely prohibits women this useful and healthy outlet for the outrage that almost every women eventually feels as a result of living in a sexist patriarchal society. Indeed, we live in a culture that punishes women for even thinking or talking about expressing their rage in this way.

This must change, and men, who after all have an obligation to help redress thousands of years of unearned patriarchal privilege, also have a moral obligation to help solve this problem.

To this end, we propose a community-based Open Source Swift Kick to the Balls Project (OSSKBP).

Like other Open Source projects, the OSSKBP relies on a wide pool of volunteers working together for the common good.

The Project has very simple parameters and it basically works like this: Men who are open to being given a swift kick in the balls need do nothing. Women will simply assume that any man not clearly indicating his position vis-a-vis being kicked in the balls with an approved OSSKBP badge or pin is open to being kicked in the balls, as any progressive, free-thinking, feminist man ought to be, by any woman who wishes to do so.

However, we also recognize and affirm that not all men will be so willing to serve. Therefore the OSSKBP provides two other options.

1. Men who would like to be asked for permission before a woman administers one or more swift kicks to their balls shall wear the official OSSKBP "Ask First Pin" at all times. This is a black lapel pin with a lavender question mark on it.
   Because of the serious and comprehensive respect with which women's desires vis-a-vis having their bodies touched by others are uniformly greeted in our culture, women will sometimes abide by any given Ask First Pin wearer's stated preference about getting a kick in the balls at the time that he is asked. At other times, however, women may make their own decisions as to whether or not to give him a quick kick in the nuts regardless of the male's expressed preference. Fair's fair.
2. Men who do not wish to be kicked in the balls at all must wear a large visible official "No Kicks, Thanks" badge at all times, including when swimming, showering, and sleeping. They may also wish to avoid areas where large numbers of women are present, particularly at night. Some men may also wish to invest in assertiveness training, sympathetic female bodyguards, body armor, or sessions with a personal self-defense trainer to increase their ability to resist undesired kicks. As these methods have long been considered completely adequate for women who wish to avoid sexual predation we feel that they are all that is necessary here.

Men choosing the "No Kicks, Thanks" option should be aware that they will be ridiculed publicly for their sexism and misogyny and their indefensible, self-serving, anti-female pursuit of their own selfish bodily autonomy. (It's not like getting kicked in the nuts does them any lasting harm, for heaven's sake.) Men who comply with all of the above and still end up getting kicked in the balls will be advised that they were asking for it, and that women can't be blamed for what happens when a man walks by with his crotch just hanging out there where it becomes a target of opportunity. (Besides, if a man weren't really willing, deep down, to get kicked in the balls, he wouldn't have stood still for it. Everyone knows that.)

Thank you for your participation in the Open Source Swift Kick to the Balls Project.

Originally published at: http://misia.livejournal.com/1055120.html. A parody of The Open-Source Boob Project proposal, which is at: http://theferrett.livejournal.com/1087686.html.

Hanne Blank is a feminist writer, historian, and activist whose books include *Virgin: The Untouched History* (Bloomsbury) and *Unruly Appetites* (Seal Press). She believes that a good stout pair of Corcoran cap-toe jump boots go with anything.

The Open Source Backup Project

Vito Excalibur

This is not a joke. This is not satire. This is not a test.

While the Open Source Swift Kick to the Balls Program is easy and fun to read and write about—I'm not really going to go around asking anyone if I can kick them in the crotch.

There is a difference between the Internet and the real world.

That is an Internet solution to a real world problem.

I would like to propose a little real world help for a real world problem.

If you're tech-savvy enough to know about the benefits of open source, then you also know how crucial it is to back your shit up frequently. If you don't back it up, you know, you're going to lose it.

I would like to start the Open Source Women Back Each Other Up Program. Here's my pledge: if I see somebody groping you in public, and you're not moaning Yes! Yes! Yes!, I will break through your Somebody Else's Problem invisibility field and come over and ask if you're okay. If your situation looks dangerous enough that I can't help on my own, I will call over friends or, if it's a situation in which I think the cops would be on your side, I will call the cops. If you're being harassed by a guy, you can say so to me, even if you don't know me. I pledge I will distract him so you can get away, or I will tell him that he needs to leave, or whatever I can do to the best of my ability. I pledge that yes, actually, because you are a woman I will give you the benefit of the doubt. If you tell me that a guy just did something shitty to you I will not refuse to look at any evidence and tell you that I know him and he's a great guy and you must have been imagining things. I have great loyalty to my male friends, but I will not allow that to blind me to the fact that none of us are saints and even my best friends can screw up and may need to be called on it. I pledge that I will walk you to your car if you don't feel safe walking alone at night, and then you can drive me to mine.

Yes, even at WisCon. I pledge that even if I don't know you, if there is a creepy guy following you around, you can say so, and I will not say to you go hide in your room; I will say to him go find another party, or if necessary, go home. I will come with you if you need to talk to the con organizers. I will not make you feel like your right to control over your own body is not a big deal.

And I will do this whether or not I like you, or even know you. It's not about liking you. It's about the fact that we need to back each other up, and I will need you to do this for me some day.

And I say this knowing that the first thing that is going to happen is that someone is going to start talking about how if everyone did this then women could just lie about men and get them kicked out of places. Well, obviously I don't want that to happen. I realize that this is open to abuse. You know what else is open to abuse? THE FUCKING STATUS QUO. If the choice is between the possibility of men worrying that if they offend a woman she can easily get them kicked out of a con and the actuality of women quietly staying home from cons in droves because they don't want men to harass them, quietly saying nothing about their harassment because they know people will tell them it's no big deal, or it's never happened to them and so frankly they don't believe in it, I am going to deal with the problem that actually exists first. Should we somehow get to the point where the stereotype of an sf con is wall-to-wall women in razorwire bras, and men don't show their faces because they're afraid of being arrested; we can go ahead and work on that problem then.

And, in a situation in which it seems like a little OSSKBP might help, I pledge to be willing to do some work under a Creative Commons license. If you know what I mean.

Now it's your turn.

What will you do?

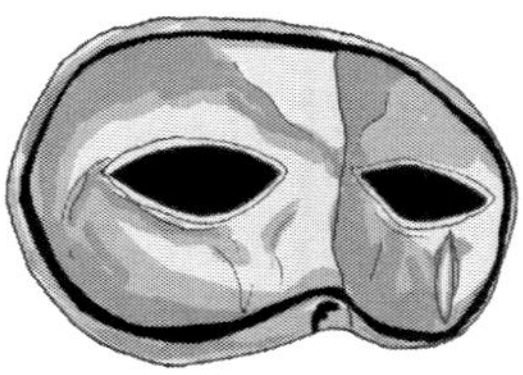

Vito Excalibur has been enjoying the hell out of WisCons since 1996. She blogs at http://vito_excalibur.livejournal.com.

HERE'S MY PLEDGE:

If I see somebody ***groping***
harassing
intimidating
threatening you,

I will back you up.

You are not Somebody Else's Problem.

I will come over and ask if you're okay. If you're being harassed, you can tell me. **Even if you don't know me**. I will distract him so you can get away; I will tell him that he needs to leave; I will do whatever I can do to the best of my ability.

If your situation looks dangerous enough I can't help on my own, I will call over friends. If *(and only if)* I think the cops would help, I will call the cops.

If you don't feel safe walking alone at night, I will walk you to your car, and then you can drive me to mine.

I will not make you feel like your right to control over your own body is not a big deal.

(Yes, actually, **because you are a woman,** I will give you the benefit of the doubt.)

If you tell me that a guy just did something shitty to you I will not tell you: I know him (or) he's a great guy! (or especially) you must be imagining things

I will listen to you.

Even if he is a friend, I will call him on his shit. And I will do this **whether or not I like you**. I will do this **whether or not I know you**. This is not about me liking you. It's about the fact that **we need to back each other up**. It's about the fact that **I will need you to do this for me some day.**

I pledge that even if I don't know you, if there is a creepy guy following you around, you can tell me. I will not tell you to go hide in your room. I will tell him to find another party; or I will tell him to go home. I will come with you if you want to talk to the authorities.

backupproject.org